A Brief History of Buddhist Studies in Europe and America

A Brief History of Buddhist Studies in Europe and America

by

J. W. de Jong

KŌSEI PUBLISHING CO. • Tokyo

Cover design by NOBU. The text of this book is set in a computer version of Palatino with a computer version of Optima for display.

First English edition, 1997
Second Printing, 1998

Published by Kōsei Publishing Co., 2-7-1 Wada, Suginami-ku, Tokyo 166-8535, Japan. Printed in Japan.

ISBN 4-333-01762-9 LCC Card No. applied for

Contents

Publisher's Preface to the Unified Edition

A Brief History of Buddhist Studies in Europe and America was originally published in four instalments over the course of sixteen years. The first instalment (covering the present author's preface and chapters 1 and 2) appeared in *The Eastern Buddhist* 7/1 (May 1974), pp. 55–106. Chapters 3 and 4 then appeared in the next issue of that same journal (October 1974), pp. 49–82. Ten years elapsed before chapter 5 appeared, in *The Eastern Buddhist* 17/1 (Spring 1984), pp. 79–107. Finally, chapter 6, which appeared in *Chūō Gakujutsu Kenkyūjo Kiyō* 20 (1990), pp. (1)–(60), brought Professor de Jong's survey of Buddhist studies up to the year 1990.

In putting together these four separately published instalments of a single survey, Kōsei Publishing Company hopes to make this highly reputed treasure trove of information more conveniently available to the many people around the world presently engaged in the study of Buddhism—scholars and students alike. Students in particular not only will benefit from the overview it gives of previous scholarly work but also may find in it indicators of the paths their own future research might take.

Unifying the four parts of the survey has necessitated some changes. First of all, the four instalments did not follow the same format throughout: the first three instalments were heavily footnoted, whereas the fourth had a bibliography at the end instead of footnotes. For this unified edition it was decided to use the author-date system of citation, so that footnotes could be reduced to a minimum, so that book titles, cities of publication, page numbers, and other source references did not interfere too much with the thrust of the main information, and so that at the end we would have one bibliography that would embrace all the major works cited in the survey. Secondly, the text has been partially rewritten. Some of these minor revisions, which do not affect the substance of what Professor de Jong originally wrote, were necessitated by the change in format; thus, for example, where the original may have had something like "In 1972 so-and-so published a new edition of . . . ," now the text might run "So-and-so published a new edition of . . . (1972)." Others of these minor revisions were necessitated by the change in perspective: from 1974, or 1984, or 1990, when the various instalments were composed, to 1996, when the present unified edition was being prepared; as a result, time expressions like "recently," "in the past five years," "is now working on," "in the near future," and so on, had to be modified. The perspective was also changed by the desire to reach a wider readership, with the result that, occasionally, scholarly shorthand that would be readily understood by the specialist had to be expanded or rephrased so as to be clear to the novice as well.

In keeping with a venerable tradition, this edition will incorporate within the text bracketed page references indicating where each next page began in the original publication. Even if the text in the original ended with a hyphenated word, and the rest of the word began the next page, then this edition will hyphenate that same word in exactly the same place and place the bracketed page reference after the hyphen. An example of this appears on the first page of Professor de Jong's original preface, where we find the combination "ex-[56]plained." Since the original pagination varied from instalment to instalment (see the first paragraph of this preface), these bracketed page numbers will "jump" after chapters 2, 4, 5. Still, these page references will enable the reader to locate, in the present edition, any passages of the main body of text referred to by authors who are citing the original edition.

While the perspective from which this edition was prepared was the present (1996), this does not mean that the work has been updated to 1996. Such was never the intention, and, as Professor de Jong's remarks in 1984 and 1990 make abundantly clear, would have been nigh unto impossible anyway, given the proliferation of publications on Buddhism in the last few decades. A few, very few, publications will appear in the text or bibliography with dates later than 1990, but these tend to be continuations of some series that began earlier.

One other point that needs to be mentioned is that, though we adopted an author-date (citation note) format, the format itself shows somewhat more variety than is customary. Where an author's name is already mentioned in the sentence, only the year of publication is given within parentheses, thus: (1875). But sometimes the year of publication and the author's name are both already mentioned in the sentence, and in such a case we usually do not add anything within parentheses; this was done, again, to avoid cluttering the text and interfering with the thrust of the message.

Preface

There seems little necessity to justify an attempt to sketch briefly the history of Buddhist studies. There is an abundance of material available in the writings of scholars, but no single work has yet been devoted to a systematic study of the history of Buddhist studies. Windisch's unfinished work (1917–20, 1921) contains much information on Buddhist studies in Europe in the first half of the nineteenth century, but very little on the following decades. Henri de Lubac, a Jesuit priest, has written a book on the meeting of Buddhism and the West (1952), but he is more interested in the reaction of the Western world to Buddhist ideas than in the history of Buddhist studies. For Buddhist scholars the most important chapter of his book is the one that deals with the information on Buddhism that can be found in the writings of missionaries in the sixteenth, seventeenth, and eighteenth centuries. A more recent work, *Buddhist Nirvāṇa and Its Western Interpreters,* by G. R. Welbon (1968), attempts to show how Western scholars have ex-[56]plained the meaning of Nirvāṇa. The usefulness of this book is diminished by the fact that the author was not sufficiently equipped for this difficult task.* Apart from these three books there are of course many other publications that contain useful information. The most important will be mentioned in due time.

The first chapter deals very briefly with Buddhist studies up to about 1825; although important work had been done before that date, most of it remained unpublished and became known much later. More space is devoted to the years 1826–77, in which Eugène Burnouf is the dominating figure. The second chapter begins in 1877 and ends in 1942; this period witnesses the work of such great scholars as Sylvain Lévi, Louis de La Vallée Poussin, Hermann Oldenberg, Theodor Stcherbatsky, and the

* For a review of his work, see *Journal of Indian Philosophy* 1 (1972): 396–403.

Rhys Davidses. The third, fifth, and sixth chapters deal with approximately the next five decades; the fifth and sixth represent updates added to the original brief sketch of Buddhist studies that I first published in 1974, in *The Eastern Buddhist.* Following chapter three there is a short chapter sketching some of the tasks that will require the attention of scholars in coming years.

In this short treatment it is of course impossible to deal adequately with all aspects of Buddhist studies. The main emphasis has been put on philological studies. From a geographic point of view India is the principal country dealt with, but developments in the Theravāda countries and in China and Tibet have not been entirely neglected. No attempt has been made to include studies on Japanese Buddhism and the history of Japanese Buddhist studies. This is a topic that can only be adequately treated by Japanese scholars.

A Brief History of Buddhist Studies in Europe and America

CHAPTER ONE

The Early Period (300 B.C.–1877)

Long before Alexander the Great's time, information about India reached Greece (Reese 1914). After Alexander's conquests (362–323 B.C.) much more became known about India. The most important source for this knowledge is the work of Megasthenes, who about 300 B.C. visited Pāṭaliputra as an envoy. Megasthenes's work has not been preserved, but many Greek and Latin authors have made use of it.[1] Megasthenes mentions brahmans and śramaṇas. Some scholars have considered the śramaṇas to be Buddhists, but this is not warranted by the use of the word in the inscriptions of Aśoka and in the Pāli texts. The first time Buddhism is mentioned in a Greek source is five hundred years after Megasthenes. Clement of Alexandria, who wrote his *Stromateis* about A.D. 200, mentions Indians who follow the precept of Boutta and venerate him as a god.[2] It is not surprising to find this information in an author living in Alexandria. In a discourse to the citizens of Alexandria, Dion Chrysostomos mentioned that among his audience [59] there were Bactrians, Scythians, and some Indians (Ad Alexandrinos 32, 40). Dion Chrysostomos died in A.D. 117. During the early centuries of our era there was no lack of contact between South India and Ceylon on the one hand and Alexandria and Rome on the other (Filliozat 1949; Lamotte 1953; Delbrueck 1955–56; Schwarz 1972). Clement could have been particularly well informed about India, if it is true that his teacher Pantainos travelled to India, as is told by Eusebius (H. eccl. 5, 10). Several scholars believe that Alexandria is mentioned in Pāli texts. The name Alasanda is found four times in the *Milindapañha* (ed. V. Trenckner 82.23–24, 327.27, 331.18 and 359.29), twice in the *Mahāniddesa* (Pali Text Society ed. 155.5 and 415.11), and once in the *Mahāvaṃsa* (29.39)(de Lubac 1952, 13–16; *CPD*

1. The most careful study of Megasthenes's work is Timmer 1930. More recent literature on Megasthenes is given by Derrett 1969.
2. Strom. I.15.71. Cf. Timmer 1930, 84–86 and Dihle 1964, 60–70.

1: 441–42). Scholars have not been able to agree, however, on whether this Alasanda refers to Alexandria or not.

About two centuries after Clement, Buddha is mentioned by Hieronymus, who tells us that Buddha was born from the side of a virgin.[3]

In the following centuries no knowledge of Buddhism seems to have reached the West. In mediaeval times Christendom venerated two saints, Barlaam and Josaphat. The legend of these two saints was very popular, and versions in many languages (Greek, Latin, French, German, Italian, Spanish, Provençal, Romaic, Dutch, and Scandinavian) circulated in medieval Europe. When the legend of Buddha became known in Europe, the resemblance to the legend of Saint Josaphat was soon noticed. The first to point it out was an unknown editor of Marco Polo's work, who added the following remark to Marco Polo's account of the legend of Buddha: "This is like the life of Saint Iosaphat, who was son of the king Avenir of those parts of Indie, and was converted to the Christian faith by the means of Barlam, according as is read in the life and legend of the [60] holy fathers" (cf. Benedetto 1928, clxxxvii, n. 1; and Moule and Pelliot 1938, 410). The Portuguese writer Diogo do Couto, who about 1612 described the exploits of his countrymen in India, remarked that Josaphat "is represented in his legend as the son of a great king in India, who had just the same upbringing, with all the same particulars that we have recounted in the life of Buddha . . . and as it informs us that he was the son of a great king in India, it may well be, as we have said, that *he* was the Buddha of whom they relate such marvels" (Lang 1957, 12). However, not until the nineteenth century was the Buddhist origin of the legend of Josaphat discovered by scholars (Laboulaye 1859; Liebrecht 1860). Since 1859 much has been written on this topic. At the end of the last century Ernst Kuhn (1894) provided a full survey of the work done by scholars since 1859. Recent discoveries of Georgian manuscripts have led to new discussions of the history of the legend. D. M. Lang and Georgian scholars have pointed out that there are two Georgian versions, an older and more complete version that was probably written in the ninth or tenth century, and a shorter one, based upon the more complete version. Both versions have been translated into English by Lang (1957, 1966). There seems to be no doubt that the older Georgian version is a Christian adaptation of an Arabic text. Probably towards the end of the eighth century "A Book of the Buddha," a "Book of Balauhar and Budhasaf," and a "Book of Budhasaf by Himself" were translated from Pehlevi into Arabic. The most complete extant text of the Arabic story

3. Hier. adv. Iov. I, 42. Cf. Dihle 1965, 38–41; Foucher 1949, 357: Traditur quod Buddam, principem dogmatis eorum, e latere suo virgo generârit.

was published in Bombay in 1888. This version was translated into Russian by Victor R. Rozen (1947) and published by Kračkovskij. Nothing is known of the Pehlevi versions mentioned above. Lang supposes that the Barlaam and Josaphat legend first developed in Central Asia among the Manichaeans. An Old Turkish fragment relates the encounter of Prince Siddhārtha with a sick man. As to the Indian sources of the legend, it has been pointed out that many of the parables are not of Buddhist origin but can be found in the *Pañcatantra* [61] and the *Mahābhārata*. It is quite possible that the Chinese translations of Buddhist texts contain episodes that have found their way into the legend. I hope that Japanese scholars will study the oldest accessible versions of the legend (the old Georgian version and the Arabic version) and compare them with the Buddhist texts in Chinese that have not been consulted by scholars in the past. (The Georgian version, in its turn, was translated into Greek about A.D. 1000. From Greek it was translated into Latin [A.D. 1048], and from Latin into many Western languages.)

The first contacts of the Western world with Buddhism in Asia took place in the thirteenth century, when Pope Innocent IV sent Franciscan and Dominican friars as envoys to the Mongol khan. The Italian Franciscan friar John of Pian di Carpino (d. 1252) left Lyons in 1245, the following year reached the Mongolian camp in Central Mongolia, and in 1247 returned to France and wrote the *Ystoria Mongalorum*. He speaks of the religion of the Kitai in Christian terms:

> Kytai autem, de quibus superius diximus, homines sunt pagani, qui habent litteram specialem; et habent Novum et Vetus Testamentum, ut dicitur, et habent Vitas Patrum, et heremitas, et domos quasi ecclesias factas, in quibus ipsi orant temporibus suis; et dicunt se quosdam sanctos habere. Unum Deum colunt, dominum Jesum Christum honorant, et credunt vitam aeternam, sed minime baptizantur; Scripturam nostram honorant et reverentur, christianos diligunt, et eleemosynas faciunt plures; homines benigni et humani satis esse videntur.
>
> (Wyngaert 1929, 57–58)

According to Henri de Lubac this passage refers to Chinese Buddhists and not to Nestorian Christians (H. de Lubac 1952, 35-6). Information about Buddhists is given by Willem van Ruysbroeck, a Flemish Franciscan friar, who spent six months in Karakorum in 1254. In his *Itinerarium* he describes Tibetan lamas rather accurately and even mentions the formula "Om mani padme hūm" ("Ou man haetavi" or "On man baccam," in Wyngaert 1929, 230). However, the most comprehensive account of Buddhism is to be found in Marco Polo's *Description of the*

World (*Divisament dou Monde*). Marco was in China from 1275 to 1291. Arriving in Sa-chau (Tun-huang), he meets Chinese Buddhists:

> It (Sa-chau) lies in a province called Tangut, whose inhabitants are all idolaters, except that there are some Turks who are Nestorian Christians and also some Saracens. The idolaters speak a language of their own. They do not live by trade, but on the profit of the grain which they harvest from the soil. They have many abbeys and monasteries, all full of idols of various forms [62] to which they make sacrifices and do great honour and reverence.
>
> (Latham, 1958, 54–55)

In his book Marco Polo mentions Tibetan Buddhists. However, it is in a chapter dealing with Ceylon that he gives a fairly accurate summary of the life of the Buddha. He mentions Adam's Peak: "The Saracens say that it is Adam's grave, but the idolaters call it the monument of Sakyamuni Burkhan (Sagamoni Borcan)." Marco Polo tells us that he was the son of a king; he mentions two of his encounters, one with a dead man and one with a very old man, and how he left the palace and "spent the rest of his days most virtuously and chastely and in great austerity." Marco Polo knows about the reincarnations of the Buddha: "And they said that he had died eighty-four times. For they say that when he died the first time he became an ox; then he died a second time and became a horse" (Latham 1958, 255–57).

While Marco Polo was returning from China, Pope Nicholas IV was sending Friar John of Monte Corvino (1247–1328) to the Mongols. He arrived in Khanbaliq (Peking) in 1294. He lived for many years in China, whence he sent two letters, the first dated 8 January 1305, the second 13 February 1306, in which he mentions the idolaters. John of Monte Corvino was appointed Archbishop of Khanbaliq in 1307 and died in 1328. In the same year the Franciscan friar Odoric de Pordenone (d. 1331) arrived in Peking. In 1330 he returned to Padua, where he dictated the story of his travels (*Relatio*). The last papal envoy was John Marignolli, who was sent to China in 1339 by Pope Benedict XII. He arrived in Khanbaliq in 1342, where he remained for three years. He returned in 1352 by way of Ceylon.[4]

The travels of the friars aroused much interest in Europe. The most popular work, which contains many legends in addition to information obtained from the writings of the friars, is John Mandeville's *Voyages*, written in 1365. About 300 manuscripts of this work are extant; it was

4. The texts of the writings of the papal envoys have been published by Wyngaert (1929). Translations of the most important are to be found in Dawson 1955. For further bibliographical references see de Rachewiltz 1971.

translated into most European [63] languages and printed 22 times between ca. 1470 and the end of the eighteenth century (see Letts 1953, 1949).

Henri de Lubac summarizes the knowledge that the Western world acquired during the thirteenth and fourteenth centuries, in the following words: "Quelques récits curieux, quelques détails extérieurs, quelques descriptions de la vie des bonzes et des lamas, c'était donc à peu près tout. La grande religion d'Orient n'apparaissait pas dans son individualité; elle n'était même pas nommée. De ses doctrines, autant dire qu'on ne savait rien" (1952, 47).

Vasco da Gama's voyage to India in 1497–98 inaugurated a new chapter in the history of the relations between the West and Asia. In the sixteenth century missionaries went out to China, Japan, Ceylon, Siam, and Indochina. In 1542 Francis Xavier (1506–52), a Spanish Jesuit, left for India. In the following year he arrived in Goa, which had been occupied by the Portuguese in 1510. In 1547 he met a Japanese merchant, named Yagiro, and brought him back to Goa. Yagiro explained to Xavier and other missionaries the history of "Xaca" (i.e., Śākya), his cult, and the life of the bonzes. Information obtained from Yagiro was sent to Europe in letters written by Xavier himself (22.6.1549), by Cosme de Torrès (25.1.1549), by the Jesuits of Goa, and by Father Nicolas Lancilotto (26.12.1548)(see Schurhammer and Wicki 1945, 151–53; Schurhammer 1932; and Postel 1552).

Xavier left Goa for Japan in 1549. He died three years later. It is not possible to study here in detail the work of missionaries in Japan and other Asian countries in the sixteenth, seventeenth, and eighteenth centuries. Henri de Lubac has given some information on the knowledge of Buddhism that they obtained in these countries. No detailed study has been made by Buddhist scholars of the many reports sent by missionaries and of the publications that are based upon these reports. Only a detailed investigation will reveal the extent to which the information contained in these publications is reliable. A study of this kind is made difficult, however, by the fact that many of these publications are found in only a very few libraries. Furthermore, many reports and letters have not yet been published and are kept [64] in manuscript form in libraries and collections. Very few have been critically edited, and those that have, have for the most part not been annotated by Orientalists. In these circumstances it is difficult to get a clear idea of the extent and the accuracy of the information on Buddhism that reached Europe in the sixteenth to eighteenth centuries. Missionaries came into contact with Theravāda Buddhism in Ceylon, Burma, Siam, and Indochina and with different forms of Mahāyāna Buddhism in China and Japan. Their knowledge was based upon what they observed, and on discussions with Buddhist priests, but very rarely on the study of the Buddhist literature itself. For these reasons it must have been very difficult to gain a clear notion of the main Buddhist teachings. A religion like Buddhism, which is based upon principles that are very different from the guiding principles of Christianity, cannot be understood without a thorough study of its scriptures.

There is perhaps only one important exception to the generalization that the missionaries were not well versed in Buddhist literature. Curiously enough, the most accurate information on Buddhism obtained in this period comes from a country that was more inaccessible than other Buddhist countries: Tibet. At the end of the sixteenth century Jesuit missionaries believed that Christians lived in Tibet (Toscano 1951, 19; Petech 1952–53, 1: xviii). The first missionary to enter Tibet was the Portuguese Jesuit Antonio d'Andrade (1580–1634), who in August 1624 arrived in Tsaparang (rTsa-braṅ), the capital of the kingdom of Guge. After his return to Agra he wrote a report of his voyage; this report is dated 8 November 1624. It was published in Lisbon in 1626, under the title *Novo Descobrimento do gram Cathayo ou Reinos de Tibet pello Padre Antonio de Andrade da Campanhia de Jesu, Portuguez, no anno de 1626.*[5] Translated into French in the following year, this report aroused great interest in Europe. However, the success of the mission in Tsaparang did not last long. In 1635 the last two missionaries were expelled. A new attempt to enter the country in 1640 led to the imprisonment of Manoel Marques. The last news from him reached India in 1641, and most probably he died in captivity. The efforts of the Jesuits to establish missions in other parts of Tibet had even less success. Estevão [65] Cacella and João Cabral travelled in 1627–28 via Bhutan to Shigatse (gŽis-kartse). Cacella arrived at Shigatse on 20 January 1628, and left there at the end of January. On 28 February 1630 he returned to Shigatse, where he died on 6 March. After a first stay in Shigatse in 1627–28, Cabral returned there in March 1631, but the same or following year he left again. Thirty years later, the Austrian Johann Grüber and the Belgian Albert d'Orville arrived in Lhasa from Peking. Their stay was of short duration (8 October to the end of November, 1661) but noteworthy, because it was due to these two Jesuits that the first information on Lhasa reached Europe (Kircher 1667; Wessels 1940).[6]

Of greater importance are the missions established in Lhasa by Italian Capuchins and Jesuits in the 18th century. The Capuchins remained in

5. There is an annotated translation in Toscano 1951, 47–76; the Portuguese text can be found in Esteves Pereira 1921.

6. On the Jesuit missionaries in Tibet and Central Asia see Wessels 1924.

Lhasa during the greater part of the first half of the eighteenth century (1707–11; 1716–33; 1741–45). Only one of them acquired a good knowledge of the Tibetan language: Francesco Orazio della Penna (1680–1745), who from 1717 to 1721 applied himself with great energy to the study of Tibetan. Della Penna, who lived in Lhasa from 1716 to 1732, compiled a great Tibetan dictionary (of about 35,000 words) that was later translated into English by F. C. G. Schroeter: *A Dictionary of the Bhotanta or Boutan Lan-guage* (1826). Della Penna also translated several Tibetan works, among which must be mentioned Tsoṅ-kha-pa's *Lam-rim chen-mo* and the *Prātimokṣasūtra.* These translations have not been preserved, but Della Penna's chronological summary of Tibetan history was published by Antonio Giorgi in his *Alphabetum Tibetanum Missionum Apostolicarum commodo editum* (1762). Giorgi's work also contains other material based upon the writings of Della Penna.[7]

On 24 September 1714, two Jesuit priests, Ippolito Desideri (20.12. 1687–14.4.1733) and Manuel Freyre, left Delhi for Lhasa. On 26 June 1715 they [66] arrived in Leh, the capital of Ladakh, and the following year, on 18 March, they finally arrived in Lhasa. Freyre returned to India, but Desideri remained in Lhasa until 28 March 1721. During the five years of his stay in Lhasa, Desideri studied in Tibetan monasteries and acquired an excellent knowledge of the Tibetan language and the Tibetan religion. He made excerpts of many Tibetan works, first of all of the *Lam-rim chen-mo.* He left India in 1729 and, during his return journey, began writing an account of his travels and of Tibetan customs and religion. The manuscript remained unpublished until 1904, when extracts were published by Carlo Puini, who had discovered the manuscript in 1875. An incomplete English version was published in 1931 by Filippo de Filippi: *An Account of Tibet; The Travels of Ippolito Desideri of Pistoia, S.J., 1712–1727.* A complete and beautifully annotated edition of the original Italian version was published later by Luciano Petech (1954–56). In this edition, the account consists of four books. The third book (Petech 1954–56, 6: 115–309) is devoted entirely to a description of Tibetan religion. Petech characterized it thus: "A stupendous description of the lamaist religion, penetratingly and profoundly understood in its essential nature as few European scholars have been able to do in the two centuries that have followed." And Giuseppe Tucci remarked: "The work of Desideri was ahead of his time: the secrets of the speculations of Mahāyāna Buddhism that began to be revealed by Orientalist erudition in the last years of the last century are already clear in the logical scholastic architecture of his *Relazione*"

7. A definitive edition of all documents relating to the Capuchin mission in Tibet has been published by Luciano Petech (1952–53).

(see Petech 1954–56, 5: xxvi–xxvii). An English version of the complete text of the *Relazione* and of the precious notes by Luciano Petech is an urgent desideratum.

It is only in the nineteenth century that the Indian sources of Buddhism in Pāli and Sanskrit began to be studied. The first Pāli grammar to be published in Europe was written by E. Burnouf and C. Lassen: *Essai sur le Pali, ou langue sacrée de la presqu'île au-delà du Gange* (1826). In the first chapter Burnouf sketches the history of Pāli studies up to 1826. According to him the first to mention Pāli was Simon de La Loubère, who visited Siam in 1687–88 as envoy of King [67] Louis XIV. In 1691 he published a *Description du royaume de Siam* (see Windisch 1917–20, 125; de Lubac 1952, 99). La Loubère's book contains a translation of the life of Devadatta (La vie de Thevetat, le frère de Sommona-Lobom, traduite du Bali, 2: 1–6) and an abstract of the *Pātimokkha* (2: 35–57). He also drew attention to the similarity of the names of the days of the week in Pāli and Sanskrit (2: 75). Burnouf adds: "Dans l'état d'imperfection où se trouvaient ces études, il y avait quelque mérite à faire ces rapprochements que Chambers a reproduits depuis." Nevertheless, Burnouf gives the honour of having discovered the connection between Sanskrit and Pāli not to William Chambers but to Paulinus a Sancto Bartholomaeo, an Austrian, whose civil name was J. P. Wesdin (1748–1806)(Windisch 1917–20, 20–22, 203; de Lubac 1952, 109 and 11). In 1793 he published a catalogue of the manuscripts of the Museum of Velletri: *Musei Borgiani Velitris codices manuscripti Avenses, Peguani, Siamici, Malabarici, Indostani,* in which he remarked that Pāli is "a dialect or a daughter of Sanskrit, the most ancient language of India" (quoting Bechert 1970, 1). According to Burnouf, Chambers repeated this in his article "Some Account of the Sculptures and Ruins at Mavalipuram" (1788); this article is dated 17 June 1784. It is of course impossible for Chambers to have repeated in a work published earlier, a remark published in a later work. Just the opposite was true. In his *Systema brahmanicum* (published in 1791, and not in 1792 as stated in Windisch 1917–20, 21), Paulinus refers expressly to Chambers: "D. Chambers in libro *Asiatick Researches tom.* I, *pag.* 160 & seq., ubi defendit linguam Balicam seu Pali vel Bali, qua liber Kammuva scriptus est, a Samscrdamica descendere, aut saltem unam cum altera intimam affinitatem habere, allatis etiam multis exemplis, quae ibi vide" (Paulinus 1791, 117). Chambers discovered Sanskrit elements in Tamil and concluded that: "*Shanscrit* [was] common to both that [i.e., Tamil (Tamulic in his spelling)] and the *Balic.*" Chambers observed that the "*Shanscrit* word *Mâha,* which signifies *great,* is constantly used in the *Balic* language in the same sense. And the names of the days are most of them the same in *Shanscrit* and in *Balic.*"

Apart from the texts translated by La Loubère, the first Pāli text to become [68] known in Europe was the *Kammavācā.* In his *Systema brahmanicum* Paulinus quoted an Italian translation in the Library of the Propagation of the Faith made from the Pāli original in 1776.[8] Another translation was described by Paulinus two years later in the catalogue already mentioned (1793).[9] According to him this text is accompanied by a commentary. It is not clear whether the commentary accompanying the text was based upon a Pāli text or on oral explanations.[10] Paulinus quotes several passages from the Peguanus codex (Burmese manuscript) of the *Kammuva* and adds explanations that were given by an "erudite interpreter" (eruditus interpres). The explanations, quoted by Paulinus, are obviously added to the translation by the Italian translator. Only an examination of the manuscript, which has been in the Library of the Vatican since 1902, will be able to show whether or not the explanations are due to the translator.[11] Perhaps it will also be possible to discover whether the Italian translator has used a Pāli text or whether his translation is based upon a Burmese version of the original. Another translation was made in Burma by Father Vincente Sangermano (1758–1819) (see Windisch, 1917–20, 17). His translation was published in English (1799) by Francis Buchanan, who received from a Captain Symes three Latin translations made by Sangermano: 1. a cosmography, extracted from various Burmese writings (pp. 167–256); 2. a summary of the religion of Godama written by a late Tarado or king's confessor (pp. 265–73); [69] 3. the book of ordinations (pp. 280–89). Burnouf says that these three treatises were based upon Pāli books, but from Buchanan's description it seems obvious that, most probably, the second and also the first were written in Burmese. It is not clear whether Sangermano translated the *Kammavācā* from the Pāli or from a Burmese version. Buchanan himself did not know Pāli or Burmese, but his long article is not only useful for the information it presents for the first time, but also for some perspicacious comments by Buchanan. For instance, he states categorically that Nirvāṇa is not annihilation: "Annihilation . . . is a very inaccurate term.

8. According to Burnouf the manuscript also contains the Pāli text. Cf. Feer 1899, 115.

9. "Kammuva, o sia Trattato dell'ordinazione dei Talapoini del secondo ordine, detti *Pinzen,* 30 pp." (Paulinus 1793, no. 6, 84).

10. "*Kammuva, o sia trattato della ordinazione dei Talapoini in carattere Pali o Bali sopra ole dorate.* Traduzione fatta per commissione di Monsignor Stefano Borgia segret. di Propag. nel 1776" (Paulinus 1791, 114, n. 2). According to Burnouf the explanations quoted by Paulinus (1791, 115: Innanzi a tutto, etc.) are to be found in the manuscript in the library of Velletri, but in his *Systema* Paulinus seems to refer only to the manuscript in the library of the Propagation of the Faith.

11. See the remarks on the commentary by Buchanan (1799, 280) and by Spiegel (1841, xi). I have not been able to consult Paulinus's catalogue, p. 84, to which Buchanan refers.

Nieban implies the being exempted from all the miseries incident to humanity, but by no means annihilation" (p. 180). Amusing is a remark by a Siamese painter on Devadatta: "Devadat, or as he pronounced it, Tevedat, was the god of the *Pye-gye*, or of *Britain*; and . . . it is he who, by opposing the good intentions of Godama, produces all the evil in the world" (p. 268). The translation by Sangermano and Buchanan of the *Kammavācā* was of use to Burnouf and Lassen, who were able to compare it with a Pāli manuscript in the Royal Library in Paris. The first reliable translation of the Pāli *Kammavācā* is one in English by a Wesleyan missionary in Ceylon, Benjamin Clough (1834). The Paris manuscript was used by Friedrich von Spiegel, who published the *Upasaṃpadā-Kammavācā* in Devanāgarī together with a Latin translation and notes: *Kammavākyaṃ: Liber de officiis sacerdotum buddhicorum* (1841). Three years later Otto von Böhtlingk published the *Kaṭhina-Kammavācā* (1844) and the next year Spiegel published three other *Kammavācā*s in his *Anecdota Pâlica* (1845, 68–71).

In the year following the publication of the *Essai sur le Pali*, Burnouf published a small brochure of 30 pages, entitled *Observations grammaticales sur quelques passages de l'essai sur le Pali de MM. E. Burnouf et Ch. Lassen* (1827), in which he quotes the *Mahāvaṃsa* and the Pāli dictionary *Abhidhānappadīpikā*. Burnouf continued his Pāli studies until his death. He collected a large amount of material for a grammar and a dictionary that have yet to be published. He planned to study in detail the canonical Pāli texts in the second volume of his *Introduction à l'histoire du Buddhisme* [70] *indien* (1844), but his untimely death prevented him from carrying out his plan. The twenty-first appendix of his translation of the *Lotus Sūtra*, which was published in October 1852, is entitled: "Comparaison de quelques textes sanscrits et pâlis" (1852, 859–67). Burnouf was able to complete only the first pages of this essay when, in the first days of March, illness forced him to abandon his work. He died only a few weeks later, on 28 May 1852. Burnouf had made a careful study of a manuscript of the *Dīghanikāya*. The appendices of his translation of the *Lotus Sūtra* contain a complete translation of the *Samaññaphala* and *Mahānidāna* Suttas (1852, 449–82, 534–44) and a translation of the beginning of the *Tevijja Sutta* (490–94).

When Burnouf and Lassen wrote their *Essai sur le Pali*, they did not know that a Pāli grammar had already been published. In 1824 Benjamin Clough, the Wesleyan missionary, published in Colombo *A Compendious Pali Grammar, with a Copious Vocabulary in the Same Language*. This work was first undertaken by W. Tolfrey. Clough's book consists of three parts: a grammar based on the Pāli grammar *Bālāvatāra*; a collection of roots based on the *Dhātumañjūsā*; and a vocabulary based on the *Abhi-*

dhānappadīpikā. The work seems to have reached Europe only after a long delay. On 11 January 1832 A. W. von Schlegel wrote to Lassen that, according to Brockhaus, only two copies had arrived in Europe (Kirfel 1914, 217).

Important work on Pāli was also done in Ceylon by George Turnour, who entered the Civil Service of Ceylon in 1818. In 1837 he published the text and translation of the first 38 chapters of the *Mahāvaṃsa* (1837). At the same time he contributed a series of important articles to the *Journal of the Asiatic Society of Bengal* (Turnour 1836, 1837–38). In the same period another Wesleyan missionary, D. J. Gogerly, began to publish articles on Pāli literature; his collected writings were published in two volumes in Colombo (Bishop 1908). They contain many translations of Pāli texts, for instance, a translation of the *Pātimokkha,* which was first published in 1839 in the *Ceylon Friend* (reprinted in 1862 in *JRAS* 19). [71]

In 1821 the Danish linguist Rasmus Kristian Rask visited Ceylon and collected many Pāli and Sinhalese manuscripts. Rask studied Pāli and Sinhalese there with the assistance of B. Clough. He also wrote a Pāli grammar that was largely based upon the *Bālāvatāra,* but this was never published. His manuscript collection made Copenhagen one of the most important centres of Pāli studies in Europe. The Pāli manuscripts were described by Niels L. Westergaard in collaboration with Friedrich von Spiegel in the catalogue of the Indian manuscripts of the Royal Library: *Codices indici Bibliothecae Regiae Havniensis* (1846). From 1859 till 1865 the French consul in Ceylon, Paul Grimblot, collected a large number of Pāli manuscripts; these have been described by J. Barthélemy-Saint-Hilaire (1866). Grimblot planned the publication of many texts in a Bibliotheca Pālica, but death prevented him from carrying out his plans. Léon Feer published his *Extraits du Paritta* in 1871 (Grimblot 1871). The first scholar to make good use of the manuscripts collected by Grimblot was I. P. Minaev, who published the text of the *Pātimokkha* with a translation and many extracts from Buddhaghosa's *Samantapāsādikā,* the *Kaṅkhāvitaraṇī,* etc. (1869). He published a Pāli grammar that was translated into French and English (1872, 1874, 1883).[12] Spiegel was the first to publish Pāli texts from the Copenhagen collection in his *Anecdota Pâlica* (1845), which contains the first four stories of the first *vagga* of the *Rasavāhinī* and the *Uragasutta* from the *Suttanipāta.* In 1855 Viggo Fausbøll published the *Dhammapada* with a Latin translation and extracts from the *Dhammapadaṭṭhakathā.* Albrecht Weber translated the *Dhammapada* into German (1860). Both Fausbøll and Weber also published some *jātaka*s from the

12. On Minaev see Alexandra Schneider, "Professor J. P. Minayeff," *Indian Historical Quarterly* 10 (1934): 811–26; and *Ivan Pavlovič Minaev. Sbornik statej* (Moscow, 1967).

jātaka collection (Fausbøll 1861, 1871a, b, 1872; Fausbøll and Weber 1862; Weber 1858). Of other texts published before 1877 [72] mention must be made of R. C. Childers's editions of the *Khuddakapāṭha* (1870) and the *Mahāparinibbāna Sutta* (1875–76), and Senart's edition and translation of Kaccāyana's grammar (1871). Book 6 of this grammar had already been translated (1863) by the Sinhalese scholar James D'Alwis.[13]

As mentioned before, Burnouf's Pāli dictionary was never published. In 1845 Spiegel announced a compilation of a Pāli dictionary on which he continued working for many years up to 1865. Bechert has given some information about the manuscript of Spiegel's dictionary, which he received from a great-grandson (1970, 2). Pāli scholars had to wait till 1875 to see the first Pāli dictionary published in Europe: *A Dictionary of the Pāli Language* by R. C. Childers. With the publication of Childers's dictionary and Minaev's grammar, and thanks to the presence of good collections of Pāli manuscripts in European libraries, the conditions were created for fruitful work in Pāli philology. From 1877 onwards Pāli texts began to be published and translated in great number, as we shall see in the next chapter.

In 1837 the Société Asiatique received from Brian Houghton Hodgson in Kathmandu 88 manuscripts of Sanskrit Buddhist texts. Immediately Burnouf began reading the manuscripts. On 5 June 1837 he wrote to Hodgson that from 25 April he had devoted all his spare moments to reading the *Saddharmapuṇḍarīka* (Feer 1899, 158). Burnouf's translation of this text was completed in 1839 (Feer 1899, 169). It was printed in 1841 but did not appear until after his death in 1852.

Burnouf translated many Buddhist Sanskrit texts. His translations from the *Divyāvadāna*, the *Avadānaśataka*, and other texts were published in his *Introduction à l'histoire du Buddhisme indien* (1844), but many others were never pub-[73]lished. Among his posthumous papers are an almost complete translation of the *Aṣṭasāhasrikā Prajñāpāramitā* and translations of the *Kāraṇḍavyūha* (which took him only ten days to complete) and the *Sumāghāvadāna* (Feer 1899, 63 and 65). Burnouf carefully read many other texts, even such difficult and voluminous texts as the *Mahāvastu* and the *Abhidharmakośavyākhyā*. The amount of work done by Burnouf in the last fifteen years of his life is staggering. Not only did he study many Sanskrit Buddhist manuscripts, but he also continued his studies of Avestan and Pehlevi texts as well as his translation of the *Bhāgavata Purāṇa*. In connection with his Pāli studies he undertook the study of Sinhalese, Burmese, and Siamese translations and commentaries. Moreover, he did not neglect modern Indo-Aryan languages such as Bengali, Marathi, and

13. For more on D'Alwis, see Seneviratne 1939.

Gujarati. For most of these languages he had to compile his own dictionary. All this was done without neglecting his duties as professor at the Collège de France, and when he was often in poor health.

Burnouf stressed the fact that Indian Buddhism had to be studied on the basis of the Sanskrit texts from Nepal and the Pāli texts from Ceylon (1844, 12). According to him it would be possible to find the fundamental and ancient elements of Buddhism in that which was common to both the Sanskrit and the Pāli texts (p. 31). Burnouf was well aware of the fundamental importance of the study of the texts for the history of Buddhism (p. 123). His ideas with regard to India at the time of the Buddha, the doctrine of the Buddha and its later development, the relation of Buddhism to castes, etc.—all of which he develops in the *Introduction*—are based on a careful study of the texts. It is only because of the progress in the study of Buddhist literature that some conclusions he arrived at have had to be modified. However, even after 150 years, his *Introduction* and his translation of the *Saddharmapuṇḍarīka* are works that one can never read without learning something. A detailed survey of the contents of these two works can be found in Windisch 1917–20 (131–39).

Burnouf appreciated the importance of Tibetan translations for the study [74] of Sanskrit Buddhist texts. When he began to study these texts in 1837, Buddhism had already been studied by scholars among the Kalmyks, who lived between the Volga and the Don. Benjamin Bergmann translated several Kalmyk texts and noted his observations of Kalmyk customs. His *Nomadische Streifereien unter den Kalmüken in den Jahren 1802 und 1803* (1804–5)[14] is still an important source for the study of the Kalmyks and Lamaism in general. Bergmann realized that, in order to understand Lamaism, it would be necessary to study the Mongolian literary language and Tibetan. This program was executed by Isaak Jakob Schmidt, who lived among the Kalmyks during the years 1804–1806. Schmidt became the founder of Mongolian and Tibetan studies in Russia (Babinger 1920). In four long articles, published from 1832 to 1837 in *Mémoires de l'Académie*, he studied Tibetan sources of Mahāyāna Buddhism (Schmidt 1832, 1834a, b, 1837). In the last of these four articles he translated the *Vajracchedikā Prajñāpāramitā* from the Tibetan version. At roughly the same time Alexander Csoma de Körös published an analysis of the Kanjur and an abstract of the contents of the Tanjur (1836–39). The Tibetan version of the *Lalitavistara* was studied by Philippe Édouard Foucaux, who published the Tibetan text and a French translation (1847–48). Schmidt published the Tibetan text and a German translation of the "Sage and the Fool," a collection of tales told in the Hu language in

14. See *IIJ* 14 (1972): 265–67.

Khotan shortly before 445 (1843).[15] Franz Anton von Schiefner trans-[75]lated many stories from the Tibetan version of the *Mūlasarvāstivāda-vinaya* and published the Tibetan text and a German translation of Tāranātha's *History of Buddhism in India* (1868, 1869, 1882). Also based on Tibetan sources is V. P. Vasil'ev's work on Buddhism, which was published in Russian in 1857 and in German and French translations in 1860 and 1865.[16]

Of great importance for the study of Indian Buddhism is the work done by Sinologists. Abel Rémusat, who in 1815 became the first professor of Chinese at the Collège de France, translated Fa-hsien's *Fo-kuo-chi*. It was published after his death by Klaproth and Landresse (Rémusat 1836). His successor, Stanislas Julien, translated the life of Hsüan-tsang and his *Hsi-yü-chi* (1853, 1857–58).

I mentioned the study of Buddhism among the Kalmyks by Bergmann and Schmidt. Buddhism in the Theravāda countries also became better known through the Wesleyan missionary R. Spence Hardy, who published several works based on Sinhalese sources (1850, 1853, 1866). In Burma the Roman Catholic bishop P. Bigandet studied Burmese sources on the life of the Buddha (1858), and in Siam Henry Alabaster translated several Siamese texts (1871).

In the period 1800 to 1877 knowledge of Buddhism greatly increased in the West. Very few Pāli texts were published during this period, but the publication of a grammar and a dictionary and the presence of collections of [76] manuscripts in several centres of Oriental studies would make intensive work possible in the following period. Burnouf laid solid foundations for the study of Sanskrit Buddhist texts. Important work was done on the Tibetan sources in this period, but this area would be left relatively neglected in the coming decades. Finally, Abel Rémusat and Stanislas Julien made known important texts for the history of Buddhism in India, but in this area, too, progress was less conspicuous.

15. For some bibliographical notes see de Jong 1968, 23, n. 39 and Takahashi 1970.

16. On Vasil'ev see Z. I. Gorbačeva, N. A. Petrov, G. F. Smykalov, and B. I. Pankratov, "Russkij Kitaeved Akademik Vasilij Pavlovič Vasil'ev (1818–1900)," *Očerki po istorii russkogo vostokovedenija*, vol. 2 (Moscow, 1956), 232–340.

CHAPTER TWO

The Middle Period (1877–1942)

It is of course not possible to make a sharp distinction between the early period of Buddhist studies up to 1877 and the following one, but 1877 can be taken as the point of departure for a new era in Buddhist studies for several reasons. [77] First of all, from 1877 many Pāli texts were edited. Secondly, Buddhist Sanskrit texts began to be published in increasing number from 1881 onwards. Perhaps most important is the fact that significant works on Indian Buddhism began to appear in the next few years, most of them written by scholars who were to contribute much to Buddhist studies in the decades that followed.

In 1877 Fausbøll published the first volume of the *jātaka* book. The seventh volume, containing Andersen's index, appeared in 1897. Oldenberg's edition of the Vinayapiṭaka appeared from 1879 to 1883. In 1881 T. W. Rhys Davids founded the Pali Text Society. With the exception of the texts mentioned above, almost all Pāli texts published in Europe after that date have been published by the Pali Text Society. Already in the 1880s a beginning was made with the publication of all five Nikāya. In 1882 the first volume of the *Journal of the Pali Text Society* was published. By 1930 all five Nikāya were published and publication of the *Aṭṭhakathās* had begun. As far as the non-canonical Pāli texts are concerned, mention must be made of Oldenberg's edition of the *Dīpavaṃsa* in 1879, and of Trenckner's edition of the *Milindapañha* in 1880. At the same time many Pāli texts were translated, beginning with the *Pātimokkha,* the *Mahāvagga,* and the *Cullavagga,* which were translated jointly by Rhys Davids and Oldenberg (1881–85). In 1899 Rhys Davids published the first volume of his translation of the *Dīghanikāya* (1899). By 1894 he had already completed his translation of the *Milindapañha* (1890–94).

After Burnouf's death in 1852, little work had been done in the field of Sanskrit Buddhist literature. The only important text published between 1852 and 1880 was the *Lalitavistara,* of which Rajendralal Mitra published a very unsatisfactory edition (1853–77). The last fascicle of this edition appeared in 1877. In 1882 Émile Senart published the first volume of his edition of the *Mahāvastu* (1882–97), still one of the most important works in the field of Buddhist studies. In 1881 Max Müller published the Sanskrit text of one of the most famous texts of Mahāyāna Buddhism, the *Vajracchedikā.* Two years later he published the texts of the *Smaller* and *Larger Sukhāvatīvyūha* (1883), the sacred texts of the Pure Land School in China and Japan. The *Divyāvadāna,* already well known through Burnouf's translations in his *Introduction,* was carefully edited by E. B. [78] Cowell and R. A. Neil in 1886. Five years later, in 1891, Hendrik Kern published the *Jātakamālā* as the first volume of the Harvard Oriental Series. In 1888 Sarat Chandra Das and Hari Mohan Vidyabhusan began the publication of Kṣemendra's *Avadānakalpalatā* (1888–1918). In 1890 Minaev published Śāntideva's *Bodhicaryāvatāra.* Louis de La Vallée Poussin published the ninth chapter of Prajñākaramati's commentary (1898, 233–388) and later the complete text (1901–14). In 1893 Cowell published the *Buddhacarita.* The first volume of a new edition of the *Lalitavistara* by S. Lefmann was printed in 1882 but did not appear until 1902 (Lefmann 1908, v).

This enumeration of the Pāli and Sanskrit texts published in this period shows how active scholars were at that time in editing Buddhist texts. During the same period great efforts were made in the interpretation of the Buddhist texts. The problems discussed in the works of the leading scholars are of basic importance; it is therefore necessary to dwell upon their work in some detail. Senart's *Essai sur la légende du Buddha* appeared from 1873 to 1875 in *Journal Asiatique,* but the second edition, which dates from 1882, deserves our special attention because it contains a revised version of the introduction and the conclusions in which the author carefully explains his method and the results obtained by it. Senart explains that the stories relating to the Buddha contain both legendary and realistic elements. Earlier scholars had considered the legendary elements as an addition to a basis of historical facts; once freed from these legendary elements, the historical truth about the Buddha would become clear. It was usual to apply this method—called the subtraction method by La Vallée Poussin—before Senart's time and also after him. It was the same method of historical criticism that was developed by New Testament scholars for studying the life of Jesus.

Senart, however, believed that the legendary, or rather the mythological, elements form a coherent system that existed even before the time of the Buddha. It is not surprising to see that Senart made great use of the *Lalitavistara.* He was unable to go back to the canonical Pāli texts, which were not yet published [79] at that time, so he relied upon such texts as the *Nidānakathā* and the *Buddhavaṃsa* and its commentary. Senart studied in detail the conception of the *cakravartin* and his seven *ratna* and that of the Mahāpuruṣa and his marks. In this way he interpreted the Buddha as the solar hero, the Mahāpuruṣa, the Cakravartin. Before his birth Buddha is the supreme god. He descends from heaven as a luminous god. His mother, Māyā, represents the sovereign creative power and is at the same time the goddess of the atmospheric mist. She dies but survives as Prajāpatī, creating and nourishing the universe and its god.

In this way Senart explains all twelve episodes of Buddha's life. He characterizes his method as historical mythology, as distinct from comparative mythology. The latter method was very popular in the nineteenth century and tended to assimilate gods and mythological figures to naturalistic phenomena, such as the sun, the clouds, lightning, etc. It will be sufficient to refer the reader to Adalbert Kuhn (1859) and Max Müller (1856, 1861–64). Senart's merit consists in the fact that, though influenced by the naturalistic mythology of his time, he tried to explain the myth of the Buddha as a product of India and its religious concepts.

In this regard his attitude is in marked contrast to that of Kern in his book on the history of Buddhism in India, which was first published in two volumes in Dutch (1882, 1884a). A German edition appeared the same years, translated from Dutch by Hermann Jacobi (Kern 1882–84). Almost twenty years later a French translation was published (Kern 1901–3). In the first volume Kern began by relating the life of the Buddha according to Pāli and Sanskrit sources—or according to Southern and Northern sources, as scholars of the time used to say. His main sources were the same as those used by Senart: the *Nidānakathā* and the *Lalitavistara* (cf. Kern 1882, 18, n. 2). After having retold the legend of the Buddha in great detail, Kern arrived at his interpretation. Like Senart, he considered the Buddha to be a solar god. However, Kern was much more astronomical in his exegesis than Senart. The twelve *nidāna* are the twelve months of the year. The six heretical teachers are the planets. The Buddha's first preaching takes place in midsummer, and this is why the Middle Way is its theme. Kern never hesitates in his identifications with stars, planets, and constellations.

Senart's system of [80] interpretation was based upon a careful examination of the Vedic and Brahmanical literature, but one finds nothing similar in Kern's book. The astonishing thing is that his categorical statements have managed to convince even such a sober-minded and cautious scholar as Auguste Barth, who was willing to consider the courtesans as mother-goddesses, the six heretical teachers as the six planets, and the rebellion of Devadatta as the struggle of the moon with the sun (1914–27, 1: 335). Barth, however, believed that the legend of the Buddha contains historical elements that had been handed down since the time of the Buddha.

Even Senart was willing to admit that historical elements had been connected secondarily with the mythical biography of the Buddha (Senart 1882, 442–44), but for him the mythical and historical elements belonged to two entirely different traditions. Senart conceded that the Pāli sources were less miraculous than the *Lalitavistara,* but according to him this does not guarantee their greater authenticity. On the contrary, this is due to the fact that they have been rewritten and simplified. Nevertheless, the mythical elements that have been preserved in the Pāli tradition show that there is no fundamental difference between the Pāli tradition and the Sanskrit sources.

Thus Kern entirely dissolved the historical Buddha into the solar god. Senart and Barth, on the other hand, did admit the possibility that reliable information had been handed down concerning the life of the Buddha, but neither of them attempted to collect these data. T. W. Rhys Davids, who in 1877 published his *Buddhism, being a sketch of the life and teachings of Gautama the Buddha* (I quote from the 14th edition, published in 1890), believed that the Pāli texts were much more reliable and complete than the Sanskrit works. He considered those statements on which both language sources agreed, as very reliable. According to him it was possible to discover the historical basis of the legend of the Buddha. On the basis of the Pāli sources Rhys Davids went on to sketch the life of Gautama. In a chapter on the legend of the Buddha he refers to Senart's theory, which he accepts "to a certain modified extent" (p. 190). He believes that "the later forms of each episode (of Buddha's life) differ chiefly from the former in the way in which they further exaggerate the details of the stories so as to make them more consistent with the imperial wealth and power ascribed to Gautama or his father by the Chakrawarti parallel; or with the belief in Gautama's omniscience and omnipotence" (p. 194). [81]

Senart's theory was rejected by Hermann Oldenberg in his *Buddha: Sein Leben, seine Lehre, seine Gemeinde,* which appeared in 1881. I quote from the second edition (1890), which refers to the second edition of Senart's *Essai sur la légende* (1882). In the chapter entitled "The character of the tradition: Legend and myth," Oldenberg defends the reliability of the canonical Pāli texts. According to him the great majority of the sacred texts were compiled before the council at Vesālī about 380 B.C. These texts were transmitted in Ceylon without undergoing the same profound changes to which the texts of other schools were subjected. Oldenberg points out that the Pāli texts used by Senart, such as the *Nidānakathā* and the *Buddhavaṃsa,* are much younger than the canonical texts. He is firmly convinced of the fact that the canonical texts contain a series of positive facts that inform us about the life of the Buddha. Oldenberg is without doubt justified in pointing out that Senart has based his theory on younger texts. However, it is difficult to accept that the Pāli Vinayapiṭaka and Suttapiṭaka are a reliable source for Buddhism during the first century after Buddha's Parinirvāṇa. Already in 1879 in the introduction to his edition of the *Mahāvagga* (1879–83, vol. 1), Oldenberg defended the historicity of the Council at Vesālī and the antiquity of the Vinaya. On this point he never changed his opinion, as one can see from a note, published in 1912, in which he declares that the essential parts of the Vinayapiṭaka and Suttapiṭaka were compiled before the Council at Vesālī (Oldenberg 1912a, 203, n. 5 [= 1967, 1021, n. 5]).

Oldenberg did not deny that the traditions concerning the Buddha contain legendary elements that go back to Vedic times or even further back and that are connected with popular ideas relating to the solar hero, the luminous example of all earthly heroes (1890 ed., 89). However, when Oldenberg related the life of the Buddha, he did not elaborate on this aspect of the legend of the Buddha. No scholar has accepted Senart's theories in their entirety, but it is interesting to see that even such eminent representatives of what came to be called the Pāli school as Rhys Davids and Oldenberg did not maintain that Senart was completely wrong. Kern's extreme view, which went so far as to deny the existence of the historical Buddha altogether, has not found any followers, but Senart's [82] theory has continued to exercise a fascination on later scholars, even though most of them followed in Oldenberg's footsteps. It has become customary to oppose Senart's mythological method to Oldenberg's rationalistic and euhemeristic method. Foucher, the author of a work on the Buddha, declares that in Senart's Buddha the human being is absent, but in the one described by Oldenberg, the god (1949, 13). This formula, first used by Barth (1914–27, 1: 344; Barth was not referring to Senart's work but to Kern's *History of Buddhism*), has often been repeated. Without doubt it underlines a very important aspect of the methods applied by Senart and Oldenberg, and it would be possible, by placing Senart (or Kern) at one end of the spectrum and Oldenberg at the other, to determine the exact place that later scholars occupy in relation to Senart or Oldenberg. Some are closer to Senart, some are closer to Oldenberg or even go beyond him. However, one aspect of the work by Senart and Oldenberg is not covered by the above-mentioned formula. Senart did not hesitate to make use of texts of much later date because he felt it was possible to reconstruct the legend of the Buddha as a system whose separate parts were indissolubly connected. To use modern terminology, Senart's approach was structuralistic, as against Oldenberg's atomistic method, which consisted in collecting bits of historical information from the oldest accessible sources. By denying Senart the right to make use of some texts of later date, by accepting only a portion of his conclusions, one does not take into account an essential aspect of Senart's method. The important point in Senart's work is the fact that he based his position upon the conceptions that the Indians had of the Buddha. Their reality is not the historical reality as conceived by nineteenth-century scholars.

Oldenberg's merit consists less in his rejection of Senart's methodological views than in his attempt to distinguish earlier and later sources. Oldenberg did important work in studying Buddhist texts from the aspect of their style. Already in his *Buddha* he draws attention to some stylistic features that prove the later date of the *Buddhavaṃsa* (1890 ed., 77, n. 1). In 1882 he distinguished earlier and later strata in the *Lalitavistara* (1882). He con-[83]tinued this line of research in his "Buddhistische Studien" (1898). Famous is his distinction between a nominal style A and a hieratic, canonical style B in Buddhist Sanskrit texts such as the *Mahāvastu,* the *Divyāvadāna,* the *Avadānaśataka,* etc. (1912 a, b). Style B closely resembles the style of canonical Pāli texts and is older than style A. Oldenberg was the first scholar to have undertaken the task that Burnouf was unable to accomplish: the comparison of Pāli and Sanskrit texts for the sake of establishing the older and common elements in both. Notable work was also done in this area by Ernst Windisch in his studies on Māra and Buddha, the birth of the Buddha, and the composition of the *Mahāvastu* (1895, 1908, 1909). Oldenberg was the first to take into account the Sanskrit fragments discovered in Central Asia at the beginning of the twentieth century. As we shall see later on, the publication of Sanskrit fragments and their comparison with parallel texts in Pāli, Chinese, and Tibetan made great progress after the mid-1930s.

Oldenberg's reliance on the Pāli texts was connected with his belief in the historicity of the Council at Vesālī and in the compilation of Buddhist texts before this Council. His examination of the traditions concerning the two first councils at Rājagṛha and Vaiśālī in the introduction to his edition of the *Mahāvagga* in 1879 stimulated, in subsequent years, an animated discussion on the Councils. A good summary of the different points of view and of the literature up to 1911 is found in L. de La Vallée Poussin's article in the *Encyclopaedia of Religion and Ethics* (1911). The inconclusiveness of the debate shows the difficulties in obtaining reliable information from the conflicting Buddhist traditions. La Vallée Poussin, who earlier published a long article on the Councils (1905a), declared that without a study of the Chinese sources no definite conclusions could be reached. However, even the transla-[84]tion and study of the Chinese sources by Jean Przyluski (1926–28) and by Marcel Hofinger (1946) did not put an end to the debate, as can be seen from subsequent studies.[1]

The introduction of Oldenberg's *Buddha* (1890 ed.) contains a chapter entitled "Indian Pantheism and Pessimism before Buddha," in which he studies the relations between Brahmanism and Buddhism. Oldenberg discovered in the older Upaniṣads ideas that are closely related to Buddhist ideas. Quoting BAU 4. 4.12: ātmānaṃ ced vijānīyāt ayam asmīti puruṣaḥ, kim icchan kasya kāmāya śarīram anusaṃjvaret (If a man should well understand the Self, saying "I am It"—seeking after what, for desire of what, should he crave after the body? [Edgerton 1965, 163]), Oldenberg pointed to the similarity to Buddhist ideas about desire, nescience, and the abolition of suffering through knowledge (1890 ed., 53). Special attention was paid by Oldenberg to the *Kāṭhaka-Upaniṣad,* in which text (pre-Buddhist according to him) the Buddhist Satan Māra figures in the form of *mṛtyu* "Death." Oldenberg believed that the Buddhists had probably not known the brahmanical texts; still, he did not hesitate to state that Buddhism had inherited from Brahmanism not only many of its important dogmas but also the general tone of religious thought and sentiments (p. 54). Since 1881 much has been written on the relations between the *Upaniṣads* and Buddhism, but without clear results. In 1925, in a preface to a new edition of his *Bouddhisme,* which was first published in 1909, La Vallée Poussin noted the arbitrary nature of judgments on the relations between the Upaniṣads and ancient Buddhism: "Sur les rapports des Upanishads et du vieux Bouddhisme, on s'en tient à des opinions arbitraires" (p. vii). La Vallée Poussin does not commit himself either way on this problem, and in his *Le dogme et la philosophie du bouddhisme* [85] he contents himself with some bibliographical notes (1930a, 165–67). Opinions have varied greatly. As La Vallée Poussin remarked, scholars who take as their point of departure the Veda and Brahmanism, consider Buddhism to be an annex of Brahmanism. The doctrines of transmigration and of the act had been invented by the brahmans. The life of a religious mendicant had been inaugurated by the brahmans and the Buddhist Nirvāṇa is nothing but an atheist deformation of Nirvāṇa in Brahman. This was how La Vallée Poussin described one extreme. Between this point of view and the other extreme, which denies any relation at all between brahmanical and Buddhist ideas, intermediate positions have been taken by most scholars. The bibliography on this topic is immense, and a critical analysis of even

1. See, for example, Demiéville 1951, Frauwallner 1952, Bareau 1955b, Lamotte 1958, 1: 136–54, 297–300, Alsdorf 1959, and Bechert 1961a.

some of the most important publications would take up too much space.[2]

In the first and second editions of his *Buddha,* Oldenberg denied any relation between Sāṃkhya philosophy and Buddhism (cf. 1890 ed., 100, n. 1). Eugène Burnouf had already discussed the relation between Buddhism and Sāṃkhya philosophy in his *Introduction* (1844), where he observed a great analogy between the primitive ontology of Buddhism as reflected in the theory of the twelve *nidāna* ("links") and Sāṃkhya philosophy (p. 511). Albrecht Weber tried to identify the *tattva*s of the Sāṃkhya with the *nidāna*s (1853, 131–33). Max Müller firmly rejected any similarity between Sāṃkhya and Buddhism (1867, 226; quoted in Oldenberg 1890 ed., 100, n. 1). However, the controversy on this problem became acute with the publication in 1896 of an article by Hermann Jacobi (1896). Jacobi believed that the *nidāna*s were based upon a preclassical Sāṃkhya system that did not know the three *guṇa*s and that was taught by Buddha's teacher Arāḍa Kālāmā, whose tenets are expounded by Aśvaghoṣa in the twelfth canto of the *Buddhacarita.* Oldenberg replied to Jacobi's theory in the third edition of his *Buddha* (1897, 443–55). The problem of the relations between Sāṃkhya and Buddhism was studied again by him in his [86] "Buddhistische Studien" (1898, 681–94), in his book on the *Upaniṣads* (1923, 254–75), and in an article on the Sāṃkhya-system (1917), in which he stated unambiguously that Buddhism was influenced by preclassical Sāṃkhya. Jacobi defended his views against Oldenberg's objections in his *Buddha* and against Senart (1896) in a second article, in which he did not fundamentally change his position (Jacobi 1898). Richard Garbe also believed that Buddhism was influenced by Sāṃkhya—not by a preclassical Sāṃkhya, however, but by Kapila's system, which he considered to be older than Buddhism (1892, 517ff.; 1894, 3–5, 14–23; 1896; 1917, 6–18). Dependence of Buddhism on Sāṃkhya ideas had also been defended by other scholars such as Joseph Dahlmann (1896, 1898, 1902) and Richard Pischel (1906). More careful in his judgment is A. B. Keith (1918 [see 1924 ed., 24–33]; 1923, 138–43). La Vallée Poussin rejected Sāṃkhya influence but did not elaborate his point of view (1898, 82; 1924 [see 1936 ed., 310]; 1930a, 182). Finally, Horsch (1968, 475) stated categorically that all attempts to derive Buddhist philosophy from a primitive Sāṃkhya (*Ursāṃkhya*) must be considered unsuccessful, but the last word on this problem has certainly not yet been said.

Kern was the first scholar to suggest a Yoga influence on Buddhism (1882, 366–405). [87] This gave rise to many discussions on the relations

2. A discussion can be found in Horsch 1968.

between Buddhism and classical Yoga or preclassical Yoga. La Vallée Poussin reacted against the definition of Buddhism as an atheist religion and devoted a chapter of his book on Buddhism (1898, 82–93) to Buddhist Yoga. Senart studied in detail the Yoga influence on Buddhism (1900, 1903), but he was unable to convince other scholars that the Yoga that influenced Buddhism was Yoga in its classical form. In his "Origines bouddhiques" he arrived at a different conclusion, according to which Buddhism was influenced by a form of Visṇuïte Yoga older than the Yoga of the epic and not yet associated with Sāṃkhya (1907).

Two scholars have stressed the importance of Yoga in Buddhism. La Vallée Poussin declared that Buddhism is essentially pure Yoga, Nirvāṇa mysticism (1937, 227). Similarly, Hermann Beckh stated that "Der ganze Buddhismus ist durch und durch nichts als Yoga" (1916, 2: 11). Oldenberg recognized the importance of Yoga in Buddhism but was not willing to consider Buddhism a branch of Yoga (1923, 275–88). For a bibliography on Yoga and Buddhism one must refer to La Vallée Poussin's publications (1930a, 182–84; 1937, 223, n. 1). La Vallée Poussin does not mention Beckh's *Buddhismus* (1916)[3] or Keith's chapter on Buddhism and Yoga in his *Buddhist Philosophy* (Keith 1923, 143–45).

While texts were being edited and translated and the problems connected with their interpretation were being studied by scholars in Europe, in India inscriptions were being discovered and edited and Buddhist monuments described and interpreted. Of all the inscriptions thus found and studied, those of Aśoka are the most important for the historian. The first attempts at deciphering them were made by James Prinsep in 1834 and the following years. Burnouf is the first scholar of Buddhism to have studied the Aśokan inscriptions. He remarked that these epigraphical monuments contain a considerable number [88] of words and expressions that belong to the language and authentic doctrine of Buddhism (1852, 653). Burnouf's careful examination of the inscriptions in the tenth appendix of his book (pp. 652–781) resulted in a more adequate interpretation of many passages. His work was continued by Kern, who in 1873 published a monograph on the "monuments of Açoka the Buddhist" (1873). In 1874 Barth published a long review of Kern's work (see Barth 1914–27, 3: 131–39). In 1877 General Alexander Cunningham, who in 1870 became director-general of the "Archaeological Survey of India," published as volume 1 of the Corpus Inscriptionum Indicarum a comprehensive edition of the inscriptions of Aśoka. Still,

3. The latest edition of this work is in one volume: Beckh 1958.

new inscriptions continued to be discovered. Senart, who in 1879 wrote a long article on Cunningham's edition, prepared a new edition of the inscriptions in a long series of articles in *Journal Asiatique,* which were published later in two volumes (1881–86). Senart's great knowledge of Middle-Indian languages enabled him to make an important contribution to the study of the language and the grammar of the inscriptions. Senart also studied the inscriptions in a larger perspective (1889); on the basis of the inscriptions, he described a popular Buddhism that attached more importance to happiness in this world and to rebirth in heaven than to Nirvāṇa and to abstruse speculations on the causal chain. According to him, Buddhism was at that time a large popular movement inspired by an elevated ethical code and reacting against ritual Brahmanism in the same way as contemporary Hinduism was. Barth, however, did not accept Senart's conclusions; he pointed out that dogmatical speculations must have originated very soon in Buddhism (1914–27, 2: 55–57). La Vallée Poussin remarked that from the beginning Buddhism was at the same time not only a religion of the masses but also of a clergy that propagated a doctrine of salvation and asceticism (1898, 31–33). In the preface of the second edition of his *Buddha* (1890), Oldenberg rejected Senart's ideas outright [89] and remarked that the true nature of Buddhism was realised not by the lay followers, but by the monks whose goal was Nirvāṇa. Oldenberg also protested against Senart's reduction of Buddhism to a branch of Hinduism and pointed out that fundamental Buddhist concepts, such as the dualism between the sufferings of human existence and deliverance, the doctrine of karman, and the ascetic way of life, were inherited from Vedism (1890 ed., iii–vii).

Though Senart's views were not accepted by these prominent scholars, his concept of Aśokan Buddhism has continued to exercise a kind of subterranean influence on Buddhist studies—and not without justification. The inscriptions of Aśoka cannot give a complete picture of Buddhism in the third century B.C., but they are of great value for the study of popular Buddhism at that time and of the influence of Buddhism among lay followers. Buddhism is not only a doctrine of monks and ascetics; it is also a religion whose followers in India for many centuries numbered in the millions. It is one of the merits of La Vallée Poussin's *Bouddhisme* (1898) that it stressed the importance of taking into account both popular Buddhism and monastic Buddhism for a better understanding of the place of Buddhism in the history of Indian religions.

Senart's *Inscriptions de Piyadasi* (1881–86) was followed by other publications of new inscriptions and by contributions to their interpretation. He also wrote several articles. Important work was also done by Georg Bühler (1887, 1909) and Heinrich Lüders (1940). Eugen Hultzsch published a new edition of *The Inscriptions of Asoka* in 1925. His work has remained the standard edition up to our days, but the many new discoveries and new interpretations that have been published since then make the publication of an entirely new edition an urgent desideratum. K. R. Norman of Cambridge University has for a number of years been engaged in this task, and it is hoped that someday his edition will be published.[4]

The Annual Reports of the Archaeological Survey, which were published from 1871 onwards by Alexander Cunningham and by James Burgess, who succeeded him in 1885 as director-general, contain much material for Buddhist archaeology. Of special importance for Buddhist studies was Cunningham's book [90] *The Stūpa of Bharhut* (1879). The monuments of Sāñchī had been studied earlier by James Fergusson in his *Tree and Serpent Worship* (1868). However, neither his work nor F. C. Maisey's *Sanchi and Its Remains* (1892) were very satisfactory. Sir John Marshall, who in 1902 succeeded James Burgess, continued the work first undertaken by Cunningham (*The Bhilsa Topes,* 1854). His guide to Sāñchī (1918) was the result of the work done by him on the site between 1912 and 1919. Then in 1940, with A. Foucher and N. G. Majumdar, he published *The Monuments of Sāñchī,* a splendid work in which Marshall studied the monuments and the art, Foucher the meaning of the sculptures, and Majumdar the inscriptions.[5]

It is not feasible to enumerate the important epigraphical and archaeological discoveries that relate to Buddhism, but mention must be made of the Aśokan inscriptions discovered in 1895 and 1896 in Nepal. The first, found near the village of Niglīva, mentions the stūpa of the Buddha Konākamana; the second, found thirteen miles away from it near the village of Paḍeria, was erected by Aśoka in the twenty-first year after his consecration to commemorate the birth of the Buddha in the park of Lummini. The discovery of these two pillars and consequently of the nearby site of Kapilavastu and of the stūpa of Krakucchanda established, as Barth pointed out (1914–27, 4: 323–35), that the legend of the Buddha was more ancient than had been previously supposed. The discoveries could not establish what was historically true in the legend of Buddha, but they made it impossible to consider Kapilavastu a mythological place without a real location, as had been done by Senart and Kern. As early as 1870 Cunningham believed that he had rediscovered the place of Buddha's Nirvāṇa near the village of Kasia, 34 miles east of Gorakhpur, but uncertainty remained. Vincent A. Smith wrote a monograph on *The Remains near Kasia* (1896) in which he rejected Cunningham's claim. It was only in

4. For a bibliography see Mehendale 1948.
5. For a survey of the archaeological work done in India up to 1938 see Cumming 1939.

1911 that an inscription discovered by Hirananda Shastri proved beyond any doubt that Cunningham had been correct in his identification (Vogel 1934, 72). [91]

The last decade of the nineteenth century inaugurated a long series of important discoveries of Buddhist manuscripts in Central Asia. The Russian consul in Kashgar, Nikolaj Fedorovitch Petrovskij, sent manuscripts in several languages to Serge Oldenburg in St. Petersburg (Oldenburg 1910). A photocopy of one leaf of a Kuchean text was published by Oldenburg (1892), and later Ernst Leumann published a transcription of it and of another leaf (1900). In the following years Oldenburg published Sanskrit fragments from Kashgar (1894a, b, c; 1899; 1902–3). In the same years manuscripts from Khotan and Kashgar were sent to A. F. R. Hoernle, who reported on them in the *Journal of the Asiatic Society of Bengal* (1893, 1897, 1899–1901). Of great importance was the discovery of a manuscript of a version of the *Dharmapada* in Prākrit. Part of the manuscript was acquired by Jules Léon Dutreuil de Rhins and Fernand Grenard in Khotan in 1892. Another part was sent by Petrovskij in 1897 to Oldenburg, who immediately published a facsimile and transcription of one leaf (1897a); in the following year Senart published a transliteration of the fragments in Paris (1898). A definitive edition of all fragments was not published until John Brough's *The Gāndhārī Dharmapada* (1962), which contains a full bibliography of all publications relating to the text.

These and other discoveries in Central Asia led to the organisation of several expeditions to Central Asia: three expeditions led by Sir Aurel Stein [92] in 1900–1901, 1900–1908, and 1913–16; four German expeditions, the first led by Albert Grünwedel and Georg Huth in 1902–3, the second by Von Le Coq in 1904–5, the third by Von Le Coq and Grünwedel in 1905–7, and the fourth by Von Le Coq in 1913–14; a French expedition led by P. Pelliot in 1906–8; three Japanese expeditions in 1902–4, 1908–9, and 1910–13; and three Russian expeditions, the first by D. Klementz in 1898, the second and third led by Serge Oldenburg in 1909–10 and 1914–15. Other expeditions are mentioned in Dabbs 1963 (chaps. 5, 6), but the ones listed above are the most important for Buddhist studies. As a result of these expeditions Buddhist manuscripts in Sanskrit, Kuchean, Agnean, Khotanese, Sogdian, Uigur, Tibetan, and Chinese arrived in great numbers in Paris, London, Berlin, St. Petersburg, and Japan. A bibliography of Central Asiatic studies was published in volume 1 of Monumenta Serindica (Ishihama et al. 1958). Waldschmidt lists all Sanskrit fragments published by German scholars from 1904 to 1964 (1965–71, 1: xxvi–xxxii) and from 1964 to 1970 (3: 275–76). Bernard Pauly has listed the publications of Sanskrit fragments brought back by Pelliot (1965a). There were no bibliographies covering the publication of Sanskrit fragments from the collections in London, Leningrad, and Japan, but most of those that were published before 1959 are to be found in Yamada Ryūjō's *Bongo Butten no Shobunken* (1959). For Kuchean and Agnean texts one must refer to Schwentner 1959; for Sogdian to Dresden 1942; for Khotanese to Dresden 1944 and Gertsenberg 1965 (16–29); for Uigur to Loewenthal 1957 and the supplementary information supplied in de Jong 1958 (81). The Tibetan manuscripts in Paris and London [93] have been catalogued by Marcelle Lalou (1939–61) and La Vallée Poussin (1962), but a bibliography of text editions does not exist.

I have mentioned the principal publications of Kern, Senart, and Oldenberg. For other studies by them the reader can refer to the bibliographies of these three scholars (Kern 1929; Finot 1929 and Guérinot 1933; Oldenberg 1967, vii–xxxv). The reviews of Auguste Barth, who especially during the period 1880 to 1900 carefully analysed many important publications on Buddhism, were published in five volumes (1914–27).[6] The bibliography of his works and the general index found in volume 5 are very useful for the study of the history of Buddhist studies.

In the 1860s a new generation of scholars was born: R. Otto Franke, Serge Oldenburg, Sylvain Lévi, T. Stcherbatsky, F. W. Thomas, E. J. Thomas, Louis de La Vallée Poussin, and Heinrich Lüders.

Sylvain Lévi's importance is not limited to Buddhism, but the work he did in this field has had a lasting influence not only in Europe but also in India and Japan. In 1927 he recalled how in 1887 Fujishima Ryōon and Fujieda Takutsū, two priests of the Nishi Honganji, became his first two pupils (Lévi 1927a, 1). They probably contributed to his attention being directed towards Buddhism. Lévi has not written any comprehensive work on Buddhism, but his genius led him from discovery to discovery, and his work has not ceased to stimulate research in many directions. Very soon he realised the importance of Chinese not only for the study of Buddhism but also for that of Indian history. He has shown by his example that Indian, [94] Tibetan, and Chinese sources are indispensable for the study of Buddhism.

Lévi was fascinated by Aśvaghoṣa. He published the text and a translation of the first canto of his *Buddhacarita* (1892), but he abandoned his plan to edit the text when he learned Cowell was already engaged in the task. Already in his earliest publications Lévi studied the historical problems related to Aśvaghoṣa, Kaniṣka, and the Indo-Scythians (1896–97). During his first journey to Nepal in 1898 he looked for the Sanskrit original of Aśvaghoṣa's *Sūtrālaṃkāra*. He obtained a copy of Asaṅga's *Mahā-*

6. For an obituary of Barth see Foucher 1916, 207–21.

yānasūtrālaṃkāra, which he edited and translated (1907–11); this marked the first publication of a text of the Yogācāra school. His researches on Aśvaghoṣa resulted in his tracing 26 stories of the *Divyāvadāna* in the Vinaya of the Mūlasarvāstivādin (1907). This article complemented the research undertaken by Édouard Huber (1904, 1906). Huber's translation of the *Sūtrālaṃkāra* (1908) was the point of departure for a long article on Aśvaghoṣa and his *Sūtrālaṃkāra* by Lévi (1908). Lévi in 1922 discovered in Nepal a manuscript of the *Dharmasamuccaya*, which contains the verses of the *Saddharmasmṛtyupasthānasūtra*. In a famous article he had already compared the description of Jambudvīpa in this work with the *digvarṇana* in the *Rāmāyaṇa* (1918). On rather tenuous grounds he connected the name of Aśvaghoṣa with the *Saddharmasmṛtyupasthānasūtra* (1925a, 36–40). The publication by Lüders (1926) of Sanskrit fragments of the *Sūtrālaṃkāra* put into doubt both the title and authorship of the work. Many scholars participated in the debate that took place in subsequent years.[7] Still, even though Sylvain Lévi [95] erred in claiming too much for Aśvaghoṣa, his devotion to him brought to light much important material.

Lévi's discovery in Nepal in 1922 of Vasubandhu's *Viṃśatikā* and *Triṃśikā* was of great importance for our knowledge of the Yogācāra school (1925b, 1932a). Some of the most important texts discovered by him were published by his pupils. Félix Lacôte edited and translated Budhasvāmin's *Bṛhatkathāślokasaṃgraha* (1908–29); this added a new dimension to the study of the famous *Bṛhatkathā*. Yamaguchi Susumu edited Sthiramati's *Madhyāntavibhāgaṭīkā* (1934–37). Sylvain Lévi also took great interest in the discoveries of Sanskrit and Kuchean manuscripts in Central Asia. Pischel's publication (1904) of a Sanskrit fragment of the *Saṃyuktāgama* inaugurated the publication of Sanskrit manuscripts discovered by the German Turfan expeditions. Lévi (1904) showed that the corresponding text was to be found in the Chinese version of the *Saṃyuktāgama*. This discovery was of great importance for the history of the Buddhist canon. In a study of the sacred scriptures of the Buddhists, Lévi underlined the importance of the discoveries of Buddhist texts of different schools for the history and comparative study of the Buddhist canon (1909).[8] For Lévi's editions of Sanskrit and Kuchean fragments we must refer to the bibliography of his writings in volumes 7–8 of the *Biblio-*[96]*graphie bouddhique* (1937, 1–64). Of his other articles we mention

7. Thus, Lévi 1927b, 1928, 1929, 1936, 80; Nobel 1928, 1931; La Vallée Poussin 1928–29, 221–24; Przyluski 1931 (and Pelliot 1931 review), 1932, 1940; Tomomatsu 1931; Johnston 1936, 2: xxii–xxiii; and Bailey 1952.

8. For Oldenberg's reaction see Oldenberg 1912a, 197–208 (= Oldenberg 1967, 1015–26).

only two that have a great bearing on the history of the Buddhist canon: his article on a precanonical language (1912) and his study of the texts recited by Koṭikarṇa (1915). In 1928 Lévi visited Bali and Java. In Bali he gained the confidence of the priests and was able to collect several *stotra,* which were published in *Sanskrit Texts from Bali* (1933). When he visited the Borobudur and inspected the lower galleries he recognized that the sculptors had made use of a text dealing with acts. A manuscript of this text had been discovered by him in Nepal during his last visit there (1932b; see also Krom 1933).

Louis de La Vallée Poussin was one of the first pupils of Sylvain Lévi, but the nature of his work is entirely different. He devoted most of his research to the study of Buddhist dogmatism, as he called it, and of the philosophical schools of Mahāyāna. His first works concern Tantrism: an edition of the *Pañcakrama* (1896a), an edition and translation of the *Ādikarmapradīpa* and a chapter on Tantrism in his *Bouddhisme: Études et matériaux* (1898, 118–232). Two years earlier he had analysed a chapter of the *Prasannapadā* (1896b), and in subsequent years he published a masterfully annotated edition of the *Prasannapadā* (1903–13), an edition of the *Bodhicaryāvatārapañjikā* (1901–14), an edition of the Tibetan text of the *Madhyamakāvatāra* (1907–12), and an incomplete translation of the same text (1907–11). His translation of the *Bodhicaryāvatāra* is still by far the most learned of all the existing translations (1907). In 1933 he wrote a long comprehensive article on the Madhyamaka (1933), but [97] his final opinion on the Madhyamaka absolute did not appear until after his death (1938). In an article on the 75 and 100 dharmas, La Vallée Poussin studied the *Abhidharmakośa* and the *Vijñaptimātratāsiddhi* (1905b). In this field his work culminated in his translation of the *Abhidharmakośa,* one of the greatest achievements in Buddhist studies (1923–31). He also translated many passages of the Abhidharma works of the Sarvāstivādin and of the *Mahāvibhāṣā,* to which he referred also in his Abhidharma studies. In the field of Yogācāra studies his greatest achievement is his translation of the *Vijñaptimātratāsiddhi* (1928–29). Even the later Buddhist school of logic was not neglected by him, as is shown by his edition of the Tibetan text of the *Nyāyabindu* together with Vinītadeva's commentary (1907–13).

Philosophical problems were taken up by him in many publications. Let us mention only his articles on the doctrine of *karman* (1902–3), the *trikāya* (1906; 1913a; 1928–29, 2: 762–813), the *pratītyasamutpāda* (1913b), and the councils (1905a, 1910). His numerous contributions to Hastings's *Encyclopaedia of Religion and Ethics* (see La Vallée Poussin's name in its index) deal with many aspects of Buddhism. If one adds to all this his publications of Sanskrit fragments (see *JRAS* 1907, 1908, 1911, 1912, 1913) and many other articles and reviews, it becomes difficult to imagine that so much could have been achieved by one scholar.[9] La Vallée Poussin also published the results of his researches in books meant for a larger (but highly intelligent) public: *Bouddhisme: Opinions sur l'Histoire de la Dogmatique* (1909); *The Way to Nirvāṇa* (1917); [98] *Nirvāṇa* (1925); *La Morale bouddhique* (1927); *Le dogme et la philosophie du bouddhisme* (1930a). Moreover, much information on Buddhism is to be found in the three volumes of his history of ancient India (1924, 1930b, 1935).

I have already mentioned several times La Vallée Poussin's *Bouddhisme,* which appeared in 1898. In this work he discussed for the first time many problems such as the value of the Pāli sources, the nature of popular Buddhism, Buddhist Yoga, etc. He was never satisfied with the results he obtained, and many of these problems were studied by him again and again over a period of forty years. For this reason it is difficult to give a general characterisation of his principal views. On some points, however, his opinions did not vary greatly. He always stressed the fact that Buddhism owed most of its ideas to brahmanical speculation and asceticism, although he pointed out that one can recognize in Buddhism a characteristic way of envisaging the problem of salvation, a coherent doctrine that can be called an orthodoxy (1909, 51). From the beginning he also underlined the importance of Yoga, and in one of his last articles he did not hesitate to consider Buddhism a branch of Yoga (1937a, 227), an opinion that was utterly unacceptable for Oldenberg (1923, 257–88), as we have seen. The problem that was always the centre of his research was the interpretation of Nirvāṇa. In his *The Buddhist Nirvāṇa and Its Western Interpreters* (1968, 256–83) G. R. Welbon has attempted to sketch the evolution of La Vallée Poussin on this point, but only a fuller treatment could do justice to this difficult problem. La Vallée Poussin always had a disinclination to study the life of the Buddha and other problems that can hardly be solved with the available materials. He preferred to analyse the views of the different schools. No scholar has contributed more to our knowledge of Buddhist Abhidharma than La Vallée Poussin.[10]

Jean Przyluski, another pupil of Sylvain Lévi, did excellent [99] work in translating, from Chinese, texts that dealt with northwestern India (1914), Buddha's parinirvāṇa (1918–20, 1920, 1936), the legend of Aśoka (1923), and the Council of Rājagṛha (1926–28). Przyluski attached much importance to geographical factors for the development of Buddhist schools. His work on the Council of Rājagṛha is inspired by some rather

9. For a bibliography of his writings see *Bibliographie bouddhique* 23-2:1–37.

10. For an excellent characterisation of La Vallée Poussin's personality and work, see Lamotte 1965a.

wild sociological ideas. Although many of his theories cannot stand the test of a serious examination, his translations will always be useful for the historian of Buddhism. In later publications he succumbed to a mania of comparatism that led him to discover non-Indian influences everywhere. Probably not much of his late work will be of any lasting value. To Przyluski belongs the great merit of having created, with Marcelle Lalou, the *Bibliographie bouddhique* (1930–67), which exhaustively analyses all publications relating to Buddhism that appeared during the years 1928 to 1958. A complete analytical bibliography of Przyluski's writings can be found in Macdonald and Lalou 1970.

La Vallée Poussin's most famous pupil is Étienne Lamotte, who prior to 1942 published translations of the *Saṃdhinirmocana* (1935), of Vasubandhu's *Karmasiddhiprakaraṇa* (1935–36a), and of Asaṅga's *Mahāyānasaṃgraha* (1938–39). A discussion of his later work has to be postponed to the next chapter.

Theodor Stcherbatsky was a pupil of Minaev, Bühler, and Jacobi. His most important work was devoted to the logic and epistemology of the later Buddhist authors Dharmakīrti and Dharmottara. In 1903 he published a Russian translation of Dharmakīrti's *Nyāyabindu* and Dharmottara's *ṭīkā.* This was followed by a study of the main concepts of the Buddhist epistemological school, published in Russian (1909) and later in German (1924) and French (1926). Both works appeared in an entirely new and enlarged version in English in the two volumes of *Buddhist Logic* (1930–32). [100] In 1918 Otto Rosenberg published a study on the problems of Buddhist philosophy, largely based on Vasubandhu's *Abhidharmakośa,* in which he advocated the view that Buddhist philosophy was based on the idea of the plurality of dharmas.[11] Stcherbatsky accepted Rosenberg's view and described Buddhism as a system of Radical Pluralism in his *The Central Conception of Buddhism and the Meaning of the Word "Dharma"* (1923), which contains an analysis of the main doctrines of the *Abhidharmakośa.* La Vallée Poussin's *Nirvāṇa* (1925) and, to a lesser degree, Keith's *Buddhist Philosophy in India and Ceylon* (1923) provoked a spirited attack by Stcherbatsky in his *The Conception of Buddhist Nirvāṇa* (1927). The second part of this book contains a translation of chapters 1 and 25 of Candrakīrti's *Prasannapadā.* The first part sketches the development of Buddhist philosophy in the schools of Hīnayāna and Mahāyāna. Stcherbatsky believed that Buddhism arose as a philosophical system that analysed matter and mind as composed of evanescent elements (*dharmas*). I cannot go into detail here on Stcherbatsky's opinions on the later development of Buddhist philosophy; his conclusion (pp. 60–62)

11. See also Pjatigorskij 1971.

summarizes briefly the results at which he arrived. Stcherbatsky had a profound knowledge of both Western and Indian philosophy. In his translations he strove to render the philosophical meaning, rather than the literal sense. In his interpretation of the epistemological school of Buddhism he tried to show parallels with Kant's transcendental philosophy. His philosophical views regarding the radical pluralism of early Buddhism and the transcendental character of later Buddhist philosophy do not do justice to the essentially religious nature of the Buddhist quest for salvation. He also carried on a heated controversy with La Vallée Poussin over the nature of the Absolute of the Madhyamaka. For further details the reader is referred to two articles published in the *Journal of Indian Philosophy* (de Jong 1972a, b). Even if Stcherbatsky's ideas are not always convincing, [101] one must recognize that, by translating and explaining for the first time some very difficult Buddhist philosophical texts, he made an important contribution to Buddhist studies.[12]

A contemporary of Stcherbatsky was Serge Oldenburg, mentioned earlier in connection with the publication of Sanskrit fragments from Kashgar. Oldenburg published many writings on Buddhist tales and Buddhist iconography. Several of his articles were translated during the 1890s.[13] He founded the Bibliotheca Buddhica series, of which the first volume was Bendall's edition of the *Śikṣāsamuccaya* (1897–1902). The thirtieth volume, Stcherbatsky's translation of the first chapter of the *Madhyāntavibhāga* (1936b), appeared in 1936. Many well-known scholars published editions of texts in this series. To mention only a few: Louis Finot (the *Rāṣṭrapālaparipṛcchā*) in 1898; J. S. Speyer (the *Avadānaśataka*) in 1902–9; H. Kern and Bunyiu Nanjio (the *Saddharmapuṇḍarīkasūtra*) in 1908–12. Another Russian scholar who has to be mentioned here is von Staël-Holstein, who edited the *Kāśyapaparivarta* (1926) and Sthiramati's commentary (1933).[14]

A pupil of Stcherbatsky, Eugène Obermiller, translated from [102] the Tibetan the *Uttaratantra*, or *Ratnagotravibhāga* (1931). His main work was devoted to the *Abhisamayālaṃkāra* (1932, 1933–43).[15]

Heinrich Lüders's importance for Buddhist studies consists in his extremely careful editions of Sanskrit fragments from Central Asia. His edition of fragments of Buddhist dramas (1911a, b) revealed for the first

12. For a bibliography of his writings see Burjatskii Institut 1968, 5–7 (to which add Über den Begriff vijñāna im Buddhismus, *ZII* 7 [1929]: 136–39). Several of Stcherbatsky's Russian articles have been published in English translation; see Stcherbatsky 1969, 1971.

13. See, for example, Oldenburg 1893a, b, 1897b, 1898 and Kern 1897 (= *Verspreide geschriften* 4 [1916]: 209–31). For a complete bibliography see P. Skačkov 1934.

14. For more information on this scholar see Elisséef 1938 and Schierlitz 1938.

15. For further information see La Vallée Poussin 1937b and Stcherbatsky 1936a.

time the fact that Aśvaghoṣa had written for the theatre, a fact of great importance for the history of Indian theatre.[16] I mentioned earlier his edition of fragments of the *Kalpanāmaṇḍitikā* (1926). Other publications of fragments have been reprinted in his *Philologica Indica* (1940). Of great importance for the problem of the precanonical language is his posthumously published *Beobachtungen über die Sprache des buddhistischen Urkanons* (Lüders and Waldschmidt 1954), in which he defended the view that the Pāli and Sanskrit Buddhist texts show traces of the existence of a primitive canon (*Urkanon*) written in an Eastern dialect, called Ardhamāgadhī or Old-Ardhamāgadhī. Lüders's work on the Sanskrit fragments was continued by his pupil Ernst Waldschmidt, who edited fragments of the *Bhikṣuṇīprātimokṣa* of the Sarvāstivādin and fragments of canonical sūtras (1926, 1932).

In the field of Buddhist philosophy important work has been done by Stanislas Schayer, Poul Tuxen, Giuseppe Tucci, and Erich Frauwallner. Schayer and Tuxen have contributed to a better understanding of the Madhyamaka philosophy by their studies on Candrakīrti's *Prasannapadā* (Schayer 1931; Tuxen 1936, 1937).[17] Schayer provoked a lively discussion [103] on the problem of precanonical Buddhism (1935, 1937; see also Regamey 1957). Tuxen wrote one of the best books on Theravāda (1928), based upon firsthand knowledge of Buddhism in Thailand. Of Tucci's work on Buddhist philosophy, one must mention above all his *Pre-Diṅnāga Buddhist Texts on Logic from Chinese Sources* (1929a), his translation of Diṅnāga's *Nyāyamukha* (1930b), and his articles on the *Vādavidhi,* Diṅnāga, Buddhist logic before Diṅnāga, etc. (1928a, b, 1929b, 1930a, 1931). Many other articles and books on Indian Buddhism were published by Tucci before 1942 (see Tucci 1971, xi–xviii). In the same period Erich Frauwallner published a series of important articles on Dignāga, Dharmakīrti, and Dharmottara that greatly increased our understanding of the role played by these thinkers in the development of Indian philosophy (see Oberhammer 1968, 9–10).

I mentioned earlier the fascination that Aśvaghoṣa exercised over Sylvain Lévi. E. H. Johnston also studied his work for many years and published exemplary editions and translations of his *Saundarananda* (1928, 1932) and his *Buddhacarita* (1936; 1937, 26–62, 85–111, 231–92). The edition and translation of the Tibetan version of the *Buddhacarita* by Friedrich Weller (1926–28) rendered great service to Johnston. Weller extensively studied Buddhist scriptures in Sanskrit, Pāli, Chinese, Tibetan, Mongolian, and Sogdian (see Schubert and Schneider 1954, xi–xiii). An

16. For a bibliography of Lüders's writings see Lüders 1973, vii–xiii.

17. For an (incomplete) bibliography of Schayer's works, see *Rocznik Orientalistyczny* 21 (1957): 24–27. For more on Tuxen, see Barr 1956.

important Mahāyāna sūtra, the *Suvarṇabhāsottamasūtra,* was edited with [104] great care by Johannes Nobel (1937; for critical remarks see Edgerton 1957a, 185–87).

I mentioned the work done by Fausbøll and the Pali Text Society for Pāli studies. Denmark has continued to be an important centre for Pāli studies. The most important undertaking in the field is *A Critical Pāli Dictionary* (*CPD*) by Dines Andersen and Helmer Smith,[18] who made use of the lexicographical materials collected by Trenckner. The first volume of the dictionary, comprising the letter *a,* was published from 1924 to 1948. In this connection one must mention the lexicographical materials collected by Wilhelm Geiger; these remained unpublished, as did the materials collected before him by Burnouf and Spiegel. However, Geiger's materials have been put at the disposal of the editors of the *CPD* and have been included in fascicles 2 and following of volume 2. Geiger's name will also always be connected with the two Pāli chronicles, *Dīpavaṃsa* and *Mahāvaṃsa,* to which he devoted many years of careful study. To Geiger is also due the best Pāli grammar: *Pāli, Literatur und Sprache* (1916). Finally, one must mention his very fine translation of the first two volumes of the *Saṃyuttanikāya* (1925–30). Together with Magdalene Geiger he wrote a detailed study of the meaning of the word *dhamma* in Pāli literature (Geiger and Geiger 1921; see also Geiger 1921).[19]

Tibetan studies relating to Buddhism can only be mentioned briefly. W. W. Rockhill made important material accessible to the scholarly world by his translations from the Tibetan of the *Udānavarga* (1883), *The Life of the Buddha,* based on the Tibetan translation of the *Mūlasarvāstivāda-vinaya* (1884), and the *Bhikṣuṇīprātimokṣasūtra* from the same Vinaya (1886).[20] Georg Huth edited and translated the *Hor-chos*-[105]*byuṅ* (1892–96; for an obituary, see Laufer 1906). Palmyr Cordier published a very accurate catalogue of the Tibetan Tanjur (1909–15; for more on him, see Chavannes 1914). Berthold Laufer published many articles based upon Tibetan materials.[21] Giuseppe Tucci undertook several expeditions to Tibet and brought back many precious materials on Tibetan Buddhist literature and art (see Tucci 1971, xi–xviii). The important work of Andrej Vostrikov on Tibetan historical literature was published twenty-five years after his death (Vostrikov 1962).

18. On Andersen see *CPD* 1: xxxv–xxxviii, and for more on Helmer Smith, *CPD* 2-1 (1960): v–viii.

19. See Bechert's article on Geiger in *CPD* 2-2 (1962): ix–xiv; a complete bibliography of Geiger's writings can be found in Geiger 1973, xi–xxxiii.

20. For obituaries of Rockhill, see Cordier 1915 and Laufer 1915.

21. These can be found in Creel 1935 and Schubert 1935–36.

Sinologists continued to study the travels of Chinese pilgrims to India. Thomas Watters prepared extensive notes on Hsüan-tsang's *Hsi-yü-chi*, which were published posthumously: *On Yuan Chwang's Travels in India* (1904–5; for a review, see Pelliot 1905). Noël Peri wrote some important articles of which we mention only two: one on the date of Vasubandhu (1911) and one on the wives of Śākyamuni (1918).[22] Two of the greatest Sinologists, Édouard Chavannes and Paul Pelliot, have made notable contributions to Buddhist studies. Chavannes translated I-tsing's work on the pilgrims to the Western countries (1894) and many Buddhist stories (1910–11, 1934). Together with Sylvain Lévi he wrote articles on some enigmatic titles in the Buddhist ecclesiastic hierarchy and on the sixteen Arhats (Lévi and Chavannes 1915, 1916; H. Cordier 1918, 226, 227, 228, 246). Pelliot's contribu-[106]tion to Buddhist studies up to 1928 has been analysed in *Bibliographie bouddhique* 4–5 (1934, 3–19). His most important publications from 1928 on were mentioned by Paul Demiéville in an article in *Paul Pelliot* (1946). Paul Demiéville continued the tradition. His article on the Chinese versions of the *Milindapañha* (1924) is the definitive work on the subject. As editor in chief of the *Hôbôgirin* (fasc. 1, 1929; fasc. 2, 1930; fasc. 3, 1937), he contributed some very long and important articles (see, for instance, the article on *Byō,* "Illness," pp. 224–70). *Choix d'études bouddhiques* (Demiéville 1973a) contains a selection of his Buddhist studies.

22. For further information on Peri, see Ed. Maitre's obituary in *BEFEO* 22 (1922): 404–17.

CHAPTER THREE

Recent Decades: A (1943–73)

By 1943 some of the greatest scholars of the preceding period had passed away; to mention only a few: Sylvain Lévi, Louis de La Vallée Poussin, and Theodor Stcherbatsky. Lüders died in 1943, but his *Beobachtungen über die Sprache des buddhistischen Urkanons* appeared posthumously and in an incomplete form only in 1954. Several scholars who had already published important work before 1943 continued their activity after that date, among whom were Friedrich Weller and Ernst Waldschmidt in Germany, Étienne Lamotte in Belgium, Erich Frauwallner in Austria, and Giuseppe Tucci in Italy. With the death of Stcherbatsky Buddhist studies declined in Russia, and only some two decades later will one observe an increasing interest in Buddhism, especially in the field of Central [50] Asian archaeology (see Bechert 1966, 138; Kotschetow 1967; Žukovskaja 1970). In other countries, however, many scholars either specialised in Buddhism or devoted much of their research to Buddhism. Although the total number of specialists in this field in the West is considerably smaller than in Japan, the future of Buddhist studies looked much brighter in the early 1970s than it did in the first postwar years.

One of the most important contributions to Buddhist studies in the first decade after the war was undoubtedly Franklin Edgerton's monumental *Buddhist Hybrid Sanskrit Grammar and Dictionary* (1953a). Edgerton embarked upon this immense task in the 1930s and a number of articles preceded the publication of this important work (1935, 1936a, b; 1937a, b, c; 1946a, b). However, only after the publication of his grammar and dictionary did Buddhist Hybrid Sanskrit become the subject of lively discussion. Yuyama (1970, 80–81) lists nineteen reviews of Edgerton's work and several articles (by Bailey, Brough, Iwamoto, Nobel, Raghavan, Regamey, and Smith) inspired by it. Edgerton defended his views in several articles and reviews and also continued his work on BHS (Buddhist

Hybrid Sanskrit) in several publications.[1] In his *Buddhist Hybrid Sanskrit Reader* (1953c) he applied his principles to the editing of several BHS [51] texts.[2] For the editing of BHS verse Edgerton's views on the metre and phonology of the *gāthās* are of fundamental importance. These views were first attacked by Helmer Smith in *Les deux prosodies du vers bouddhique* (1950), in which he severely criticised Edgerton's article in *JAOS* 66 (1946a). After the publication of Edgerton's *Grammar and Dictionary*, Smith discussed Edgerton's views in his *Analecta rhythmica* (1954) and in his "En marge du vocabulaire sanskrit des bouddhistes" (1953–55).[3] Edgerton's metrical theories were also discussed briefly by Waldschmidt (1953–56, 2: 59–62), by Heinz Bechert (1961b, 26; 1972, 70), and by Franz Bernhard (1965–68, 1: 16–20). Finally, in this connection, mention must be made of Lamotte's pages on BHS in which he draws attention to the history of epigraphic mixed Sanskrit (1958, 634–45).

Buddhist Hybrid Sanskrit was first known as Gāthā dialect because it was characteristic of the language of the verses of Mahāyāna sūtras. Wackernagel (1896, xxxix–xl) lists the publications that appeared up to 1896. Bibliographical information on the publications that appeared after 1896 was added in Renou's translation (1957, 81–85) of Wackernagel's text. Senart's edition of the *Mahāvastu* (1882–97) made it clear that the Gāthā dialect was not limited to verses. Moreover, it was found to have been used in inscriptions and in non-religious works such as the Bakshālī manuscript, a mathematical text (Kaye 1927–33), and in the Bower manuscript, a medical text discovered in 1890 near Kucha (Hoernle 1893–1912). In 1886 Senart therefore proposed the name "mixed Sanskrit" [52] (Senart 1881–86, 2: 470). Edgerton's Buddhist Hybrid Sanskrit refers only to Buddhist texts and does not include secular texts and inscriptions. The publication of Edgerton's work made it possible to study the linguistic history of India on a much more comprehensive basis than when Senart (1881–86, 2: 447–538) tried to unravel the relations between Sanskrit, "mixed Sanskrit," and Prakrit.

Edgerton's work is in the first place descriptive. He divides the BHS into three classes according to the degree of hybridization of the language. The first class contains texts of which both the prose parts and the verses are entirely in BHS. This class consists mainly of the *Mahāvastu*. One must add now the parts of the Vinaya of the Mahāsāṃghika edited by Roth (1970) and Jinananda (1969). The second class comprises texts of

1. For these reviews, see Edgerton 1952, 1953b, 1957b, and 1963; for BHS-related articles see Edgerton 1954a, b, 1955, 1957a, 1961.

2. For a complete bibliography of Edgerton's publications see *Language* 40:116–23.

3. For Smith's other publications on Pāli and Middle Indic metrics see *CPD*, vol. 2, fasc. 1, p. viii.

which the verses are in BHS but the prose parts contain few signs of Middle Indic phonology and morphology. However, the vocabulary is largely BHS. The third class consists of texts of which both prose and verse are Sanskritized. Only the vocabulary shows that they belong to the BHS tradition. According to Edgerton, BHS tradition goes back to an early Buddhist canon, or quasi-canon, which was composed in a Middle Indic vernacular that very probably already contained a dialect mixture. In his view the Prakrit underlying BHS was not an eastern dialect, as had been assumed by Heinrich Lüders, who maintained that at least parts of the works of the Pāli and Sanskrit canon were translated from Old-Ardhamāgadhī. Edgerton did not have at his disposal Lüders's *Beobachtungen* (Lüders and Waldschmidt 1954) and referred to Lüders's view that the original dialect of the *Saddharmapuṇḍarīka* was Māgadhī, solely on the ground of voc. pl. forms in *-āho*. *Beobachtungen* contains more evidence in support of Lüders's theory, but it is certainly true that all the characteristics of BHS cannot be completely explained by an Old-Ardhamāgadhī canon. It is of course possible that some texts were transmitted in Old-Ardhamāgadhī but that later additions to the canon were composed in a mixture of dialects, with the result that the older parts of the canon also were transposed into the same language. This mixture of dialects was subjected to a process of Sanskritization when BHS texts were written.

Brough (1954), Renou (1956, 209), and Regamey (1954) agree [53] with Edgerton on this point, but they are not willing to accept that the prose of the works of the second class and the works belonging to the third class belong to the BHS tradition. According to them these texts were written in a Buddhist Sanskrit that contains some elements of BHS. Edgerton rejected this opinion:

> It seems to me that hybrid forms in the prose of the second class are just what hybrid forms in the verses of the same texts are: relics of genuine BHS forms which must have been much more numerous. Similarly texts of the third class. And I hold that all the works I have classified as BHS (excepting perhaps the Jātakamālā), and some others, do constitute, on the whole, a unified tradition.
>
> (1957a, 189–90)

In his grammar (1953a, 1: 1.40–44) Edgerton pointed out that in the case of texts such as the *Saddharmapuṇḍarīka*, *Vajracchedikā*, and *Udānavarga* the Central Asian manuscripts show a more Middle Indic appearance than the Nepalese manuscripts. According to Regamey (1954, 523) these texts have not been submitted to a conscious Sanskritization but copyists have corrected the texts. However, if one compares for instance Chakravarti's edition of the *Udānavarga* with the later recensions, one observes not a mechanical Sanskritization but rather the transposition of words, or the replacement of *pāda*s with newly created *pāda*s, etc. This is certainly due to a deliberate attempt to rewrite these verses in Sanskrit.

It seems to me that it is not possible to make a universal generalization. Some texts, written in Buddhist Sanskrit with a few BHS elements, may have been composed directly in this language, but others may well be the end product of a long process of Sanskritization. It will probably be possible to arrive at a greater degree of certainty only when the available Central Asian and Gilgit manuscripts have been properly edited and accompanied by photographic facsimiles.

Another objection that has been raised against Edgerton is his use of Nepalese manuscripts. Edgerton had not himself studied any manuscripts of Buddhist texts. Scholars like Brough, Regamey, Nobel, and Waldschmidt, on the other hand, had long years of experience studying manuscripts and were more keenly aware of the possibility of scribal errors than Edgerton. It is of course often difficult to distinguish between a genuine BHS form and a scribal error. It is perhaps methodically advisable to assume first that an aberrant (from classical Sanskrit) form is a BHS form and not a scribal error. [54] However, in reacting to the practice of editors to Sanskritize their texts, Edgerton has sinned in the opposite direction. He admits the genuineness of 3rd person plural, optative, and aorist forms in *-itsu(ḥ)* and *-etsu(ḥ)* because they occur very often in the manuscripts of the *Mahāvastu*. Brough and Regamey are undoubtedly right in rejecting the evidence of the recent Nepalese manuscripts in this case. There is no doubt that Edgerton's *Grammar* contains many forms for which the manuscript evidence is slight and doubtful. It will be necessary to verify, in each case, whether the manuscript readings can be accepted as they are or whether a different reading must be assumed. Let me quote one example that was brought up by Brough. In the *Lalitavistara* one finds *anyatra karma sukṛtāt* (37.7). In 8.9 Edgerton explains *karma* as an ablative of an *a*-stem resulting from a shortening of *-ā(t)* for metrical reasons. In 17.13, however, he proposes an alternative explanation as a stem-form. Brough prefers this latter explanation. However, if one takes into account the context: *na ca saṃskṛte sahāyā na mitrajñātijano ca parivārāḥ / anyatra karma sukṛtād anubandhati pṛṣṭhato yāti*, it is obvious that *anyatra* is here not a preposition but an adverb meaning "on the contrary, only" (see Edgerton's *Dictionary*, s.v. *anyatra*). The original reading must have been *anyatra karma sukṛtaṃ*. A misunderstanding of the meaning of *anyatra* has led to the transformation of *sukṛtaṃ* into *sukṛtād*. Edgerton pointed out that a syllable ending on an *anusvāra* before a vowel is used for metrical reasons in order to obtain a long syllable.

In his critical examination of Edgerton's position Helmer Smith prefers to speak of metrical doublets: for instance *-aṃ, -ām,* or *-aṃm* before a vowel instead of *-am.* Edgerton's assumption of vowels being lengthened or shortened because the metre requires it was rejected by Nobel (1955a) with reference to Smith 1953–55. Edgerton replied by stating that "Smith thought that such changes should be recognized only when there was some historic, phonological or morphological 'justification' for them" (1957a, 187). I believe this is not an adequate presentation of Smith's opinion. In *Les deux prosodies du vers bouddhique* (1950) Smith admits lengthening of a short vowel at the end of a *pāda,* of an initial vowel preceded by a prefix (*an-ābhibhūto*), and shortening of *-e* to *-i, -ā* to *-a, -aṃ* to *-u, -o* to *-u.*

The principal point of difference between Edgerton and Smith is that, according to Smith, Middle Indic orthography admits a short vowel before a caesura where metrically a long vowel was pronounced, for instance the fifth syllable of a *triṣṭubh-jagatī,* and also in other places where the metre [55] requires a long vowel, for instance the second syllable of a *triṣṭubh-jagatī* or the third syllable of the first and third *pāda* of a *śloka.* In these places manuscripts often write *-o* for *-a.* Smith maintains that one pronounced a long *a* and not an *o.* The writing of an *-o* is a pedantic orthography. Smith, who has a profound knowledge of Pāli metres, also tries to show that there is a greater variety of metrical schemes in Middle Indic metres than in the metres of classical Sanskrit. Therefore Smith does not limit himself to stating that lengthening or shortening of vowels must be justified on historic, phonological, or morphological grounds; he maintains that metrical and rhythmical considerations also have to be taken into account.

Smith has made an important contribution to the study of Buddhist Hybrid Sanskrit metrics in his articles. It is a pity that he did not write in a more accessible form; one has to take his objections against Edgerton seriously. Still, one should not magnify the differences between the views of Edgerton and Smith. Much of what was said by Edgerton is correct, but his short article (1957a) contains statements that are too comprehensive and need to be qualified. Edgerton's metrical theories have a great bearing on the editing of BHS texts. As Smith points out, it would be wrong to try to artificially reconstruct a metrically correct text by transforming Sanskrit forms into hybrid forms. However, Smith does not indicate how an editor is to proceed when his manuscripts are partly written in a Middle Indic orthography and partly in a metrically correct but pedantic orthography. This happens not only in Nepalese manuscripts but also in older manuscripts from Central Asia and Gilgit. In these circumstances, and considering the fact that in most cases there is only one Central Asian or Gilgit manuscript available, it is certainly preferable to be conservative, i.e., to keep the manuscript readings and to correct only those that are clearly scribal errors.

In the second place it will be necessary to separate manuscripts that belong to different streams of tradition. An edition such as Kern's edition of the *Saddharmapuṇḍarīka* (1884b), which combines readings from Nepalese manuscripts with readings from the Central Asian Petrovsky fragments, is neither fish nor flesh. The *Saddharmapuṇḍarīka* is a typical example of the problems connected with the editing of manuscripts of different origin: Nepalese manuscripts and fragments from Gilgit and Central Asia. One ought to edit the fragments separately before trying to reconstruct the history of the text. Once all the fragments from [56] Gilgit and Central Asia have been properly edited, it will be possible to see how they relate to the text as transmitted in Nepal. At present only some fragments from Gilgit and Central Asia have been edited. The Nepalese manuscripts were not properly edited by Kern and Nanjio (1908–12), as Baruch pointed out in his *Beiträge zum Saddharmapuṇḍarīkasūtra* (1938). Only when a substantial part of the Central Asian and Gilgit fragments of Buddhist texts have been edited will it be possible to study in far greater detail both the metrics and the grammar of BHS. For Edgerton's work the *Mahāvastu* is of fundamental importance. The presence of an old manuscript in Nepal and the publication of parts of the *Mahāsāṃghikavinaya* will make it possible to re-edit the *Mahāvastu* and to re-examine the characteristic features of its language and metrics. Roth's edition (1970) of the *Bhikṣuṇīvinaya* will be of great help but Jinananda's edition of the *Abhisamācārikā* (1969) cannot be used because the editor failed to reproduce the manuscript readings correctly (see my review of Jinananda's edition, de Jong 1974).

It will also be one of the tasks of the future to study again the problem of the Prakrit underlying BHS. Dschi Hiän-lin (1944, 1949) has defended the view that the original Buddhist canon was written in Old-Ardhamāgadhī and any texts that show the substitution of *-u* for *-aṃ* have been influenced by the dialect of northwestern India (Bailey's Gāndhārī). Both Edgerton and Bechert (1972, 78–79) have clearly shown that Dschi's theory is unacceptable. Edgerton believes that BHS is based upon a Middle Indic vernacular that very probably already contained a dialect mixture. He finds no reason to question the essential dialectic unity of the BHS Prakrit. Bechert (1972, 76) has pointed out that the *Mahāvastu* and the *Bhikṣuṇīvinaya* of the Mahāsāṃghika belong to a different linguistic and stylistic tradition than other BHS texts such as the *Saddharmapuṇḍarīka*. Undoubtedly, future research will be able to make finer linguistic and stylistic distinctions among the texts that have been named BHS by Edgerton. Brough has already made a division into nine groups that takes into account linguistic and stylistic features.

However, there are two reasons why it will probably [57] never be possible to fully explain the Middle Indic background of the different classes of BHS and Buddhist Sanskrit texts. In the first place the Middle Indic material at our disposal (such as the Aśokan inscriptions and later inscriptions) is insufficient. Texts in Middle Indic languages were written down several centuries after Aśoka and do not allow conclusions as to their characteristic features in earlier periods. In the second place, BHS texts were submitted to a great deal of Sanskritization before they were written down; it is not possible to prove that they were originally composed orally in Middle Indic without any admixture of Sanskrit influence. Even in the case of Pāli, where the problems of text editing are far less serious than in BHS texts, it has not been possible to determine exactly which Middle Indic dialect or dialects contributed to its formation. Both for historical and linguistic reasons western India was probably the home of Pāli, but the well-known Māgadhisms in Pāli show that Pāli is not based exclusively on western dialect(s). Pāli probably reached its final form in western India only after having undergone the influence of Middle Indic dialects in other parts of India.

If much more work still has to be done on BHS, the same cannot be said with regard to the only extant Buddhist text in Prakrit, the "Gāndhārī *Dharmapada*" as it has been called by John Brough (1962). His edition contains all the fragments. Previous scholars—Senart, Lüders, Franke, Bloch, Konow, and H. W. Bailey—had been able to study only the parts published in 1897 and 1898. The language of the text had been called Northwestern Prakrit. Gāndhārī, the name Bailey proposed, was adopted by Brough. Bailey (1946) showed that this language has been of great importance for the history of Buddhism in Central Asia. Many Indian words in Khotanese, Agnean, Kuchean, and other languages of Central Asia are based on Gāndhārī forms. The same language is used in the Kharoṣṭhī versions of the Aśoka inscriptions in Shahbazgari and Mansehra, later Kharoṣṭhī inscriptions (Konow 1929), and in the Niya documents that were edited by A. M. Boyer et al. (1920–29). This language is typified by the preservation of all three Indian sibilants, and the preservation of certain consonant groups (*tr*, *br*) [58] that have been assimilated in other Prakrits. Chinese transcriptions of Indian words in the translation of the *Dīrghāgama* of the Dharmaguptakas are based upon a Prakrit dialect that, according to Bailey and Brough, must have been the

Gāndhārī language. Undoubtedly, other Chinese translations must have been made from texts written in Gāndhārī. Only a careful study of Chinese translations will make it possible to discover which translations are based upon a Gāndhārī original. It is not possible to determine to which school the Gāndhārī *Dharmapada* belonged. The Sarvāstivāda school is the one most frequently mentioned in the Kharoṣṭhī inscriptions of northwestern India. From the Central Asian manuscripts published by Waldschmidt and other German scholars it is obvious that the same school was once prevalent in Central Asia. However, Brough shows that the Gāndhārī *Dharmapada* is different from the Sarvāstivāda tradition as preserved in the *Udānavarga*. Brough gives as possibilities the Dharmaguptakas and the Kāśyapīyas, which are both mentioned also in northwestern inscriptions. He carefully compares the Gāndhārī versions of the *Dharmapada* stanzas with those of other versions in the extensive commentary (pp. 177–282) that follows his edition of the text. This commentary is of fundamental importance for the study of many linguistic and grammatical problems in the Sanskrit, Pāli, and Gāndhārī versions of the *Dharmapada*. Brough's work can without hesitation be called the definitive work on the subject. Further research and the discovery of new materials are not likely to cause any substantial changes in the main body of this work. K. R. Norman, an excellent specialist in Middle Indic, who has made a thorough study of Brough's work, has shown that only very few revisions can be suggested (1971).

In the thirty years or so after the end of the war great progress was made with the publication of the Sanskrit manuscripts that were brought back by the German Turfan expeditions. Most of the Hīnayāna fragments belong to the Sarvāstivāda school. This has been proved by comparison with Chinese translations in the case of fragments of the Vinaya and also in the case of an Abhidharma text, the *Saṃgītiparyāya*, fragments of which were published by Stache-Rosen (1968). Fragments of the same [59] text were found by Joseph Hackin in Bamiyan in 1930 (Lévi 1932c, 2 and 9–13). A manuscript, brought back from Kucha by Pelliot, was identified by Demiéville (1961) as a fragment of the *Abhidharmajñānaprasthānaśāstra*. It is more difficult to identify sūtra texts as belonging to the Sarvāstivāda school because there is no complete Chinese translation of the Sūtrapiṭaka of the different schools. It is moreover not always easy to determine to which school one should assign the texts that are extant in Chinese translation (de Jong 1968b). Popular in Central Asia was a group of six texts: *Daśottarasūtra, Saṅgītisūtra, Catuṣpariṣatsūtra, Mahāvadānasūtra, Mahāparinirvāṇasūtra,* and (probably) the *Ekottarasūtra*. Ernst Waldschmidt has analysed the *Mahāparinirvāṇasūtra* and parallel texts in *Die Überlieferung vom Lebensende des Buddha* (1944–48) and edited the Sanskrit text together with parallel passages in Pāli, Tibetan, and Chinese (1950–51). Waldschmidt has in the same way analysed and edited the *Mahāvadānasūtra,* which deals with the seven Buddhas who preceded Gautama and, in particular, with Vipaśyin (1953–56).

The third great text analysed and edited by Waldschmidt (1951, 1952–62) is the *Catuṣpariṣatsūtra,* which relates an important episode in the life of the Buddha, beginning with the invitation of the Brahmakāyikā gods to preach the doctrine and ending with the conversion of King Bimbisāra and Upatiṣya and Kolita. Waldschmidt was able also to use a manuscript from Gilgit that had been identified by Giuseppe Tucci as part of the *Saṃghabhedavastu* of the Vinaya of the Mūlasarvāstivādin. The comparison of the manuscripts from Central Asia with the Gilgit manuscript is important not only for the linguistic history of the text but also for the study of the relations between the Sarvāstivādin and the Mūlasarvāstivādin. If the *Catuṣpariṣatsūtra* is a Sarvāstivāda text, the Mūlasarvāstivādin must have incorporated great parts of it into their Vinaya, of which a considerable part was [60] found in Gilgit (see Dutt 1939–59, vol. 3). Waldschmidt's editions are exemplary. His careful editions of the fragments (1963, 1965–71) leave no doubt about the manuscript readings, which, moreover, can be checked with the help of photomechanic reproductions of the manuscripts.

By analysing parallel texts and publishing the Sanskrit fragments together with parallel passages, Waldschmidt makes available all the relevant material. It is a pity that, as Nobel observed (1955, v, n. 1), Dutt's edition of the Gilgit manuscripts is very unsatisfactory. Waldschmidt's editions have been criticised in one respect only. According to Edgerton (1952, 1957b, 1963), Waldschmidt Sanskritized many readings.[4] There is no doubt that the texts edited by Waldschmidt contain BHS elements. However, it is by no means certain this has to be explained by the fact that these texts were originally composed in BHS. From a historical point of view one would expect texts such as the *Mahāparinirvāṇasūtra* to belong to the older stratum of the Buddhist canon. However, it is possible that the Sarvāstivādin began writing down their canonical texts at a much later period, when the use of Sanskrit had already greatly replaced the use of Prakrit and BHS. Some Sarvāstivāda texts, clearly, were originally written in BHS. This is shown by the existence of an old manuscript of the *Udānavarga,* found near Kucha by Pelliot, that was partly edited by Chakravarti (1930). It seems possible that a small number of texts of the Sarvāstivāda school were written in BHS, but that later texts were written in Buddhist Sanskrit with an admixture of BHS elements. An edition

4. Also see Brough 1954, 364–65.

of the *Udānavarga* that Lüders had prepared was destroyed in the war. Franz Bernhard, whose untimely death is a great loss for Buddhist studies, edited the text of the *Udānavarga* with the help of a great number of manuscripts and [61] fragments (1965–68).[5] The text edited by Bernhard represents the vulgata, which is much more Sanskritized than the text preserved in the manuscript found by Pelliot.

Many other Sanskrit fragments of the Turfan collection were published before 1970. I mention only the edition of the *Daśottarasūtra* by Mittal and Schlingloff, Tripāṭhī's edition of the *Nidānasaṃyukta*, Härtel's edition of the *Karmavācanā*, Valentina Rosen's edition of fragments of the *Vinayavibhaṅga* of the Sarvāstivādin and of the *Saṅgītisūtra*, Schlingloff's edition of *stotras*, metrical texts, and a Yoga textbook, and Weller's edition of fragments of the *Buddhacarita*, the *Saundarananda*, and the *Jātakamālā* (see Waldschmidt 1965–71, 1: xxviii–xxxii, 3: 275–76). Waldschmidt also edited a large number of fragments in a series of articles, many of which were reprinted in a collection of his publications (1967), and in the *Sanskrithandschriften aus den Turfanfunden*, of which three volumes had been published, with more still to follow.

Sanskrit fragments from the Pelliot collection in Paris were edited by Bernard Pauly in a series of articles published in *Journal Asiatique* (1965–67). Pauly also gave a general description of the collection of Sanskrit fragments brought back by Pelliot (1965). His article contains a list of the fragments that were published prior to 1965 (pp. 116–19). These fragments also show the prevalence of the Sarvāstivādin in the region of Kucha.

I already mentioned the publication of parts of the Vinaya of the Mahāsāṃghika. Roth's careful edition of the *Bhikṣuṇīvinaya* (1970) is important not only for putting at our disposal the Indian original but also for opening up new perspectives for a renewed study of the *Mahāvastu*, a sixteenth-century manuscript of which exists in Nepal. J. J. Jones's translation of the *Mahāvastu* (1949–56) is based upon Senart's edition and upon a comparison with parallel texts in the Pāli Tripiṭaka. Some parts of the *Mahāvastu* were critically studied [62] by Alsdorf (1968a) and T. R. Chopra (1966). Ernst Leumann's translation of *Mahāvastu*, 1: 1–193.12 was published in Japan.[6] This was not available to Jones, but he could have made use of Rudolf Otto Franke's translation of *Mahāvastu* 1:

5. See also Schmithausen 1970.

6. In the *Proceedings of the Faculty of Liberal Arts and Education*, Yamanashi University, vols. 1 to 3 (1952, 1957, 1962). The translation of *Mahāvastu* 2:83.13–121.14 by Ernst Leumann and Watanabe Shōkō was published in *Indo Koten Kenkyū (Acta Indologica)* 1 (1970): 63–108.

4.15–45.16, which was published posthumously (Franke 1929, 1930). In *The Earliest Vinaya and the Beginnings of Buddhist Literature* Erich Frauwallner (1956) tried to establish that the Vinayas of the different schools derive from a work called *Skandhaka,* composed in the first half of the fourth century B.C. This theory has been accepted by several scholars but was rejected by Lamotte (1958, 194–197).

Important work on the history of early Buddhism was published by André Bareau, who made a comprehensive study of the materials that have been transmitted on the Buddhist sects and on the councils (1955a, b). Bareau has also written a large work on the biography of the Buddha that is based upon a critical examination of the information on the life of the Buddha contained in the Sūtrapiṭakas, the Vinayas of the Theravādin, the Mahīśāsaka and the Dharmaguptaka, and the Sanskrit *Mahāparinirvāṇasūtra* and parallel texts (1963–71). Bareau's work is an important contribution to the study of the "successive states of the legend of the Buddha," to use the title of a chapter of Lamotte's book in which he distinguishes five successive states in the development of the Buddha legend (1958, 718–33). A. Foucher's *La vie du bouddha* (1949) is important not for a critical examination of the literary sources of the Buddha [63] legend but for the use of archaeological materials he had studied for many decades.

Study of the Pāli canon continued during the period 1943–73. In 1960 the first fascicle of the second volume of the *Critical Pāli Dictionary* was published. The cooperation of scholars from several countries promises to ensure the stable, continued publication of this monumental dictionary. The seventh fascicle, published in 1971, brought the dictionary up to the word *ugghāṭima,* and we may expect the completion of volume 2, containing the vowels *ā—o,* in the near future. In 1952 the Pali Text Society published the first fascicle of a *Pāli Tipiṭakaṁ Concordance* (Hare 1952–); when this project is completed, a great service will have been rendered to Pāli and Buddhist studies. In the field of Pāli grammar special attention was paid to syntax by Hans Hendriksen, who wrote a *Syntax of the Infinite Verb-forms of Pāli* (1944), and by Oskar von Hinüber, who analysed the syntax of the cases in the Vinayapiṭaka (1968; see also de Jong 1973). A grammar of Pāli according to structural principles was published in Russian by Tat'iana Elizarenkova and V. N. Toporov (1965). The Pali Text Society continues to publish editions of texts and translations. Among the latter, especially noteworthy are I. B. Horner's translations of the entire Vinayapiṭaka (1938–66) and the *Majjhimanikāya* (1954–59), distinguished by their precise terminology and judicious use of the commentaries. K. R. Norman made new translations (1969, 1971b) of the *Thera-* and *Therīgāthā* that, by their penetrating analysis of metrical, grammatical, and philological problems, mark a great advance on C. A. F. Rhys Davids's translations (1909, 1937).[7] The necessity of revising older editions of Pāli texts by taking into account Oriental editions of them and analysing metrical problems was clearly brought out in several studies published by Alsdorf (1957, 1968b) and W. B. Bollée (1970). [64]

One of the most important texts of later Hīnayāna is the *Saddharma-smṛtyupasthānasūtra.* It was studied by Lin Li-kouang in his *L'aide-mémoire de la vraie loi* (1949). Lin also prepared an edition of the Sanskrit text of the verses that had been rearranged in thirty-six chapters by Avalokitasiṃha as a compendium of the Buddhist doctrine: the *Dharma-samuccaya* (1946–73). The first volume appeared in 1946 after his death. Volume 2 (containing chapters 6–7) was published in 1969, and the final volume in 1973. According to Lin's calculation the incomplete Sanskrit manuscript of the *Dharmasamuccaya* contains 2,372 verses, whereas the Chinese and Tibetan versions of the *Saddharmasmṛtyupasthānasūtra* contain about 2,900 verses. The verses are not very interesting in themselves, being nothing but dull variations of well-known themes, but they form a welcome addition to Buddhist literature in Sanskrit. The edition is based upon very bad copies, made by Nepalese scribes, and much effort will still be needed to solve textual problems.

In the field of Abhidharma there was the welcome publication of the Sanskrit text of the *Abhidharmakośabhāṣya* by P. Pradhan (1967), although the critical apparatus is practically nonexistent. Much more care has been given by P. S. Jaini to his edition of the work of an unknown Vaibhāṣika critic of Vasubandhu's Sautrāntika leanings: the *Abhidharmadīpa* (1959). A major contribution to this field were the Abhidharma studies published by Frauwallner (1963, 1964, 1971, 1972, 1973a). They are the only systematic survey of Abhidharma literature in a Western language, and it is a pity that they were not included in his *Kleine Schriften.*

In the field of Mahāyāna studies much work was done in this period. Our knowledge of a rather neglected group of texts, the Prajñāpāramitā texts, was greatly enlarged by the efforts of one scholar, Edward Conze. Since the publication of his article on the *Prajñāpāramitāhṛdayasūtra* (1948) he has published a great number of books and articles, most of them dealing with Prajñāpāramitā or the *Abhisamayālaṃkāra.* He published a comprehensive survey of the Prajñāpāramitā literature (1960); editions and translations of the *Abhisamayālaṃkāra* (1954), the *Vajracchedikā* (1957, 1958b), the *Aṣṭasāhasrikā* (1958a, 1973a), the *Pañcaviṃśatisāhasrikā* (1961, 1964), and the *Aṣṭādaśasāhasrikā* (1962a); and a dictionary of Prajñā-

7. Norman 1969 is reviewed by me in *IIJ* 13 (1972): 297–301.

pāramitā literature (1967a). Conze also published extensively [65] on many other aspects of Buddhist studies (for example, 1951, 1962b, 1967b).

The greatest work ever undertaken by a Buddhist scholar in the West is undoubtedly Lamotte's translation of the *Mahāprajñāpāramitāśāstra* or *Prajñāpāramitopadeśa* (1944–80).[8] The author of this work treats so many topics that it requires a scholar of great learning to do full justice to its richness. Nobody could have been more qualified than Lamotte. The notes, which take up much more space than the translation itself, constitute a treasure-house of learning in all things Buddhist unequalled in Western Buddhist studies. An extensive index becomes an ever more urgent desideratum with the publication of each new volume. During the period under review, Lamotte published three volumes, to bring the translation to the end of the 27th *chüan*. As we shall see later, volumes four (1976) and five (1980) completed the translation of the first *parivarta* (*chüan* 1–34), the most important part of the work.

Johannes Nobel continued his work on the *Suvarṇaprabhāsa* (1944–50), the Sanskrit text of which he had edited in 1937. In 1944 he published the Tibetan translation, in 1950 a Tibetan-German-Sanskrit dictionary, and finally a translation of I-tsing's version and the Tibetan translation of that same version (1958; see also Conze 1967b, 18). Lamotte translated the *Vimalakīrtisūtra* from the Tibetan and Hsüan-tsang's Chinese version (1962),[9] and another important text, the *Śūraṃgamasamādhisūtra* (1965b).[10] [66] Friedrich Weller, who earlier published indices of the Tibetan translation and Indian text of the *Kāśyapaparivarta* (1933, 1935), continued his work on this text with translations of the four Chinese versions (1964, 1966a, b, 1970) and the Indian text (1965) and an edition of the Mongolian version (1962). The *Rāṣṭrapālaparipṛcchā* was translated by J. Ensink (1952).[11]

A manuscript brought back by Rāhula Sāṅkṛtyāyana and manuscript fragments from the Turfan collection in Berlin were used by D. R. Shackleton Bailey for his editions and translations of Mātṛceṭa's *stotras* (1948, 1950–51, 1951).[12] Fragments of the *Varṇārhavarṇa* were edited by Pauly (1964; see also de Jong 1967), and Schlingloff published photomechanic facsimiles of the fragments of Mātṛceṭa's *stotras* in Berlin (1968).

During this period much work was done in the field of Mahāyāna phi-

8. The first 2 vols. are reviewed by Demiéville in *JA* (1950): 375–95 (= *Choix d'études bouddhiques*: 470–90). The 3d vol. is reviewed by me in *Asia Major* 17 (1971): 105–12.

9. Reviewed by R. H. Robinson in *IIJ* 9 (1966): 150–59.

10. I reviewed this work in *Orientalistische Literaturzeitung* 65 (1970), cols. 72–83.

11. Reviewed by D. R. Shackleton Bailey, *JRAS* (1954): 79–82, and by myself, *JA* 241 (1953): 545–49.

12. For my review of Bailey 1951, see *T'oung Pao* 42 (1954): 397–405.

losophy. Jacques May's excellent translation (1959b) of chapters 2–4, 6–9, 11, 23–24, 26–27 of the *Prasannapadā* supplements the translation of the other chapters by Stcherbatsky (1927), Schayer (1931), Lamotte (1935–36b), and de Jong (1949).[13] Nāgārjuna's *Vigrahavyāvartanī* with the author's commentary was [67] edited by E. H. Johnston and Arnold Kunst (1951) and translated into English by Kamaleswar Bhattacharya (1972). T. R. V. Murti's *Central Philosophy of Buddhism* (1955) is based upon the available Sanskrit texts of the Mādhyamika school. An important review by Jacques May (1959a) criticizes the Kantian bias of Murti's approach. And, finally, Friedrich Weller published a Tibetan-Sanskrit index of the *Bodhicaryāvatāra* (1952–55).

The Chinese Buddhist canon has preserved important materials for the early history of the Yogācāra school. These were studied by P. Demiéville (1954) in a long article on the *Yogācārabhūmi* of Saṅgharakṣa. The publication by V. V. Gokhale (1947) of fragments of the Sanskrit text of Asaṅga's *Abhidharmasamuccaya* has led to further studies of this basic Abhidharma work of the Yogācāra school. Prahlad Pradhan reconstructed the Sanskrit text with the help of Hsüan-tsang's Chinese version (1950), and Walpola Rahula translated the entire work into French (1971).[14] Paul Demiéville translated a chapter of the *Bodhisattvabhūmi* from the Chinese (1957a), and Nalinaksha Dutt published a new edition of the text (1966). Alex Wayman published *Analysis of the Śrāvakabhūmi Manuscript* (1961), while L. Schmithausen made a very thorough study of a small section of the *Yogācārabhūmi* on Nirvāṇa (1969a). G. Tucci (1956) published Asaṅga's summary of the *Vajracchedikā:* the *Triśatikāyāḥ prajñāpāramitāyāḥ kārikāsaptatiḥ.* An excellent survey of the history and doctrines of the Yogācāra school was made by Jacques May (1971). [68]

The main work of the Tathāgatagarbha school, the *Ratnagotravibhāga,* was edited by E. H. Johnston (1950) and translated by J. Takasaki (1966).[15] The doctrine of the *tathāgatagarbha* was studied on the basis of Indian and Tibetan materials by David Seyfort Ruegg (1969),[16] who is not the first scholar to have studied Indian Buddhist philosophy in the light of the Tibetan philosophical tradition. (Obermiller, for instance, made use of works written in Tibet.) However, nobody before him has studied Tibetan works on such a large scale.

13. See my review of May 1959b in *IIJ* 5 (1961): 161–65.

14. Rahula's translation is reviewed by me in *T'oung Pao* 59 (1973): 339–46. See also Schmithausen 1972.

15. I reviewed Takasaki's translation in *IIJ* 11 (1968): 36–54. See also Schmithausen 1971.

16. The work is reviewed by Masaaki Hattori in *Journal of Indian Philosophy* 2 (1972): 53–64.

Much work was also done on the epistemological school of Buddhism, first by Frauwallner (1959, 1968) and other scholars of the Vienna school. Masaaki Hattori translated the first chapter of the *Pramāṇasamuccaya* (1968). As regards Dharmakīrti, one must mention the texts published by Rāhula Saṅkṛtyāyana (see Yamada 1959, 142–43). An excellent edition of the first chapter of the *Pramāṇavārttika* was published by Raniero Gnoli (1960). Tilmann Vetter translated the first chapter of the *Pramāṇaviniścaya* (1966) and wrote on epistemological problems in Dharmakīrti (1964). Frauwallner studied the order in which the works of Dharmakīrti were composed (1954). Ernst Steinkellner published the Tibetan text of the *Hetubindu,* a reconstruction of the Sanskrit text, and a richly annotated translation (1967). He also wrote two articles on Dharmakīrti's philosophy (1968, 1971). I shall refrain from mentioning publications [69] relating to later philosophers such as Devendrabuddhi, Dharmottara, Arcaṭa, Jitāri, Durvekamiśra, Ratnākīrti, Jñānaśrī, Ratnākaraśānti, and Mokṣākaragupta. Publications in this area that appeared up to 1965 are listed in Karl H. Potter's *Bibliography of Indian Philosophies* (1970), and a supplement (1972) covers a few more years.

Tantrism is still the most neglected branch of Buddhist studies. Tucci's *Tibetan Painted Scrolls* (1949) contains much information on Indian and Tibetan Tantrism. David Snellgrove published an excellent edition and translation of the *Hevajratantra* (1959), and Ariane Macdonald made good use of Tibetan sources in her study of the second chapter of the *Mañjuśrīmūlakalpa* (1962).

During this period only one comprehensive work on Indian Buddhism was published: Lamotte's history of Indian Buddhism (1958) to which I have referred several times. This work gives evidence of Lamotte's great knowledge of the Buddhist scriptures and their historical background. He has been successful in analysing the historical and geographical factors that determined the history of Buddhism from its beginning to the end of the first century A.D. His work will stand for many years, as the basic work on the history of Buddhism during this period.

To end this brief survey of the research accomplished during the period under review, a few words must be said on Tibetan and Chinese Buddhism, because Indian Buddhism cannot be studied without knowledge of its developments in Tibet and China. It is not necessary to dwell in detail upon the great contributions made by Tucci in this field. A complete bibliography of his writings from 1911 to 1970 (Tucci 1971, xi–xxiv) shows how much he has accomplished. Herbert V. Guenther has made notable contributions to the study of Tibetan philosophy (1959, 1963, 1966, 1969, 1972a, b), although his interpretations are not always acceptable. Lessing and Wayman published a translation of Mkhas-grub rje's *Fundamentals of the Buddhist Tantras* [70] (1968), which is a systematic survey of Tantrism by one of Tsoṅ-kha-pa's main pupils.

In the field of Chinese Buddhist studies the leading scholar is Demiéville. His work on the Council of Lhasa is of great importance for the history of Buddhism in India, Tibet, and China (1952; see also Tucci 1956–71, pts. 2 and 3). Many of Demiéville's articles on Buddhism were published recently in *Choix d'études bouddhiques* (1973a), which also contains a bibliography of his publications. To this must be added his translation and study of the ninth-century Ch'an master Lin-chi (1972). Other contributions by Demiéville to Buddhist studies are found in *Choix d'études sinologiques 1921–1970* (1973b). Erik Zürcher wrote a comprehensive study of the early period of Chinese Buddhism from its beginnings in the first century to the early fifth century (1959). A reprint with additions and corrections was published later (1972). Kenneth Ch'en wrote the first history of Buddhism in China in a Western language: *Buddhism in China* (1964). In a compact article Demiéville sketched the main lines of development of Chinese Buddhism (1970). This article gives a select bibliography of the most important publications in Western languages on Chinese Buddhism.

CHAPTER FOUR

Future Perspectives

[71] It is not my intention to speculate about the future of Buddhist studies. Nobody can foresee at present in which direction Buddhist studies will develop in the years to come. Much will depend on the conditions that will prevail in the universities in which most of the research is undertaken. Even more important, perhaps, is the human factor. Will Buddhist studies be able to continue to attract capable young scholars to engage in a field of study that promises little material gain and that to many seems of no relevance in the world of today?

There seems little point in trying to answer these questions. However, it is not impossible to offer some reflections on the tasks that lie ahead of us. In the preceding pages I have tried to sketch briefly some aspects of Buddhist studies *in the West.* In order to arrive at a more complete picture of the present state of Buddhist studies as a whole, it would be necessary to look also at the results obtained by Japanese scholars since the beginning of the Meiji period, when the first Japanese scholars went to Europe to study Buddhist Sanskrit texts. It would be presumptuous on my part to try to do this. Much more work has been done by Japanese scholars in Japan in the last hundred years than by Western scholars in the West. Moreover, even the best libraries in the West contain only a small fraction of the Japanese publications on Buddhism. It is very difficult for a scholar in the West to know what is being published in Japan. This brings me to the first point I would like to discuss.

In the past Western scholars have made little use of Japanese publications, whereas many Japanese scholars are very well informed about the research being undertaken in the West. First of all, this is due to the fact that few Western scholars know Japanese. Most Western scholars begin by studying Sanskrit and Pāli and later acquire sufficient knowledge of Tibetan and Chinese to read Tibetan and Chinese texts translated from

Sanskrit or other Indian originals. Their knowledge of Chinese enables them to make use of Japanese dictionaries such as Mochizuki's *Bukkyō daijiten* (1932–36) and Akanuma's *Dictionary of Indian Buddhist Proper Names* (1930–31), etc., [72] but this knowledge is not sufficient for reading Japanese books and articles. Secondly, in the West Buddhist studies are orientated more towards philological and grammatical problems. The West has been nurtured in a long tradition of editing, translating, and analysing Latin and Greek texts. The methods developed by classical scholars have been applied to the study of Sanskrit and Pāli texts. In Japan, however, the Chinese Buddhist canon has for many centuries been the basic source for the study of Buddhism. This canon has been printed many times in China and Japan since the tenth century, and for this reason Japanese Buddhist scholars in the past were not obliged to study and edit manuscripts in the same way as Western scholars had to edit manuscripts in Latin and Greek, or study the grammar of these languages, etc. When Western scholars began a serious study of Buddhist texts, their first task was the editing and translation of Sanskrit and Pāli texts and the study of Sanskrit and Pāli grammar.

It is not surprising, in view of the different traditions in which Western and Japanese scholars have been educated, that Buddhist studies have developed in different directions in the West and in Japan. However, it will certainly be detrimental to Buddhist studies in the West if Western scholars remain largely ignorant of the work done by their Japanese colleagues. It will always be a daunting task for Western scholars to learn enough Japanese to read Japanese publications, but this is an obstacle that must be overcome. Western Sinologists are very well aware of the importance of the work of Japanese scholars, and nowadays most Western Sinologists make good use of Japanese studies. It is undoubtedly necessary for Western Buddhist scholars to follow the example of the Sinologists. Even though a Western scholar has to spend many years acquiring a good knowledge of Sanskrit, Pāli, Tibetan, and Chinese, it will not be impossible to also learn enough Japanese to be able to read Japanese publications.

Still, once a scholar has learned enough Japanese, he or she is faced with another problem, a very practical problem. Each year Japanese scholars publish not only many books, some of which run to 600 or more pages, but also numerous articles in hundreds of periodicals. A Japanese scholar can go to his university library and find all the articles that are important for his research. In the West this is out of the question. Even in the best-funded universities the Western specialists in Buddhist studies can make only a modest claim on the financial resources of their libraries for the purchase of publications in [73] their field of research. They have to be very selective in advising the library with regard to the purchase of books and subscriptions to periodicals. Secondly, Western scholars whose knowledge of Japanese will always be limited will not be able to make a rapid selection of the books and articles that are most useful for their research, and scholarly advice from Japanese colleagues will be of great help to them. Of great assistance would be bibliographies that are analytical, critical, and systematic.

The only Western bibliography that took into account Japanese publications, the *Bibliographie bouddhique,* is defunct. Japanese scholars have done excellent work in publishing systematic bibliographies of articles on Buddhism, such as the bibliographies published by Ryūkoku University, but no information is given on the contents or on the scholarly value of the articles. Annual bibliographies like those published by the Jimbun Kagaku Kenkyūjo in Kyoto and Tōhō Gakkai in Tokyo are useful, but they are not an answer to the requirements of Western specialists. For one thing, there is a need for systematic and critical surveys of the work done in the different branches of Buddhist studies over the last seventy to eighty years. One would like to suggest that a group of leading Japanese scholars plan a series of bibliographical surveys relating to such topics as Early Buddhism, the schools of Hīnayāna Buddhism, Early Mahāyāna, Madhyamaka, Yogācāra, etc. These surveys should not limit themselves to an enumeration of titles of books and articles; rather, they should critically analyse the contents of the most important of them, so that a reader might see not only what has been done but also what still has to be done. Once a series of such bibliographical surveys has been published, it would be possible to publish regular surveys of current research, adding, insofar as possible, information on the research projects that are being undertaken by individual scholars or by institutes and universities. It will be necessary to give exact references for the page numbers of books and journals and the date and place of publication, indications that are not always given in Japanese bibliographies. It would certainly be asking too much to expect that such surveys be published in English, but this is not necessary, although it would be helpful for librarians in Western universities. Publishing them in Japanese, however, would be both easier for Japanese scholars and also cheaper to produce. [74] At the same time such bibliographical surveys would be useful for young Japanese scholars.

It may seem that this proposal is only meant to assist Western scholars to find their way in the overwhelming mass of Japanese publications and therefore would be of less interest to Japanese scholars. This is not true; such systematic bibliographical information would not only be useful to Japanese scholars as well, it would also help bring about a greater exchange of ideas and methods between Western and Japanese scholars, to the profit of both sides. If Western scholars could make greater use of Japanese publications and react to them, it would benefit Japanese scholars. It is exactly because Japanese and Western scholars have been brought up in different worlds that an exchange of opinions between them would be fruitful. For instance, Japanese scholars would be able to learn from the philological methods developed in the West, whereas Western scholars would have much to learn from Japanese scholarship in the study of Chinese Buddhist texts, which have been closely scrutinized by Japanese scholars for many centuries. The number of Buddhist scholars in the West is limited, and will probably always be limited. Most of them are working more or less in isolation; there are very few universities where one can find more than one or two specialists in this field. Moreover, Western scholars are scattered over many countries and write in several languages, so it is not easy for them to collaborate in research projects. (Some important works have been produced through international cooperation, despite the difficulties involved; the publications of The Pali Text Society, the Bibliotheca Buddhica, and the *Bibliographie bouddhique* are some examples. At present the *Critical Pāli Dictionary* is one of the most important undertakings of this nature.) Japanese scholars have produced some lasting collaborative achievements. One must be extremely grateful for the great energy of Junjirō Takakusu in organizing the publication of such epoch-making works as the *Taishō Shinshū Daizōkyō*, the *Nanden Daizōkyō*, and the *Kokuyaku Issaikyō.* And thanks to the tireless energy of Shōson Miyamoto and his collaborators, the *Index of the Taishō Shinshū Daizōkyō* is published at regular intervals.

The fact that Japanese scholars have in the past been able to produce such collective works of lasting value to Buddhist studies, and continue to do so at present, justifies the hope that it will be possible to organise other projects of similar scope. The *Taishō Shinshū Daizōkyō* is still the basis for serious study of the Chinese Buddhist canon. Even so, its [75] editors have not been able to make full use of all the existing materials. Moreover, although many variant readings are given in the footnotes, the *Taishō Shinshū Daizōkyō* cannot be said to be a truly critical edition of the Chinese texts. It is one of the traditions of Western scholarship that the study of philosophical, religious, and historical problems in ancient Rome and Greece must be based first of all on a sound philological basis. The same applies to the study of Buddhism, which has produced such an enormous literature in many languages. One can expect that the publication of Sanskrit manuscripts will continue both in the West and in Japan. A critical study of the Chinese Buddhist texts can only be undertaken in

Japan by Japa-nese scholars. It will be necessary to collect systematically the printed editions of the Chinese canon. Some of them, for instance the very important Chi-sha (磧砂) edition, had not even been discovered when the *Taishō Shinshū Daizōkyō* was being published. Furthermore, many old manuscripts are still preserved in Japanese temples and libraries. Last but not least, the Tun-huang manuscripts are now more accessible, with many of the collections being catalogued. The fact that at present many more manuscripts are available is of great importance for the study of the transmission of the Chinese texts. In ancient manuscripts many characters were written in a way different from the way they are written now, and this accounts for confusion between characters and for scribal errors that have been perpetuated in the printed editions. Just as editors of San-skrit manuscripts have to pay careful attention to the script in which a manuscript is written and to the errors the scribe may have committed in copying a manuscript written in a different script, in order to establish a correct text, so in the same way the editors of Chinese Buddhist texts will have to take into account historical and personal peculiarities in the writing of Chinese characters.

It is obvious that such an undertaking will demand many years and will require the collaboration of many scholars. It will probably be best to begin with texts that are rather short and whose textual history is not too complicated. This also depends, of course, on the number of manuscripts available. The publication of a small number of critical text editions will make it possible to gradually work out a system of editorial methods before undertaking the editing of more difficult texts on a larger scale. The result will be a slowly increasing corpus of critical text editions that will form the essential basis for further comparative study of the Chinese texts with Indian originals [76] and Tibetan translations. The publication by the Suzuki Research Foundation of the Peking edition of Kanjur and Tanjur has greatly stimulated the study of the Tibetan canon. In this case, too, it will now be necessary to compare other editions and Tun-huang manuscripts and to publish critical editions. Some of the Tun-huang manuscripts contain archaic translations that have been revised by the editors of the Kanjur and Tanjur. In some cases these archaic translations are closer to the Indian original than the revised texts in the Kanjur and the Tanjur. Critical editions of Chinese and Tibetan translations are an essential prerequisite for the publication of synoptic editions of the various translations of the same text. Von Staël-Holstein's edition of the *Kāśyapaparivarta* is a good example of the way a synoptic edition has to be planned. The ideal goal of Buddhist philology must be the publication of synoptic editions of Buddhist texts in Sanskrit, Tibetan, and

Chinese or in Tibetan and Chinese. Of course, where there is no Indian original and no Tibetan translation, only a critical edition of the Chinese text will be possible.

The Chinese Buddhist texts are of fundamental importance for Buddhist studies for two reasons. In the first place the Chinese canon has preserved many Indian texts, especially ancient Indian texts that have not been translated into Tibetan. In the second place the Chinese texts have been translated from the second century A.D. onwards and enable us to study older recensions of Indian texts. The fact that many texts have been translated more than once in different periods in China makes it possible to study the development of these texts. This is not possible just with the aid of Tibetan translations, which generally represent the Indian text in its final form.

However, the study of Chinese translations is often complicated by the fact that the attribution of a translation to a translator is wrong or doubtful. The Chinese canon contains many catalogues of translations, Tao-an's catalogue dating from A.D. 374 being the first. Yet they often contain conflicting information. Japanese scholars—I mention only Daijō Tokiwa and Tomojirō Hayashiya—have done much work in studying these catalogues critically. Also, a study has been made of the terminology used by the translators. This internal criterion is certainly the most important. Generally speaking, however, scholars have studied the terminology of one text in the course of their research and limited themselves to a number of technical terms. In this field of research much more work still needs to be done. It will be neces-[77]sary to study, not a single text, but the work of one translator, and in a systematic fashion. Tomojirō Hayashiya has realised the importance of a systematic study of the terminology used by translators, but he has not been able to carry out his plans. It will be necessary to avoid limiting oneself to the terminology and to take into account also the vocabulary used by the translator and the characteristic features of his style. Terminology by itself is not always a reliable guide, because translations of Buddhist terms are often taken from translations already in existence. Moreover, one must be aware that the printed editions of the Chinese canon do not always transmit a text in exactly the same form as it was written by the translator and his collaborators. Translations were copied by hand for many centuries before they were printed for the first time. It is quite possible that later copyists changed the renderings of Buddhist terms to bring them into line with equivalent expressions current in their time. It is much more difficult, however, to change vocabulary and style. As mentioned before, Tunhuang fragments of Tibetan translations of Buddhist texts contain archaic translations that, in some cases, were subject to extensive revision by the editors of the Kanjur and Tanjur. There is no evidence to prove that the organisers of the first printed editions of Chinese translations made large-scale revisions to existing translations, but it is quite possible that copyists made some changes in the texts. A systematic examination of the Chinese Buddhist texts, translated by An-shih-kao (安世高) and his successors, will make it possible to determine the peculiarities of each translator. Traditionally a distinction is made between archaic, old, and new translations. But this distinction is not sufficient for a critical examination of the existing translations. We first of all need to know in much greater detail the terminology, the vocabulary, and the style of the principal translators. Once these are better known, it will become possible to decide with greater certitude whether a certain text is rightly or wrongly attributed to one of these translators. Then, once we have studied the work of the principal translators, it will be easier to study carefully the translations made by those translators who have translated only a few texts.

A careful study of the language in which the Chinese Buddhist texts are written is necessary in order to determine the date of each translation and the name of the translator. In this way it will become possible to solve many problems relating to the history of the Chinese Buddhist canon, problems [78] that are of great importance for the history both of Indian Buddhism and of Chinese Buddhism. A better and more precise knowledge of the language of the Chinese translations will also lead to a greater knowledge of the Indian originals. Many Indian texts are only known through a Chinese translation. Even where an Indian original exists, often it is not the same text as that translated in China but a later text that differs from it, because in the course of its transmission in India it was subjected to alterations and accretions. Of great importance for the knowledge of the language of the Indian original are the transcriptions of Indian names and terms. In recent years John Brough has shown that the language of northwestern India, the so-called Gāndhārī, has to be taken into account when explaining Chinese transcriptions of Indian names. Thanks to the work of Karlgren, Pulleyblank, and other scholars, it is possible to reconstruct with a fair degree of certainty the pronunciation of Chinese characters in T'ang and pre-T'ang times. On the Indian side more is now known about Buddhist Hybrid Sanskrit and Gāndhārī through the work of Edgerton and Brough. Continued study of Chinese transcriptions and of Indian texts that are not written in pure Sanskrit will be required in order to obtain a better picture of the linguistic aspects of the texts that have been translated into Chinese.

In recent decades many scholars have done excellent work in publishing detailed Tibetan-Sanskrit indices of Buddhist texts, but there still are very few Chinese-Sanskrit indices. It is of course more difficult to compile indices of Chinese translations than it is of Tibetan translations, because the Tibetan translators generally adhered to a well-determined terminology, even though sometimes one Sanskrit word is rendered by many different Tibetan words, as can easily be seen by consulting Lokesh Chandra's Tibetan-Sanskrit dictionary. Nevertheless, it is certainly possible to compare Indian texts with Chinese translations and to compile Chinese-Sanskrit dictionaries. These dictionaries would be of great help in the study of Buddhist texts. Once a number of these dictionaries or indices have been published, it will be possible to compile a comprehensive Sanskrit-Chinese dictionary that will allow us to see how a certain Sanskrit term has been translated by An-shih-kao, Dharmarakṣa, Kumārajīva, etc. Probably there will be less uniformity in the renderings of terms by the translators of Indian texts in China than is the case in Tibet. Chinese translators, especially those in older periods, did not [79] always use the same equivalents. This is perhaps partly due to the fact that they did not always have the same Chinese collaborators to polish the Chinese style. The range of variation in the use of terminology by one translator is one of the many important facts that can only come to light by the compilation of Chinese-Sanskrit and Sanskrit-Chinese dictionaries.

In the past much work has been done in translating Buddhist texts written in Sanskrit, Pāli, and Chinese. Much more still has to be done. Many translations of Sanskrit texts by Western scholars were done in the nineteenth century, but they were not based on critical editions, and very few contain sufficient notes. Now, however, we have some excellent translations: Johnston's translations of the *Buddhacarita* and the *Saundarananda,* for example. Johnston's translations are based upon critical editions and an extensive study of Buddhist literature in Sanskrit and Pāli. He paid great attention to the stylistic and lexical characteristics of these two Sanskrit texts. A scholar who is well acquainted with the Chinese Buddhist literature could probably add much to the commentary, and it is always possible to improve upon Johnston's translation in some points, as was shown by Claus Vogel in his study of the first chapter of the *Buddhacarita* (1966). Nevertheless, Johnston's translations remain a splendid achievement, and they show how Buddhist texts should be translated. Many Pāli texts, too, have been translated into English, but new critical translations are an urgent desideratum. As an example of such a critical translation, accompanied by lengthy notes, I would like to mention K. R. Norman's translation of the *Theragāthā* (1969). In this translation the commentary takes up much more space than the translation itself. Norman's work clearly demonstrates how Pāli texts have to be translated and studied.

The translations by Johnston and Norman are translations of literary texts. It is not surprising, therefore, that they have concentrated their efforts first of all on the language and the style of the texts, as is obvious from the notes to their translations. In the case of texts of philosophical or historical significance, the translation ought to be accompanied by a commentary dealing with these aspects. It is not difficult to give an example of a translation that contains a commentary discussing in great detail all important items in the text itself: [80] Lamotte's translation (1944–80) of the *Ta-chih-tu-lun* (大智度論). His work is a fine example of Buddhist scholarship. There is no doubt that Japanese scholars, too, could provide us with translations of Chinese Buddhist texts accompanied by commentaries of similar scope. Most of the translations in the *Kokuyaku Issaikyō* are only sparingly provided with notes. However, it is not sufficient to translate a text and to explain briefly some technical terms; both the introduction to, and the commentary on, a translation ought to provide full information on all matters relating to the text.

When it comes to translations of Chinese Buddhist texts, Western translators are forced to translate each character into English or another Western language. Japanese translators often do not really translate the Chinese text but rather indicate how each sentence has to be analysed and constructed. All important words and terms are left untranslated, because the Japanese language allows the translator to keep the same Chinese characters as those found in the Chinese text. However, such translations fail to do justice to the original texts. It will often be necessary to translate Chinese characters by other Chinese characters. Sometimes, however, it will be difficult to find good equivalents, and then it will be necessary to retain the same characters, but in such cases one should provide a note to explain the exact meaning and value of these terms in the Chinese text. Critical translations of Chinese Buddhist texts into Japanese must be based on a searching analysis of the style, vocabulary, and terminology of the Chinese text. In the case of Chinese Buddhist texts translated from original Indian texts, it will be necessary to try to determine, as far as possible, the Indian terms that occur in the original text.

Problems of a different nature arise when one has to translate original Chinese Buddhist texts. In many instances the authors of these texts have used Buddhist terms, but not in the same meaning that those terms have in Indian texts. In the early period of Chinese Buddhism, Taoist ideas clearly exercised a great influence. Often it is difficult to know whether a certain term reflects a Taoist idea or has to be interpreted as a Buddhist idea rendered by a Taoist term. A Japanese translator will be tempted to retain the same Chinese characters without trying to solve this difficulty.

In such cases an English translation would be far more enlightening. Let me quote one example. Seng-chao's work has been studied and translated by a group of scholars from Kyoto in the *Jōron Kenkyū*, a splendid publication that shows the excellent [81] results that can be obtained by the combined efforts of a group of scholars in the study of one text. In a review of this work in *T'oung Pao*, Paul Demiéville has expressed his great appreciation of the work done by these scholars (1957b). Still, he has not omitted to point out that the Japanese translation of the text does not solve all the problems related to the interpretation of the text, mainly because difficult terms have not been translated. Demiéville remarks that, in translating the same text into English, Liebenthal (1948) had to decide in each single instance how to render a Chinese term into English. Undoubtedly, the ideal solution would be for Japanese and Western scholars to work together in order to translate such texts into English, to the benefit of both Japanese and Western scholarship.

In what I have said up to now, the main emphasis has been put on philological problems, such as critical editions of texts, analysis of style and language, critical translations, etc. Buddhist studies, of course, embrace much more than philology, but philology is of basic importance. Once texts have been properly edited, interpreted, and translated, it will become possible to study the development of religious and philosophical ideas. Indian Buddhism has produced a very rich literature, of which much is preserved in Sanskrit and Pāli, but even much more in Tibetan and Chinese translations. Moreover, Buddhist monuments show another important aspect of Buddhism. The great wealth of literary and archaeological sources for the study of Buddhism in India will occupy many scholars for centuries to come. However, this mass of material must not make us forget that Indian Buddhism cannot be studied in isolation from its context. It is also necessary to study Vedic and Brahmanical literature, Jainism and other Indian religions, Dharmaśāstras, etc. The study of Indian Buddhism has first of all to be seen as a branch of Indology. In Japan the study of Buddhism has for many centuries been based exclusively on Chinese Buddhist texts. In the last one hundred years Japanese scholars have added to the study of Chinese texts the study of Sanskrit, Pāli, and Tibetan texts, and much has been done by them to enhance our knowledge of Indian Buddhism. However, other branches of Indological studies have not developed to the same extent. Recent years have seen an increasing interest among Japanese scholars in the study of the six *darśana*s. It is to be hoped that many scholars [82] will become interested in other aspects of Indian culture as well. Scholars like Zenryū Tsukamoto have brilliantly demonstrated that Chinese Buddhism can only be understood when seen against the background of Chinese history and culture. In the same way, Indian Buddhism has to be studied in relation to Indian culture, as one of the manifestations of Indian spirituality. This can only be achieved when scholars are actively engaged in the study of all aspects of Indian culture. The cultures of India, China, and Japan cannot be understood without knowledge of Buddhism. Similarly, Buddhism cannot be understood without knowledge of the cultures of India, China, and Japan.

Allow me to conclude with the wish that future generations of scholars, both in Japan and in the West, will work closely together in the study of Buddhism.

CHAPTER FIVE

Recent Decades: B (1973–83)

In the first place it is my sad duty to mention the names of the scholars who passed away during the next period under review.

Frank-Richard Hamm died in 1973 (see Hahn 1975a), Erich Frauwallner the following year (see Oberhammer 1976a, b). Ludwig Alsdorf passed away in 1978 (see Bruhn 1979, Oberhammer 1979, Alsdorf 1974, v–xix); 1979 witnessed the death of Paul Demiéville (see Gernet and Hervouet 1979, Hervouet 1981), Edward Conze (see de Jong 1980),[1] [80] and Christiaan Hooykaas (see Swellengrebel 1980). In 1980 Valentina Stache-Rosen (see Waldschmidt 1982) and Friedrich Weller (see Rau 1982) passed away. The following year Isaline Horner (see Cousins et al. 1974, ix–xi; Iggleden and Iggleden 1974) and Arnold Kunst died.[2] In 1982 Jean Filliozat (see P. Filliozat 1983, Filliozat 1974, xi–xxv) and Constantin Regamey[3] passed away, and in May 1983 Étienne Lamotte departed this life. It is not necessary, I believe, to describe here the accomplishments of these scholars, as their books have been mentioned in previous chapters or will be referred to in the course of this chapter. Apart from Frank-Richard Hamm and Valentina Stache-Rosen, who died at a relatively young age, all the scholars mentioned died in their seventies or eighties or even in their nineties, and their contributions to Buddhist studies are well known. I would like, however, to say a few words about Étienne

1. For bibliographies of Conze's works see Conze 1975b, 222–34; 1978, 127–37; 1979, 154–57; and Lancaster 1977, 419–33.

2. Kunst's main work was the translation of the *anumāna* (18th) chapter of the *Tattvasaṃgraha* (Kunst 1939) and the edition of the Tibetan translation of the same chapter (Kunst 1946–47). He also published, together with E. H. Johnston, the Sanskrit text of Nāgārjuna's *Vigrahavyāvartanī* (*MCB* 9: 99–152).

3. Regamey's publications are listed in *Asiatische Studien/Études asiatiques* 35/2 (1981): 9–17.

Lamotte, who was able to complete his translation of the first *parivarta* (*chüan* 1–34) of the *Mahāprajñāpāramitāśāstra* or *Prajñāpāramitopadeśa* with two more volumes during this period. The complete work, which contains more than two thousand five hundred pages, is of a scope without parallel in the history of Buddhist studies in the West. It is difficult to realise that these five large volumes constitute only a part of his achievement. To him we also are indebted for excellent translations of five important works: *Saṃdhinirmocana* (1935), *Karmasiddhiprakaraṇa* (1935–36a), *Mahāyānasaṃgraha* (1938–39), *Vimala*-[81]*kīrtinirdeśasūtra* (1962), and *Śūraṃgamasamādhisūtra* (1965b), and in addition a comprehensive history of Indian Buddhism up to the Śaka era (1958). His many articles and reviews are listed in the bibliography that Daniel Donnet (1980) contributed to a volume of Indian and Buddhist studies published in honour of Étienne Lamotte.

During the period under review several scholars were honoured with the publication of a felicitation volume: Isaline Horner (Cousins et al. 1974), Ernst Waldschmidt (Museum für Ind. Kunst 1977), Herbert Guenther (Kawamura and Scott 1977), Edward Conze (Lancaster 1977 [sic: it actually appeared only in 1979]), and Étienne Lamotte (Institut Orientaliste 1980). Volumes in memory of Richard Robinson (Kiyota 1978) and Ludwig Alsdorf (Bruhn and Wezler 1981) were also published. Particularly welcome was the publication of collected articles of Wilhelm Geiger (1973), Ludwig Alsdorf (1974), Jean Filliozat (1974), R. Otto Franke (1978), H. von Glasenapp (1980), and Erich Frauwallner (1982). We can only hope that, notwithstanding difficult economic conditions, the "*Kleine Schriften*" of eminent scholars will continue to be published, because there is no better way to honour scholars than by making their work more accessible. In this connection one can have nothing but praise for the von Glasenapp Stiftung, which since 1967 has been responsible for publishing the *Kleine Schriften* of many scholars.

Although on the one hand Buddhist studies suffered serious losses with [82] the passing away of so many eminent scholars, on the other hand the ranks were filled again by young scholars who published excellent work and in this way contributed to the continued prosperity of Buddhist studies. In most countries of Europe and in America, universities faced great difficulties maintaining their existing programmes, yet Buddhist studies continued—in some instances, on an even larger scale. More scholars were engaged in the study of Buddhism in Europe and America than ever before.

My survey of Buddhist studies will mainly be concerned with studies relating to Buddhist texts in Indian languages or translated from these languages into Tibetan and Chinese. Without any doubt, the study of Indian Buddhist texts deserves a central place in Buddhist studies because it forms the basis for any serious work in the study of religion, philosophy, history, or art.

First of all, then, I draw attention to the fact that a great number of facsimile editions of Buddhist Sanskrit manuscripts were published during this period. In the past, editions of Sanskrit fragments of Buddhist texts were often accompanied by facsimiles, but facsimiles of complete manuscripts or of large fragments were rare, although one must mention that already in 1926 a facsimile edition of a Sanskrit manuscript brought back by Ekai Kawaguchi was published in Japan (1956). W. Baruch pointed out that this manuscript was written in 1069/1070 (1938, 1). H. Toda has published a romanised transliteration of the entire manuscript (1980, 1980–85). The publication of facsimiles makes it possible to check the readings adopted by editors of texts. This is not the only advantage of facsimiles, however. It is absolutely necessary to study texts as much as possible on the basis of facsimiles of manuscripts because this is the only way to understand the mistakes that have been and can be committed by scribes. Moreover, it is only by taking into account the fact that texts were often successively written in different scripts that one can fully understand the often complicated history of a text in the course of its transmission. For [83] this reason the facsimile editions published during this decade are extremely welcome.

Of particular importance for the history of Buddhist literature are the manuscripts from Central Asia and Gilgit. Most of the manuscripts from Central Asia represent only fragments. German scholars have published a great number of facsimiles of these manuscripts, either together with text editions or separately, since the first publications by Pischel in 1904 (Waldschmidt 1965–71, 1: xxvi–xxxii, 3: 275–76; Sander and Waldschmidt 1980–85, 4: 353–54). An almost complete manuscript of the *Saddharmapuṇḍarīka* was published in facsimile in Lokesh Chandra 1976 and in romanisation in Toda 1981. This "Kashgar" manuscript, as it is called, is described by Heinz Bechert in his foreword to the facsimile edition. Heinz Bechert also edited nine folios of this manuscript (1972). Readings of this manuscript were made known for the first time in 1912 by Hendrik Kern in the edition of the *Saddharmapuṇḍarīka* published in Bibliotheca Buddhica (Kern and Nanjio 1908–12), but we had to wait till 1976 for the publication of a facsimile edition of this very important manuscript. The *Saddharmapuṇḍarīka* is undoubtedly one of the most interesting texts for the study of the history of Buddhist texts, because manuscripts of it have been found in Central Asia, Gilgit, and Nepal. Many of the Sanskrit manuscripts discovered in Gilgit—those kept in the National Archives in Delhi—were published in facsimile by Raghu Vira and Lokesh Chandra in ten volumes (1959–74). Two groups of manuscripts of the *Saddharmapuṇḍarīka* (A and B) were published in facsimile and in romanisation by S. Watanabe (1972). Two folios of group B and manuscripts of group C were published in facsimile by Raghu Vira and Lokesh Chandra (1959–74). They were not included in the facsimiles published by Watanabe, but H. Toda published a romanised text of these folios (1979), thereby complementing Watanabe 1972. In 1982 Oskar von [84] Hinüber edited folios 45–74 of another Gilgit manuscript (K) of the *Saddharmapuṇḍarīka* (1982c). In his introduction he showed that the Gilgit manuscripts of the *Saddharmapuṇḍarīka* can be divided into two families, one comprising the manuscripts of group A, the other the manuscripts B, C, and K. The relations of these two recensions to the Central Asian materials on the one hand and to the Nepalese manuscripts on the other proved to be much more complicated than scholars had thought in the past.

Although it is my intention to limit this survey to work done by scholars in Europe and America, sometimes, as here, it is necessary to mention the works of Indian or Japanese scholars. It is also absolutely necessary to mention at least the publication by the Institute for the Comprehensive Study of the Lotus Sutra (Risshō University) of facsimiles of more than thirty manuscripts of the *Saddharmapuṇḍarīka* from Nepal, Gilgit, and Central Asia in fifteen volumes, of which twelve have been published since 1977. It has thus become possible to make an exhaustive study of the different recensions of the *Saddharmapuṇḍarīka* and to analyse in detail the grammatical and lexicographical characteristics of each recension. When writing his *Buddhist Hybrid Sanskrit Grammar and Dictionary* (1953a), Franklin Edgerton had only very unreliable text editions of the *Saddharmapuṇḍarīka* at his disposal. It will be one of the main tasks of Buddhist philology eventually to replace Edgerton's monumental work with one that is based upon reliable editions of texts, but it will be a long time before such an undertaking is feasible. At present the most important work to be undertaken is the editing of all texts published in facsimiles and the study of different recensions and their grammatical and lexicographical characteristics. What we need are not only grammars of single texts but also grammars of one single recension of a text, along the lines of the grammar of Sanskrit Recension A of the *Prajñāpāramitāratnaguṇasaṃcayagāthā* published by Akira Yuyama (1973; see also 1976).[4] The same applies to lexicographical studies. Only when a sufficient number of grammars and [85] lexicons have been published in

4. Yuyama 1973 and 1976 were reviewed by G. Schopen in *IIJ* 20 (1978): 110–24.

this way will it become possible to undertake the compilation of a comprehensive grammar and dictionary of Buddhist Hybrid Sanskrit.

The publication of facsimiles of Gilgit manuscripts has made it possible to prepare new editions of the texts previously edited in a very unsatisfactory way by Nalinaksha Dutt. Hinüber 1979a presents an excellent survey of the history of the studies on the Gilgit manuscripts. It contains a bibliography of editions of manuscripts published in facsimile by Raghu Vira and Lokesh Chandra. In a recent article on the importance of the Gilgit manuscripts (1982b; see also 1980a and 1981c), von Hinüber deals with different problems relating to these manuscripts, such as the colophons, which contain interesting information on the presence of Sakas in Gilgit and on the Paṭola-ṣāhi dynasty. He also examines the different recensions of the *Saṃghātasūtra,* of which eight manuscripts have been found in Gilgit. Of great importance is the almost complete manuscript of the *Vinayavastu* of the Mūlasarvāstivāda school. The text of three *vastus* (*Saṃghabheda-, Śayanāsana-,* and *Adhikaraṇavastu*) was published by Raniero Gnoli (1977–78, 1978). It is very much to be hoped that the manuscript used by Gnoli will also be published in a facsimile edition.

Another important collection of manuscripts and photocopies is the Patna collection of the manuscripts from Tibet photographed or copied by Rāhula Saṅkṛtyāyana in 1929–38. Several texts were published by Indian scholars from 1973 (Shukla 1973; Thakur 1974; Tatia 1976a, b; Jaini 1979; Shukla 1979; Shastri 1979). However, some of these editions are very unsatisfactory, and the publication of facsimiles would be highly desirable.[5] Gustav Roth (1980, 93–135) edited the text of the [86] *Dharmapada,* which was also edited by N. S. Shukla (1979). K. R. Norman and Margaret Cone continued working on a new edition and critical study of this text, which is of great importance for the study of the different recensions of the *Dharmapada.*[6] Chinese versions of the *Dharmapada* and *Udānavarga* were studied by Charles Willemen (1974, 1975a, 1978). I might mention here the useful (for Western scholars as well) publication of the *Dharmapada* studies of K. Mizuno (1981).

The fourth volume of the catalogue of Sanskrit manuscripts from Central Asia (Sander and Waldschmidt 1980) lists the editions of texts published in the period 1970–80. Also very useful is the systematic survey of the manuscripts described in the first four volumes of the catalogue. The contents of the manuscripts of Buddhist literature are divided into seven sections: 1) Vinaya; 2) Sūtra; 3) Anthologies of Religious Poems and Narratives; 4) Abhidharma, Buddhist Technical Terms, Com-

5. See my review of K. Shukla's edition of the *Śrāvakabhūmi* in *IIJ* 18 (1976): 307–10, and Schmithausen 1982a.

6. Personal correspondence to the author from K. R. Norman, dated January 4, 1982.

mentaries, Yoga; 5) Cult; 6) Mahāyāna-Sūtras; 7) Poetry. In recent years German scholars have been active in photographing Sanskrit manuscripts in Nepal for the Nepal-German Manuscript Preservation Project. A few publications based upon these manuscripts have already appeared (see Harrison 1982 and Hahn 1982a). This project will undoubtedly be of great importance for the study of Sanskrit Buddhist texts, but as long as no list or catalogue is available it is difficult to know which new materials have been uncovered.

Thus far I have discussed mainly the publication of facsimile editions and the contents of manuscript collections from Central Asia, Gilgit, Tibet, and Nepal. Next it might be useful if I sketch developments in the study of Buddhist texts in a systematic way, beginning with the texts of the Hīnayāna schools. I mentioned above the editions [87] of parts of the Vinaya of the Mūlasarvāstivāda school and of the so-called Patna *Dharmapada.* Fragments of sūtras from the Turfan collection were edited by Waldschmidt in the fourth volume of the catalogue of the Sanskrit manuscripts from Central Asia, and in separate publications (see Sander and Waldschmidt 1980–85, 4: 353–54). Fragments of the *Abhidharmaprakaraṇabhāṣya* were edited by J. Imanishi (1975). J. Takasaki (1965) identified fragments of the *Dharmaskandha* among the Gilgit fragments edited by Sudha Sengupta. Candrabhāl Tripāṭhī identified fragments of the *Ekottarāgama* among these same fragments, and was engaged in preparing a new edition (see Hinüber 1979a, (6)332). Mention should also be made here of a romanised text of the *Ekottarāgama* published in Japan by Yūsen Ōkubo (1982).

Western scholars have paid relatively little attention to Abhidharma literature. The one great exception was, of course, La Vallée Poussin. It comes, therefore, as no surprise that two important Abhidharma texts were translated by two of his pupils. José van den Broeck translated Ghoṣaka's *Amṛtarasa* from the Chinese (1977b).[7] The translation is preceded by a long and interesting introduction that outlines the place of the *Amṛtarasa* in the development of the Sarvāstivāda school. Marcel van Velthem translated Skandhila's *Abhidharmāvatāraśāstra* from the Chinese and edited the text of the Tibetan version (1977).[8] Another important Abhidharma text, the *Abhidharmahṛdaya,* or *Abhidharmasāra,* by Dharmaśrī, was translated into English by Charles Willemen (1975b) and into French by I. Armelin (1978).[9] The same text was also studied in several articles by Leon Hurvitz (1977, 1978, 1979).[10] [88]

7. See my review in *T'oung Pao* 66 (1980): 277–83.

8. See my review in *T'oung Pao* 65 (1979): 294–303.

9. See a review by me in *The Eastern Buddhist* 13/1 (1980): 151–58.

10. On Hurvitz 1978 see my remarks in *The Eastern Buddhist* 12/2 (1979): 159–60.

In the field of Prajñāpāramitā studies Edward Conze, the great pioneer who did so much in this neglected field, continued his work. In 1978 he published a revised and enlarged edition of his book *The Prajñāpāramitā Literature* (1960).[11] Other works published by him in this period include a translation of the short Prajñāpāramitā texts (1973b), an edition of chapters 70 to 82 of the Gilgit manuscript of the *Aṣṭādaśasāhasrikā-Prajñāpāramitā* (1974), and another volume of collected articles entitled *Further Buddhist Studies* (1975b). In the volume in honour of Conze, *Prajñāpāramitā and Related Systems* (Lancaster 1977), most contributions deal with one aspect or other of the Prajñāpāramitā literature. This volume shows clearly that Conze's example stimulated younger scholars to engage in the study of the Prajñāpāramitā literature.

I have mentioned already some of the many publications of facsimiles and romanised editions of the *Saddharmapuṇḍarīkasūtra.* Paul Harrison published an edition of the Tibetan text of one of the earliest Mahāyāna sūtras, the *Pratyutpanna-buddha-*[89]*saṃmukhāvasthita-samādhi-sūtra* (1978). In 1965 Friedrich Weller published a German translation of the *Kāśyapaparivarta;* another German scholar, Bhikkhu Pāsādika, translated the same text into English (Pāsādika 1977–79). It will be very useful to compare these two translations carefully when studying the *Kāśyapaparivarta.* Bhikkhu Pāsādika also "restored" the Sanskrit text of the *Vimalakīrtinirdeśasūtra* from the Tibetan version (Pāsādika and Joshi 1981), arriving in several instances at interpretations that differ from those found in Lamotte's French version, which was also translated into English (Boin 1976). A very good, readable translation of the same text was published by Robert Thurman (1976).[12] Pierre Python, O.P., translated the *Vinayaviniścaya-upāli-paripṛcchā* into French (1973); the book also contains a translation of Mātṛceṭa's *Sugatapañcatriṃśatstotra.*[13] A text that is one of the scriptural authorities for the Tathāgatagarbha school, the *Śrīmālāsiṃhanādasūtra,* was translated from the Tibetan and the Chinese by Alex and Hideko Wayman (1974).

Much work was done on the Madhyamaka school. To David Seyfort Ruegg we owe the first comprehensive treatment of the literature of the Madhyamaka school (1981). Another important work is Christian Lindtner's *Nagarjuniana: Studies in the Writings and Philosophy of Nāgārjuna* (1982a), in which he studies the thirteen texts that, according to him, can be safely attributed to Nāgārjuna: the *Mūlamadhyamakakārikā, Śūnyatāsaptati, Vigrahavyāvartanī,* [90] *Vaidalyaprakaraṇa, Vyavahārasiddhi,*

11. For additions see von Hinüber's review in *IIJ* 22 (1980): 73–74.

12. I reviewed Pāsādika and Joshi 1981 in *IIJ* 25 (1983): 160–61, and Thurman 1976 in *IIJ* 22 (1980): 254–56.

13. See my review in *IIJ* 19 (1977): 131–35.

Yuktiṣaṣṭikā, Catuḥstava, Ratnāvalī, Pratītyasamutpādahṛdayakārikā, Sūtrasamuccaya, Bodhicittavivaraṇa, Suhṛllekha, and *Bodhisaṃbhāra[ka].* Finally, one must mention Jacques May's article (1979) on *Chūgan* in the fifth fascicule of the *Hōbōgirin.*

One of the most difficult problems in Madhyamaka studies is the great number of works that are attributed to Nāgārjuna. Christian Lindtner adopts internal and external criteria of authenticity. He considers the *Mūlamadhyamakakārikā*s to be his magnum opus. Those works that agree with it in regard to style, scope, and doctrine and that are explicitly ascribed to Nāgārjuna by the testimony of "trustworthy witnesses," such as Bhavya (Bhāvaviveka), Candrakīrti, Śāntarakṣita, and Kamalaśīla, are considered by him to be genuine. Seyfort Ruegg takes as his point of departure the *Mūlamadhyamakakārikā*s together with any other texts ascribed to the same author that are doctrinally related, namely the *Yuktiṣaṣṭikā, Śūnyatāsaptati, Vaidalyaprakaraṇa, Vigrahavyāvartanī,* and *Ratnāvalī.* As to the other seven texts attributed to Nāgārjuna by Lindtner, Seyfort Ruegg is much less confident, and with regard to most of them he mentions only that they are ascribed to him. As regards the *Bodhicittavivaraṇa,* Seyfort Ruegg is inclined to attribute it to a Vajrayānist master, Ārya Nāgārjuna, who was most probably also the author of a commentary on the *Guhyasamāja* and of the *Pañcakrama.*

It seems that all scholars agree in considering the *Mūlamadhyamakakārikā*s to be the most important work of Nāgārjuna, and it was accordingly made the subject of many studies. New manuscript material made it possible to publish a new edition (de Jong 1977a). Another edition was published by Lindtner (1982b), who also translated the text into Danish (pp. 67–135, 175–215). Lindtner is critical of previous English translations of this work by Streng (1967, 181–220) and by Inada (1970), but praises Gnoli's Italian translation (1961). It is to be hoped that a good English translation of this work will be published in the near future. [91]

Of particular importance is the fact that recent scholars have concentrated their attention on the *Mūlamadhyamakakārikā*s in order to analyse Nāgārjuna's philosophy. In his book Seyfort Ruegg uses this text as the basis for his sketch of some important points of philosophical interest in Nāgārjuna's thought. Also based exclusively upon it are two articles by Tilmann Vetter (1982a, b) and a very detailed study of the logic and dialectics of Nāgārjuna by Guy Bugault (1983).

Lindtner published in his *Nagarjuniana* (1982a) an edition of the Tibetan text of the *Śūnyatāsaptati,* of the Sanskrit text and the Tibetan version of the *Vigrahavyāvartanī,* and of the Tibetan version and the Sanskrit fragments of the *Yuktiṣaṣṭikā* and of the *Bodhicittavivaraṇa.* The book also contains the first edition of the Sanskrit text of the *Lokātītastava* and the *Acintyastava*. Lindtner maintains that the four hymns of Nāgārjuna are the *Lokātītastava, Niraupamyastava, Acintyastava,* and *Paramārthastava,* because these four are found in four MSS and are often quoted. Moreover, the same four hymns are found in Amṛtākara's *Catuḥstavasamāsārtha* (see Tucci 1956a, 236–37 and Lamotte 1944–80, 3: xliii). Lindtner's *Nagarjuniana* (1982a) also comprises English translations of the *Śūnyatāsaptati, Yuktiṣaṣṭikā, Lokātītastava, Acintyastava, Bodhicittavivaraṇa,* and *Bodhisaṃbhāra[ka].* In another book (1980), Lindtner has translated into Danish the *Ratnāvalī, Yuktiṣaṣṭikā, Niraupamyastava,* and *Paramārthastava,* while his *Nāgārjuna's filosofiske værker* (1982b) contains a Danish translation of the *Bodhicittavivaraṇa, Lokātītastava, Acintyastava, Mūlamadhyamakakārikās, Śūnyatāsaptativṛtti, Vigrahavyāvartanī,* and *Bodhisaṃbhāra[ka].* Moreover, this latter book also contains an edition of the Tibetan text of the *Śūnyatāsaptativṛtti.*

Michael Hahn published a new edition of Nāgārjuna's *Ratnāvalī* (1982a). [92] The work also contains the text of the canonical Tibetan version and a photocopy of the Chinese translation by Paramārtha. (Ajitamitra's commentary was critically edited and analysed by Hahn's pupil, Y. Okada [1990].) Nāgārjuna's *Sūtrasamuccaya* was translated from the Tibetan version by Bhikkhu Pāsādika (Pāsādika 1978–82). Hsueh-li Cheng translated the *Twelve Gate Treatise* from the Chinese (1982). This work is ascribed to Nāgārjuna in the Chinese tradition, but is probably a later compilation based upon Nāgārjuna's work.[14]

Āryadeva is generally considered to be a direct disciple of Nāgārjuna. His most important work is without doubt the *Catuḥśataka,* of which parts have been preserved in Sanskrit. Before World War II Vidhushekara Bhattacharya had already published the Sanskrit and Tibetan texts of chapters 8–16 (1931). Only recently, however, have Western scholars undertaken the study of this important work. One must mention in the first place Jacques May's translation of the ninth chapter, in which permanent entities are refuted; his work consists of a translation of the text and Candrakīrti's commentary, and of an edition of the Tibetan version of those portions for which the Sanskrit text has not been transmitted (May 1980, 1981a, b, 1982, 1984). Lindtner announced an edition of the *Catuḥśataka* (1982a, 278, n. 260). The *Akṣaraśataka* and its *vṛtti* are attributed to Āryadeva by the Chinese tradition. A new edition by Holten Pind was being readied for publication in *Indiske Studier* 5 (see Lindtner 1982a, 15, n. 33). The *Hastavālaprakaraṇa* and its *vṛtti* are attributed to

14. See my review in *IIJ* 28 (1985): 228–30.

Āryadeva or to Dignāga; the authors of the most recent translation, Fernando Tola and Carmen Dragonetti (1980), are inclined to attribute the work to Āryadeva.

As regards the commentaries on the *Mūlamadhyamakakārikās*, Lindtner translated the eighteenth chapter of Buddhapālita's com-[93]mentary (1981a) and Mervyn Sprung several chapters of Candrakīrti's *Prasannapadā* (1979). However, the latter translation did not find favour with reviewers.[15]

Early in the twentieth century La Vallée Poussin published his incomplete translation of Candrakīrti's *Madhyamakāvatāra* and his *bhāṣya* (1907–11). Helmut Tauscher (1981) continued La Vallée Poussin's work by translating the last part of chapter six, which had not been translated by him.[16] Christian Lindtner published the Tibetan text of Candrakīrti's *Pañcaskandhaprakaraṇa* (1979).

One of the most popular works of the Madhyamaka literature is Śāntideva's *Bodhicaryāvatāra,* of which several new translations appeared: in English by Stephen Batchelor (1979), in German by Ernst Steinkellner (1981a), in Danish by Christian Lindtner (1981b, 36–162), and in Dutch by Ria Kloppenborg.[17]

Among the later Madhyamaka scholars one of the most important is Kamalaśīla, the disciple of Śāntarakṣita, on whose *Tattvasaṃgraha* he wrote a very extensive commentary. He is also the author of three *Bhāvanākramas* that have been much studied in recent years.[18] J. van den Broeck published a French translation of the first *Bhāvanākrama* (1977a), [94] which was also translated into Spanish by Luis Gómez (1977). Gómez also translated the third *Bhāvanākrama* into Spanish (1972), and an English translation of the same text was produced by Robert Olson and Masao Ichishima (1979). Kamalaśīla's *Bhāvanāyogāvatāra* was rendered into Spanish by Gómez (1979).

The two other philosophical Mahāyāna schools, the Yogācāra and the Tathāgatagarbha, received less attention from Western scholars in the period under review. Important articles on both schools were published by Lambert Schmithausen. His book on the *Vijñaptimātratā* and the *Ālayavijñāna* (1987), which was his "Habilitationsschrift," had not yet been published, but many problems were discussed by him in articles on the *Viṃśatikā* and *Triṃśikā* (1967), and the *Abhidharmasamuccaya* (1972,

15. See my review in *IIJ* 23 (1981): 227–30 and Ernst Steinkellner's review in *JAOS* 102 (1982): 411–14.

16. See the review by me, *IIJ* 25 (1983): 214–15.

17. Ria Kloppenborg's translation is mentioned in Lindtner 1981b, 7 n. 2; Lindtner also refers to an Italian translation by A. Pezzali.

18. See A. Yuyama, *IIJ* 17 (1975): 265–70 and de Jong, *IIJ* 25 (1983): 154–55.

1976a). According to Schmithausen, "the thesis of universal idealism originated from the *generalization* of a situation observed in the case of objects visualized in meditative concentration, i.e., in the context of *spiritual practice*" (1976b, 247). Schmithausen earlier had published on the literary history of the oldest texts of the Yogācāra school (1969b). The names of Maitreya, Asaṅga, and Vasubandhu are attached to these texts but it is not possible to accept the traditional ascriptions. It is only through detailed textual studies such as the ones undertaken by Schmithausen that it will become possible to trace the history of the early Yogācāra school. A new edition of the *Bodhisattvabhūmi* was published by N. Dutt in 1966, but Gustav Roth [95] showed convincingly that Dutt's edition is not to be relied upon; Roth published a new edition of the beginning of the text, corresponding to Dutt's edition p. 1–p. 2, line 3 (1977). The Tattvārtha chapter of the *Bodhisattvabhūmi* was translated by Janice Dean Willis (1979), but this work is completely unsatisfactory.[19]

In 1969 David Seyfort Ruegg published his great work on the doctrines of the *tathāgatagarbha* and the *gotra* (1969); it was reviewed in a long article by Schmithausen (1973). Seyfort Ruegg published a translation of Bu ston's treatise on the *tathāgatagarbha* (1973); his book contains a long introduction on Bu ston's sources and on the doctrine of the *tathāgatagarbha* according to Bu ston's school. Thanks to the studies of Takasaki and Seyfort Ruegg it has now become possible to understand the importance of this school of thought.

Much work was done by Frauwallner on the study of the epistemological school of Buddhism founded by Dignāga, but reaching its culmination with Dharmakīrti. Ernst Steinkellner published an edition of the Tibetan version and the Sanskrit fragments of the Svārthānumāna chapter of Dharmakīrti's *Pramāṇaviniścaya* (1973). His annotated translation followed later (1979a). Meanwhile he published a verse index of the Tibetan versions of Dharmakīrti's works (1977a). Mention must also be made of his articles on works by Dharmottara (1976), Karṇakagomin (1978, 1979b), Jñānaśrīmitra (1977b), Jinendrabuddhi (1980), and Śākyamati (1981b). Finally, Steinkellner sketched [96] the spiritual place of the epistemological tradition in Buddhism in a lecture given at several universities in Japan (1982). A student of Steinkellner, Gudrun Bühnemann, translated Ratnakīrti's *Sarvajñasiddhi* (1980).[20] In 1930 Frauwallner had translated Dignāga's *Ālambanaparīkṣāvṛtti* into German; the same text was finally translated into English by Fernando Tola and Carmen Dragonetti (1982).

19. See my review in *Orientalistische Literaturzeitung* 80 (1985): 195–98.

20. See my review in *IIJ* 25 (1983): 155–58.

Alex Wayman was active in the field of Tantric studies. He published a collection of articles (1973) and a book on the Yoga of the *Guhyasamājatantra* (1977).[21] Christopher S. George edited and translated the first eight chapters of the *Caṇḍamahāroṣaṇatantra* (1974), of which La Vallée Poussin had edited the sixteenth chapter in 1897. Published also was a book by T. Skorupski on the *Sarvadurgatipariśodhanatantra* (1983). Many Sanskrit Tantric manuscripts are kept in manuscript collections and still await editing. It is a pity that in the West few scholars seem to be interested in the philological study of Tantric texts. We owe to a Japanese scholar, Kanjin Horiuchi, the edition of one of the most important tantras, the *Sarvatathāgatatattvasaṃgraha* (1974–83). Per Kværne published a very thorough study of the *Caryāgīti* (1977).[22] His book contains the text of the *Caryāgīti* and of Munidatta's commentary, and an edition of the Tibetan versions. The concept of *sahaja*, which plays an important role in these Tantric songs, was studied by him in a separate article (1975).

In the field of Buddhist literature remarkable work was done by [97] Michael Hahn. He published the Tibetan version and a translation of Candragomin's *Lokānandanāṭaka* (1974a; see also 1974b, 1977a). He also studied the *Jātakamālā*s of Haribhaṭṭa and Gopadatta (1977b). The Tibetan version of four *jātaka*s from the *Haribhaṭṭajātakamālā* were edited and translated by Hahn over several years (1973–80). In another article (1981) he studied the date of Haribhaṭṭa, who according to him was active in the first half of the fifth century. He also published a new edition of the *Subhāṣitaratnakaraṇḍakakathā* (1982b), which had previously been studied very carefully by Heinz Zimmermann (1975), especially with regard to the very defective Tibetan version. Hahn also made a contribution to the study of the first canto of *Buddhacarita* by studying the Tibetan version of the verses missing in the Sanskrit manuscripts (1975b).

Another text studied was Kṣemendra's *Bodhisattvāvadānakalpalatā* (de Jong 1979, 1977b, 1981), of which many readings in the Bibliotheca Indica edition were shown to be incorrect. Especially useful was a Cambridge manuscript dating from 1302. Buddhist epistolary literature was studied by Siglinde Dietz in a voluminous thesis (1980) that was later published as Dietz 1984a. The *Suhṛllekha* was [98] translated into Danish by Lindtner (1981, 19–35) and into English by Kawamura (1975) and by Jamspal et al. (1978).

Of great importance for the history of Buddhism in India are inscriptions, particularly the Aśokan inscriptions. Ulrich Schneider published a

21. This latter work was reviewed by Per Kværne in *IIJ* 22 (1980): 242–47.

22. See Norman's review in *Acta Orientalia* 41 (1980): 105–9.

critical edition and translation of the rock edicts (1978).[23] K. R. Norman has made many contributions (see Schneider 1978, 180) in a series of articles (1976d, 1978a). Since the end of World War II the Aśokan inscriptions have been studied by many scholars, and a systematic bibliography, to supplement the one in Mehendale 1948, would be very welcome. T. Damsteegt studied the so-called epigraphical Hybrid Sanskrit (1978).[24]

In 1881 the Pali Text Society was founded by T. W. Rhys Davids (Norman 1981a). To commemorate the centenary of its foundation, the Pali Text Society published volume 9 of the *Journal of the Pali Text Society*, to which fifteen scholars contributed articles.[25] Under the guidance of I. B. Horner and K. R. Norman, who succeeded Horner as president, the Pali Text Society continued its publication of texts, translations, indexes, etc. Horner produced new translations of the *Vimānavatthu*, and the *Bud-*[99]*dhavaṃsa* and *Cariyāpiṭaka* (1974, 1975). Her last work was a translation of her own edition of the *Buddhavaṃsa* commentary (1978). Bhikkhu Ñāṇamoli translated the *Paṭisambhidāmagga* (1982). In 1982 the Pali Text Society published a very useful index of the *Kathāvatthu*, compiled by a group of Japanese scholars (Tabata et al. 1982). A new translation of the famous *Vessantara-jātaka* was published by Oxford University Press (Cone and Gombrich 1977). Norman published some important notes on the text of this *jātaka* (1981b). Ludwig Alsdorf wrote an article on the *Bhūridatta-jātaka* in which he suggested corrections in the text (1977). Finally, mention must be made of Norman's comprehensive survey of Pāli literature (1983a).

One of the most important publications is that of the Burmese recension of a collection of fifty *jātaka*s by P. S. Jaini (1981–83). An important cosmological text, the *Lokapaññatti*, was edited by Eugène Denis, who examined in detail the relations of this text to other texts in Pāli, Sanskrit, Chinese, and Tibetan (1977). According to Denis the *Lokapaññatti* was probably translated into Pāli, or compiled in Pāli making use of Sanskrit sources, in Burma in the eleventh or twelfth century. Jacqueline Ver Eecke edited and translated two later Pāli texts, the *Dasavatthupakaraṇa* (1976) and the *Sīhaḷavatthupakaraṇa* (1980). Her editions are based mainly

23. For reviews see Norman, *Acta Orientalia* 40 (1979): 346–53 and Colette Caillat, *IIJ* 27 (1984): 133–37.

24. See the reviews by Norman, *Lingua* 48 (1979): 291–94 and Gérard Fussmann, *JA* 268 (1980): 420–26.

25. The editor of the journal is K. R. Norman, and articles in vol. 9 were written by A. Bareau, H. Bechert, L. S. Cousins, R. Gombrich, O. von Hinüber, I. B. Horner, P. S. Jaini, J. W. de Jong, D. J. Kalupahana, É. Lamotte, K. R. Norman, Walpola Rahula, D. Seyfort Ruegg, H. Saddhātissa, and A. K. Warder.

upon Sinhalese editions. H. Saddhātissa wrote a number of articles on Pāli literature in Thailand (1974, 1976), Cambodia (1980, 1981), and Laos (1979). Oskar von Hinüber showed the [100] importance of the Pāli tradition in Burma for the transmission of the Pāli texts (1983a). Both Norman (1976a, b, c, 1977, 1978b, 1979a, b, c, 1980a, b, c, 1981c, d, 1982a, b, 1983b) and von Hinüber (1974, 1975, 1976, 1977a, b, 1978a, b, 1979b, 1980b, 1981a, b, 1982a, 1982–83) made detailed studies of etymological and philological problems in Pāli texts. [101] A structural grammar of Pāli was produced by Tat'iana Elizarenkova and V. N. Toporov (1976).

Of great importance for the study of texts are dictionaries, catalogues, and bibliographies. A new Sanskrit dictionary of the Turfan Buddhist manuscripts, of which the first three fascicles appeared during this period, also includes, from the third fascicle on, manuscript materials from collections other than the Berlin collection.[26] It comprises mainly texts belonging to the Sarvāstivāda school, but also some Dharmaguptaka and Mūlasarvāstivāda texts. Five more fascicles (8 to 12) of volume 2 of the *Critical Pāli Dictionary* were published from 1973 to 1982.[27] After the death of Ludwig Alsdorf the task of editing the dictionary was entrusted to K. R. Norman. The *Hōbōgirin,* correctly called an encyclopaedic dictionary, is a work well known to Japanese scholars; a fifth fascicle, containing many important articles, appeared in 1979. A new catalogue of the Taishō edition, this time including all one hundred volumes, was published in 1978.[28]

I mentioned already the catalogues of the Turfan manuscripts. Important for Pāli studies are the catalogue of Ceylonese manuscripts in the Royal Library in Copenhagen, by the late Godakumbura (1980), and the catalogue of Burmese manuscripts by Heinz Bechert et al. (1978). Tibetan blockprints and manuscripts in German collections were described by D. Schuh (1973–81) [102] and by F. Wilhelm and J. Losang Panglung (1979).[29]

26. *Sanskrit-Wörterbuch der buddhistischen Texte aus den Turfanfunden,* fasc. 1 (1973), fasc. 2 (1976), fasc. 3 (1981). Göttingen: Vandenhoeck & Ruprecht. See reviews by Seyfort Ruegg, *JAOS* 97 (1977): 550–52 and 99 (1979): 160–61; Schmithausen, *ZDMG* 132 (1982): 407–14; Hahn, *Göttingische Gelehrte Anzeigen* 231 (1979): 273–88; and W. Thomas, *Indogermanische Forschungen* 80 (1975): 232–37 and 84 (1979): 297–302.

27. Fasc. 8 (1973): ugghāṭiyati–udaka-sakuṇika; fasc. 9 (1975): udaka-saṅkhāta–upakkama; fasc. 10 (1979): upakkama–uparima; fasc. 11 (1981): uparima–uposathakiriyā; fasc. 12 (1982): Uposathakumāra–uḷumpa. For bibliographical details on reviews see Oskar von Hinüber's review of fascicles 6 to 10: Bemerkungen zum CPD II, *KZ* 94 (1980): 10–31.

28. *Répertoire du canon bouddhique sino-japonais.* Compiled by P. Demiéville, Hubert Durt, and Anna Seidel. Paris: Librairie d'Amérique et d'Orient, 1978.

29. See my reviews in *IIJ* 20 (1978): 317–18 and 25 (1983): 158–60, and in *IIJ* 23 (1981): 232–34.

Another important publication is the descriptive catalogue of the Korean Buddhist canon, compiled by Lancaster (1979).

Some attempts were made to revive *Bibliographie bouddhique*, but unfortunately without success. The last fascicle to appear covered the years 1954 to 1958, and as yet no publication has emerged to fill this gap in our bibliographical information. Still, we must be thankful for some very useful systematic bibliographies, as, for instance, A. Yuyama's very exhaustive bibliography of the Vinaya literature (1979) and H. Nakamura's comprehensive bibliography of Indian Buddhism (1980). A bibliography of translations of Pāli texts was published by Russell Webb (1975). Also very useful are the bibliographies contained in the reprint of the Dbu-ma, Sems-tsam, and Tshad-ma sections of the Derge Tanjur.[30] Another very detailed bibliography comprising both Kanjur and Tanjur was scheduled for publication as a supplement to the edition of the Nyingma edition of the Tibetan Buddhist canon that was published by Dharma Publishing in 1981. Finally, a bibliography of translations of Mahāyāna texts into Western languages was produced by Peter Pfandt (1983).

Thus far I have dealt mainly with Buddhist studies relating to Indian texts. It is not possible to mention even briefly the work that has been done with relation to texts from Tibet, China, and the Theravāda countries. Even less could I do justice to studies in the fields of philosophy, religion, history, and art. Still, it may be useful to mention a few publications as an indication of the kind of work that is being done in these fields by Western scholars. Since 1959 Tibetan studies have developed immensely, with many publications relating to Tibetan Buddhism and, indirectly, to Indian Buddhism. Michel Strickmann [103] made available an excellent survey of Tibetan Buddhist studies (1977). Of the many publications published after his survey, mention must be made of one, Helmut Eimer's edition of the Tibetan version of the *Pravrajyāvastu* of the Vinaya of the Mūlasarvāstivāda school (1983). Eimer paid great attention to the different Kanjur and Tanjur editions and showed how important it is to consult as many of these as possible. His edition of the *Pravrajyāvastu* is based upon no less than six blockprint editions and five manuscripts. As regards studies on Theravāda countries, attention should be drawn to the symposium on Buddhism in Ceylon and on religious syn-

30. These have appeared in 53 volumes (20, 17, and 16, respectively) between 1977 and 1984. The chief editors were Kyōshō Hayashima, Jikidō Takasaki, and Zuihō Yamaguchi, and the publisher was Sekai Seiten Kankō Kyōkai, Tokyo. The Japanese title of the series is *Deruge-ban: Chibetto Daizōkyō* (some reference works give it as *Chibetto Daizōkyō, Deruge-ban*); the English title is given as *Tibetan Tripiṭaka*. See my reviews in *IIJ* 22 (1980): 260–61 and 25 (1983): 154–55.

cretism in Buddhist countries (Bechert 1978). Much information on Buddhism in Cambodia is to be found in the studies published since 1976 by François Bizot (1976, 1980, 1981). C. Hooykaas, who died in 1979, also made important contributions to the study of Buddhism in Bali (Goudriaan and Hooykaas 1971, Hooykaas 1973).[31]

Very interesting for the study of the texts of the Hīnayāna schools is Schmithausen's study on the recensions of the *Udānavarga* (1970). Seyfort Ruegg published an important article on the chronology of the Madhyamaka school (1982). Based upon very careful study of the Pāli texts and the Chinese versions of Hīnayāna texts are the studies of André Bareau (1974a, b, 1975, 1979, 1980a, b, 1981, 1982a); these have shed much light on the history of early Buddhism. [104]

For the study of Buddhist philosophy one must mention the work of Schmithausen on the *smṛtyupasthānas*, on the threefold *duḥkhatā,* and on liberating insight (1976c, 1977, 1978, 1981, 1982b), and Seyfort Ruegg's beautiful study on *catuṣkoṭi* (1977). A monograph on self and non-self in early Buddhism is known to me only through a reference in an article by Tilmann Vetter (Pérez-Remón 1980). The two truths in Buddhism and Vedānta were studied by several scholars in a volume edited by Mervyn Sprung (1973).

How important it is to study again identifications made in the past has been shown by Dieter Schlingloff, who in a series of important articles has published the results of his studies of the wall-paintings of Ajanta and of other Buddhist monuments (1971, 1972a, b, 1973a, b, c, 1975a, b, 1976, 1977a, b, c, d, 1981a, b, c, 1982). His work is based upon a careful study of the monuments and upon a profound knowledge of Buddhist narrative literature. [105]

Another field of study in which important work has been done in recent years is anthropology. Scholars working in this field have directed their attention to the Tibetans in India and Nepal and to the Theravāda countries. It must be left to a specialist in this field to make a survey of the results obtained by anthropologists.

I hope that I have been able to give some idea of the work that has been done in this period of approximately ten years by Western scholars in the field of Buddhist studies and, above all, with regard to the study of Buddhist texts in India. It is of course impossible for one man to give an adequate survey of the work being done in so many branches of Buddhist studies, and I can only hope that others will supplement the bibliographical information I have given.

31. For a complete bibliography see Swellengrebel 1980.

CHAPTER SIX

Recent Decades: C (1984–90)

Introduction

It is not without some misgivings that I am attempting to give a survey of Buddhist studies during this seven-year period. The reason is that it has become more and more difficult to keep oneself informed of all that is being published in so many languages and in so many countries. This survey would have been much more incomplete if I had not benefited from [2] the kindness of colleagues who have generously sent me copies of their publications. The library of the Australian National University has been a good source of information, but financial restrictions prevented the library from acquiring all the publications I would have liked to see. Especially regrettable was the cancellation of subscriptions to several journals. Thus it is possible that some important publications may have escaped my notice. However, even if a person could have access to all the books and periodicals that have been published in these seven years, it would still not be possible to list all the books, not to mention articles, published in this period. Moreover, it would be well-nigh impossible for any single individual to inspect and read so many publications, even if the selection, as in earlier chapters, is limited mainly to philological publications relating to Indian Buddhism. Perhaps someday it will be possible to fill in the gaps in a future publication, and for this reason I would be much obliged if readers would take the trouble to point out to me important publications that ought to have been mentioned.

Buddhist studies suffered a great loss by the untimely death on 9 January 1984, of John Brough. He had a critical mind and a great knowledge of Sanskrit, Pāli, Prakrit, Tibetan, and Chinese. His work *Gāndhārī Dharmapada* (1962) was one of the most important works in the field of Buddhist studies published since World War II. He wrote many articles that deserve publication in a volume of collected papers (see Burton-

Page 1985).[1] In 1984, also, Giuseppe Tucci passed away; his numerous publications on Indian and Tibetan Buddhism are well known to all scholars of Buddhism (see Gnoli 1984, Webb 1983–84, and esp. Petech and Scalpi 1984). In 1985 Ernst Waldschmidt died; to him we owe a great many editions of Buddhist Sanskrit fragments from Central Asia and several volumes of a catalogue of Sanskrit manuscripts from Central Asia (see Härtel 1985a, b, Sander and Waldschmidt 1980–85; Waldschmidt 1965–71, and esp. Waldschmidt 1989, xiii–xli).[2] Two prominent Japanese scholars passed away during this period: Hakuyū Hadano, who published widely on Indian and Tibetan Buddhism, and Shinten Sakai, a specialist in Tibetan translations of Indian Tantric texts. Other scholars who passed [3] from the scene are David Friedmann, who translated the first chapter of Sthiramati's *Madhyāntavibhāgaṭīkā* (1937; see Gelblum 1985), Eugène Denis, the author of a two-volume book on the *Lokapaññatti* (1977; see Bareau 1987),[3] and Hermann Kopp, who edited several Pāli commentaries (see Webb 1987, 143). In 1986 A. L. Basham passed away. Most of his publications relating to Buddhism aim at a more general public. No complete bibliography of his writings has as yet been published; S. N. Mukherjee published a bibliography (1982) that does not go beyond 1976, and the same bibliography was faithfully reproduced several years later, misprints and all (with the addition of a few more) by S. K. Maity (1988, 14–18). Russell Webb produced a useful survey of Basham's publications relating to Buddhism (1986); it is, however, not complete and does not mention, for instance, his article "The Evolution of the Concept of the Bodhisattva" (1982).[4]

Collected papers and felicitation volumes

Several volumes of collected papers were published during this period. The seventieth birthday of Gustav Roth saw the publication of a volume of his Indian studies (1986). The *Kleine Schriften* of Friedrich Weller were published in two volumes (1987). Ernst Waldschmidt's *Ausgewählte kleine Schriften* were published (1989). On the occasion of his retirement from Kyoto University, Yūichi Kajiyama's English and German articles were published in *Studies in Buddhist Philosophy* (1989). The first volume of K. R.

1. To the bibliography one must add the following article: "Sakāya Niruttiyā: Cauld kale het," in Bechert 1980, 35–42.

2. For reviews of vols. 1–5 of the Catalogue see my reviews in *Orientalistische Literaturzeitung*, 62 (1967): 498–99; 69 (1974): 74–75; 71 (1976): 75–76; 79 (1984): 391–93; 82 (1987): 393–94.

3. See my review in *IIJ* 22 (1980): 70–73.

4. See my review in *The Eastern Buddhist* 15/1 (1982): 149–51.

Norman's *Collected Papers* was published (1990b); it comprises thirty articles first published between 1956 and 1977. The writings of both Hakuyū Hadano and Shinten Sakai were each published in four volumes: *Chibetto-Indogaku Shūsei* (1986–88), and *Sakai Shinten Chosakushū* (1984–88).

Tucci's memory was honoured by the publication of three volumes of papers, edited by G. Gnoli and L. Lanciotti (1985–88). *Indologica* [4] *Taurinensia* (14, 1987–88) published a volume in honour of Colette Caillat. Three Japanese scholars were honoured with felicitation volumes: Jikidō Takasaki (Takasaki . . . Kinenkai 1987), Masaaki Hattori (Yamakami et al. 1989), and Kōtatsu Fujita (Fujita . . . Kankōkai 1989). In 1990 Tadeusz Skorupski edited a volume dedicated to David L. Snellgrove (1990a); the volume does not include a bibliography of Snellgrove's writings, but the most important ones are mentioned in Skorupski's opening article: "The Life and Adventures of David Snellgrove" (1990b). Finally, many articles on Buddhism are to be found in the following three felicitation volumes: *Kalyāṇamitrārāgaṇam: Essays in Honour of Nils Simonsson* (Kahrs 1986); *Hinduismus und Buddhismus: Festschrift für Ulrich Schneider* (Falk 1987); and *India and the Ancient World . . . Professor P. H. L. Eggermont Jubilee Volume . . .* (Pollet 1987).

Earliest Buddhism

Is it possible to recover the original message of the Buddha? A workshop on "Earliest Buddhism" held during the 7th World Sanskrit Conference in Leiden in August 1987 showed irreconcilable opinions among scholars on this point. Three of the four papers read at the conference were later published (Seyfort Ruegg and Schmithausen 1990).[5] In his preface, Schmithausen outlined three different positions: 1) some scholars, mainly British, accept the reliability of the greater part of the Nikāyas and believe that the canonical texts give a true picture of the doctrine of the Buddha; 2) other scholars believe that it is impossible to retrieve the doctrine of earliest Buddhism, let alone the Buddha's own doctrine, be-[5]cause the Buddhist texts were transmitted for many centuries and transformed during this time before being written down, and even afterwards were not immune to changes; 3) other scholars, again, believe that it is possible to apply the methods of higher criticism to Buddhist canonical texts and to establish a relative sequence (or sequences) of textual layers and/or a sequence (or sequences) of doctrinal development.

The first position was most vigorously defended by Richard

5. Noritoshi Aramaki's paper, "Some Precursors of the Subconscious Desire in the Attadaṇḍasutta," was not available for publication.

Gombrich (1990). Gombrich stressed the importance of the oral tradition and remarked that "the kind of analysis which can dissect a *written* philosophical tradition is inappropriate for oral materials." Elsewhere he referred to an article by Lance Cousins (1983), in which Cousins remarked that "authenticity lies not in historical truth, although this is not doubted, but rather in whether something can accord with the essential structure of the *dhamma* as a whole. If it can not, it should be rejected. If it can, then it is to be accepted as the utterance of the Buddha" (Cousins 1983, 3). There is no doubt that the importance of the oral tradition has not been sufficiently understood by scholars in the past. For instance, both Hajime Nakamura and André Bareau, who have written extensively on early Buddhism, have compared Pāli canonical texts and Chinese Āgama texts without taking into account the role played by oral tradition in the transmission of these texts (Nakamura 1970–71; Bareau 1963–71). Future researchers will have to try to determine how far the oral tradition has been instrumental in shaping the wording and the contents of the canonical Buddhist texts.

Another important point raised by Gombrich is the Buddha's and his followers' knowledge of Brahmanical traditions and doctrines.[6] According to Gombrich the Buddha presented central parts of his message as a set of antitheses to Brahmanical doctrine.

Lambert Schmithausen published a long article (1981) on "Liberating Insight" and "Enlightenment" in Early Buddhism, in which he examined various and conflicting theories in the Sūtrapiṭaka and tried to sketch the outlines of a historical development. He expressed the hope [6] that his paper might stimulate further discussion, and it certainly did. A similar approach was taken in publications by Tilmann Vetter (1985, 1988), Noritoshi Aramaki (1980),[7] Johannes Bronkhorst (1986), and Konrad Meisig (1987, 1988). Both Vetter 1988 and Bronkhorst 1986 examined the meditation theories in early Buddhism, Vetter concentrating on Buddhist meditation and Bronkhorst contrasting the mainstream meditation found in early Jaina and Hindu scriptures with the meditation practices described in early Buddhist texts. Aramaki 1980 appeared a few years before the period under review. In this article he distinguished five strata: 1) an older *gāthā*-tradition starting in the early Upaniṣads; 2) the oldest stratum of the Buddhist scriptures, such as the proto-*Dharmapada*, the

6. Gombrich's paper is also published in *The Buddhist Forum*, vol. 1 (London: SOAS, 1990), pp. 5–20. The same volume contains his paper "How the Mahāyāna Began," pp. 21–30, first published as Gombrich 1988b. See further Gombrich 1984 and 1988a, and his article, "Buddhism," in the *Encyclopaedia Brittanica*.

7. The following articles by him are known to me only from bibliographical references: Aramaki 1983, 1984, 1985a, b.

Aṭṭhakavagga, and the *Pārāyaṇavagga* of the *Suttanipāta;* 3) the *Devatāsaṃyutta,* the *Mārasaṃyutta,* and the *Bhikkhunīsaṃyutta* of the *Sagāthavagga* of the *Saṃyuttanikāya;* 4) the latest of the verse sūtras, such as the *Hemavatasutta* of the *Suttanipāta;* 5) a great number of prose sūtras. Meisig compared in great detail the different recensions of the *Śrāmaṇyaphalasūtra* (1987)[8] and the *Aggaññasutta* (1988) in order to establish a stratification of the texts. In another study of the *Śrāmaṇyaphalasūtra,* Graeme Macqueen made a comparative analysis of the text and studied its main themes (1984, 1988).

At the 7th World Sanskrit Conference Norman read a paper (1990a) that Schmithausen characterized as "an attempt to reintegrate the divergencies . . . into a largely . . . coherent picture of the authentic doctrine of the Buddha as represented by the majority of the canonical sources" (Seyfort Ruegg and Schmithausen 1990, 2). It is not surprising that Schmithausen, who is one of the main defenders of the third position, arrived at the conclusion that the different approaches were hardly compatible, and wisely suggested that it "would seem reasonable to try different approaches side by side and to test the heuristic value of each of them" (p. 3).

Let us consider some aspects of the controversy. It is interesting to see that several scholars have attached great importance to the *Suttanipāta* as one of the oldest texts and as reflecting at least in [7] parts the original message of the Buddha. Some scholars, especially Hajime Nakamura, are of the opinion that such older verses as those found in the *Suttanipāta* and in other parts of the canon contain the oldest form of the Buddhist teachings. An opposite view has been expressed by Shinkan Murakami, who remarked: "We pointed out that the Buddhist canon has some . . . verses in common with the *Mahābhārata* and the Jaina sūtras. Considering also, that, in most cases, verses are not likely to convey a teaching in an accurate way and that the verse portions cannot be said to contain the whole of the early Buddhist teaching, one may question the attempt to recover the original teachings of the Buddha from the verses only" (1979, 245). The picture that Nakamura sketches of early Buddhism on the basis of the older verses in the canon is indeed entirely different from the one presented, for instance, in Norman 1990a.

It is a misconception to assume that the oldest form of the doctrine is to be found in verses that in their literary form are older and more archaic than other parts of the canon. Many of these verses have parallels in non-Buddhist texts and belong to collections of verses current among wandering groups of ascetics. These verses were incorporated much

8. See the review by Paul G. Griffiths, *JAOS* 109 (1989): 146–49.

later into the *Khuddakanikāya,* the fifth and last collection of the Suttapiṭaka of the Theravādins. The doctrines found in these verses thus became part of the Buddhist teachings, but this does not mean that they reflect the oldest form of the Buddha's message. Another frequent misconception is that a shorter version of some doctrinal development is necessarily more original than a more expanded one and that an enumeration of a few items is likewise more primitive than one in which more items are mentioned.

Probably much can be said in favour of the second position as outlined by Schmithausen. There is no reason to doubt that the Buddha preached for many years and that many of his utterances are to be found in the canonical texts. However, how can the teachings of the Buddha himself be distinguished from those preached in later times? [8] How is it possible to prove that the traditional accounts of the first sermons of the Buddha are reliable historical sources? Not long after the Nirvāṇa of the Buddha the leaders of the saṃgha tried to find criteria for assessing the authenticity of texts. We must admire their methods and their scrupulousness but it cannot be denied that they were unable to lay down infallible principles of authenticity. It is difficult to see how, more than two thousand years later, modern scholars could be more successful in this regard.

The anātman doctrine

The difficulties encountered in interpreting the canonical texts show up clearly in the continuing discussion on the *ātman* in early Buddhism. Years ago K. Bhattacharya published a book in which he tried to demonstrate that Buddhism recognised the Upaniṣadic *ātman* (1973; cf. Lamotte 1944–80, 4: 2005). Since then he has published several articles in which he adduces further arguments and documents (1975, 1979, 1980, 1988, 1989). The latest of these concludes with the following words: "The Buddha's Absolute appears to be the same as that of the Upaniṣads." A similar point of view was defended by J. Pérez-Remón (1980), but his views were refuted by T. Vetter (1983) and Steven Collins (1982a). Collins 1982b makes a detailed study of the *anātman* doctrine and arrives at quite opposite conclusions (cf. Griffiths 1983).

One of the most penetrating studies of the *ātman* problem is to be found in Oetke 1988a, where the author carefully analyses the *anātman* doctrine in the Pāli canon, the second book of the *Milindapañha* (ed. V. Trenckner, pp. 25–28) and the ninth book of the *Abhidharmakośabhāṣya.* On pp. 119–21 he discusses the famous *Alagaddūpamasutta* (*Majjhima-*

nikāya, sutta 22), which is often adduced by those who believed that the Buddhists did not deny the existence of an *ātman*. Oetke refers to discussions of this sutta by La Vallée Poussin (1930a, 100 and 197), Bhattacharya (1973, 67; 1980), and Pérez-Remón (1980, 188). It is instructive to compare their remarks with studies of the same sutta by Norman (1981d) and Richard Gombrich (1990).

Strangely enough, the *ātman* problem seems to excite the minds of [9] scholars who are not at all at home in the world of Buddhist scholarship. For instance, Frits Staal (1985) tried to show that Lamotte refrained from adopting a definite position in this regard. Staal made disparaging remarks about those who did not share his ill-founded opinion.[9] It is to be hoped that Webb-Boin's English translation of Lamotte's *Histoire du bouddhisme indien* will be able to dispel such fanciful interpretations of his ideas (see under Lamotte 1958).

Oetke 1988a has shown convincingly that most of the arguments adduced in favour of the belief in an *ātman* in early Buddhism are invalid (156–59). Whatever conclusion may be drawn from a few isolated texts, one has to take into account the fact that, as La Vallée Poussin has pointed out, the canon, in its entirety, denies the existence of any reality whatsoever apart from the impermanent *skandhas*. It is certainly rather perverse to assume that with regard to the *ātman* the Buddhists in later times adopted a position that would be entirely opposed to that found in the oldest texts.

Facsimiles

The publication of facsimiles of Sanskrit manuscripts is of great benefit for the study of texts. In the last chapter I mentioned the publication by the Institute for the Comprehensive Study of the Lotus Sūtra of a facsimile edition of more than thirty manuscripts. Twelve volumes have been published and three remain to be published. The same institute has now undertaken the tremendous task of publishing a romanized text and index of the manuscripts of the *Lotus Sūtra*. Two volumes have already been published (Institute 1986–).

A facsimile edition of a Nepalese manuscript of the *Lotus Sūtra*, dated 1082, was published in Beijing (Culture Palace 1984) and sold for the

9. For a refutation see de Jong 1987. Also, La Vallée Poussin 1930a, 101: "Quelle que soit la valeur des affirmations, claires ou voilées, de l'*âtman*, le Bouddhisme historique ne se trompe pas en confessant que le Canon, dans l'ensemble, nie l'existence de quelque réalité que ce soit en dehors des *skandhas* impermanents,–mettant à part le Nirvâna, chose en soi et éternelle."

ridiculous price of $2,500. I have not been able to consult this edition nor the romanized version that was published in 1988 (Jiang 1988). Hirofumi Toda was the first to report on it (1984a, 1985). Toda himself, meanwhile, continued to publish editions and studies of Sanskrit manuscripts of the same sūtra (cf. bibliography). Keishō Tsukamoto, one of the scholars engaged in preparing the roma-[10]nized edition of the manuscripts of the *Lotus Sūtra*, published notes on the *Saddharmapuṇḍarīka-stava*s (1985) and a study of Sanskrit manuscripts of the sūtra (1987).

An edition of 85 folios of seven manuscripts of the *Saddharma-puṇḍarīkasūtra*, accompanied by facsimiles, was published by M. Vorob'eva-Desjatovskaja; the same volume also contains editions of six fragments of the *Mahāparinirvāṇasūtra* and of an almost complete manuscript of the *Dharmaśarīrasūtra* by G. M. Bongard-Levin (Bongard-Levin and Vorob'eva-Desjatovskaja 1985).[10] The *Mahāparinirvāṇasūtra* fragments were also published in an English edition in Tokyo (Bongard-Levin 1986). New fragments of the same text were discovered by Kazunobu Matsuda in the Stein/Hoernle collection in the India Office Library (1987, 1988). Bongard-Levin and Vorob'eva-Desjatovskaja also published a survey of the Sanskrit texts from Central Asia in the Lenin-grad collection (1986).

The fifth volume of the catalogue of Sanskrit manuscripts from Central Asia (Sander and Waldschmidt 1985) contains facsimiles of the fragments described in it. However, the sixth volume (see Bechert 1989) does not contain any facsimiles. Volume five also includes a word index. In both volumes the majority of the texts consist of fragments of vinaya and sūtra texts, most of which have been identified. Additions and corrections to volumes 1 to 5 are to be found in an important appendix in volume six (pp. 209–25). Fumio Enomoto was able to identify many fragments as belonging to the *Saṃyuktāgama* (1985). He also edited several *Saṃyuktāgama* fragments found in Bamiyan and in Eastern Turkestan (1989a). In addition he showed that the Chinese *Saṃyuktāgama* belongs to the Mūlasarvāstivāda school (1986).

Very welcome was the publication of a new series, Bibliotheca Codicum Asiaticorum, the first volume of which contained facsimiles of Sanskrit manuscripts of three works of Vasubandhu (Mimaki et al. 1989). Noteworthy is the inclusion of a photocopy, [11] alas not very legible, of a Sanskrit manuscript of the *Triṃśikā* belonging to the Cultural Palace of the Nationalities in Beijing.

10. See reviews by me, *IIJ* 30 (1987): 215–21; by D. Seyfort Ruegg, *BSOAS* 51 (1988): 576–78; and by L. Sander, *Orientalistische Literaturzeitung* 84 (1989): 92–97.

Vinaya, Āgama, and Abhidharma texts

Many text editions were published during this period. Georg von Simson published an edition of manuscripts of the *Prātimokṣasūtra* of the Sarvāstivādins (1986). The final part of the same *Prātimokṣasūtra* was edited by Klaus T. Schmidt, who compared the Sanskrit and Tokharian A versions with parallel versions (1988).[11] Klaus Wille produced a very useful survey of the Gilgit manuscript of the *Vinayavastu* of the Mūlasarvāstivādins (1990), of which 405 out of the total of 523 leaves have been preserved; his book includes an edition or new edition of a number of fragments. In a postscript Heinz Bechert draws attention to an unauthorized edition of leaves 199–201 of the Gilgit manuscript of the *Vinayavastu* by Hisashi Matsumura and lists a number of misreadings in it. Claus Vogel and Klaus Wille published fragments of a Gilgit manuscript of the *Pravrajyāvastu* (1984).

Fragments of the *Dīrghāgama* of the Sarvāstivādins were published by Jens-Uwe Hartmann (1989). The same volume contains an edition of canonical verses, the *Śarīrārthagāthā* that occur in the *Yogācārabhūmi* (Enomoto 1989b), and a not very satisfactory edition of the *Āyuḥparyantasūtra* (Matsumura 1989).[12]

In the field of Abhidharma literature notice must be taken of editions of *Dharmaskandha* fragments by Siglinde Dietz (1984b; cf. Pāsādika 1986) and Kazunobu Matsuda (1986). Fragments of the *Lokaprajñapti* were also identified by Matsuda (1982; see also Yuyama 1987). Siglinde Dietz identified other fragments of the same text in a Gilgit manuscript and in the Turfan collection (1989a). According to her, 48 pages out of the 222 pages of the Tibetan translation are preserved in the Sanskrit fragments.

Buddhist literature

Jens-Uwe Hartmann's edition of Mātṛceṭa's *Varṇārhavarṇastotra* (1987) replaces the previous edition published by Shackleton Bailey in 1950. Whereas the latter had at his disposal about 58 per cent of the original [12] text, Hartmann was able to base his edition on fragments covering about 82 per cent of the original text. Hartmann also published (1988a) fragments of Aśvaghoṣa's *Buddhacarita* and *Saundarananda* and of Mātṛceṭa's *Anaparāddhastotra* and *Prasādapratibhodhava* (*Śatapañcāśatika*).

11. See my review in *IIJ* 34 (1991): 310–12.
12. Reviewed by me in *IIJ* 35 (1992): 70–72.

Carol Meadows was able to use a manuscript from the National Archives of Nepal for a new edition of Ārya-Śūra's *Pāramitāsamāsa* (1986), but without deriving full profit from it.[13]

Ratna Basu published an edition of the Sanskrit text of an anonymous commentary on the *Jātakamālā* and of the Tibetan version of Vīryasiṃha's *Jātakamālāpañjikā* (1989). Peter Khoroche made a new translation of the *Jātakamālā*.[14] This text was also translated into Japanese by Ryūshō Hikata and Shin'ichi Takahara (1990). The *Jātakamālā* was first translated into English by J. S. Speyer (1895), and thereafter into Hindi by S. Caudharī (1951 and 1971), into Russian by A. P. Barannikov and O. F. Volkova (1962), and into Italian by Raniero Gnoli (1964). Ratna Handurukande published an article on *jātakamālās* in Sanskrit (1987).

Michael Hahn, who has done so much for the study of the narrative literature of the Buddhists, published a complete edition of the voluminous *Mahajjātakamālā* (1985) accompanied by a long introduction in which he gives very useful bibliographical information about the medieval narrative literature of the Buddhists, which is still very little studied: *Aśokāvadānamālā, Bhadrakalpāvadānamālā, Dvāviṃśatyavadānakathā, Kalpadrumāvadānamālā, Ratnāvadānamālā, Vicitrakarṇikāvadānamālā, Vratāvadānamālā,* and *Saṃbhadrāvadānamālā.* Ratna Handurukande published the text and translation of five Buddhist legends in the *campū* style from the *Avadānasārasamuccaya* (1984). Tilak Raj Chopra edited the Sabhikaparivarta, which is chapter 14 of the *Bhadrakalpāvadāna* and chapter 9 of the *Saṃbhadrāvadānamālā* (1990), and Hahn edited the Puṇyarāśyavadāna, chapter 13 of the *Aśokāvadānamālā* (1990), which according to him was written by Gopadatta. Bibliographical information on the publications by Michael Hahn and his pupils has been given by Hahn in his article on Indian and Nepalese manuscripts in the Indological Insti[13]tute of Bonn University (1988). To Hahn we also owe a reprint of Gauri Shankar's edition of Śivasvāmin's *Kapphiṇābhyudaya* followed by a revised romanized version of cantos i–viii and xix (1989). Hahn describes in detail the new manuscript materials used by him (pp. i–xxxvi of the appendix).[15]

In 1930 N. P. Chakravarti published an edition of chapters 1–3 and 5–21 of the *Udānavarga.* This edition is based upon a manuscript written on wooden planks that was discovered by Paul Pelliot in a temple of Subaši near Kučā. Recently Hideaki Nakatani published a complete edi-

13. For a review of Hartmann 1987 see my review in *IIJ* 32 (1989): 243–48; for a review of Meadows 1986, see ibid., pp. 234–39.

14. For a review by me, see *IIJ* 35 (1992): 314–16.

15. For a review of Hahn 1985 see my review in *IIJ* 31 (1988): 156–58; I have also reviewed Hahn 1989 in *IIJ* 35 (1992): 54–55.

tion of the text together with parallel verses. A separate volume contains facsimiles (1987). A volume still to be published will comprise an introduction and a commentary. Prajñāvarman's voluminous commentary on the *Udānavarga* is preserved in Tibetan translation only. It has been edited by Michael Balk (1984), who also wrote a dissertation on the *Udānavarga* (1988) in which he showed the importance of the commentary for the study of the second recension of the *Udānavarga*, which belongs to the school of the Mūlasarvāstivādins.[16] A new edition of the Tibetan text of the *Udānavarga* was published by Champa Thupten Zongtse together with Siglinde Dietz (1990). This edition is based upon the text of the Lhasa Kanjur and lists in the notes the readings of other editions. Important for the study of the different recensions of the *Udānavarga* and *Dharmapada* is Margaret Cone's new edition of the Patna *Dharmapada* (1989).

The Tanjur contains the Tibetan text of thirteen letters. Three letters have been edited and translated several times: Nāgārjuna's *Suhṛllekha*, Candragomin's *Śiṣyalekha*, and Mātṛceṭa's *Mahārājakaniṣkalekha*. Nine of the remaining ten have been edited and translated by Siglinde Dietz (1984a).[17]

Abhidharmakośa

Subhadra Jha published the first volume of an English translation of the *Abhidharmakośabhāṣya* (1983) and of La Vallée Poussin's commentary. I do not know if more volumes have been published, but not [14] much good can be said of this first volume.[18] Leo M. Pruden published in four volumes (1988–90) a complete translation of La Vallée Poussin's monumental work. James Duerlinger translated the ninth chapter of the *Abhidharmakośabhāṣya* (1989). Both the first edition of the Sanskrit text by Prahlad Pradhan (1967) and the revised edition by A. Haldar (1975) leave much to be desired. Yasunori Ejima published critical notes on the text of the ninth chapter (1987) and shortly thereafter a new edition of the first chapter (1989). Ejima also announced a new edition of chapter nine by himself and one of chapter four by Toshio Sako. It is to be hoped that the other chapters will also be edited in the same way.

Tables of citations of Āgama texts in the *Abhidharmakośabhāṣya* were published by Kōtatsu Fujita (1984) and Yoshifumi Honjō (1984). Bhikkhu Pāsādika studied not only the canonical quotations but also those from Abhidharma texts and from texts written by single authors (1989). José

16. I reviewed Balk 1984 in *IIJ* 30 (1987): 236–38.
17. See my review in *Buddhist Studies Review* 3/1 (1986): 76–79.
18. Reviewed by me in *IIJ* 33 (1990): 237.

Pereira and Francis Tiso published (1987) a translation of the first chapter of the *Abhidharmakośa* (the *kārikā* text) followed by a schematic presentation of the contents of the first chapter and a Sanskrit-English glossary. The same journal publishes much interesting Abhidharma material. Of great importance is the index to Yaśomitra's *Abhidharmakośavyākhyā* by Tetsuya Tabata and Hoshiko Tabata (1986–90), of which five parts have been published so far.

A young Russian scholar, V. I. Rudoj, has undertaken a complete translation of the *Abhidharmakośabhāṣya,* the first volume of which was published during the period under review (1990). In the introduction he mentions the plan for the study of the *Abhidharmakośa* that Stcherbatsky had outlined in 1917. It is instructive to read in a recent article by J. V. Vasil'kov (1989) how his plans were frustrated by the machinations of Stalinist lackeys. All his pupils perished in camps with the sole exception of B. V. Semičov. Semičov and M. G. Brjanskij published a Russian translation of chapters 1–3 of the *Abhidharmakośabhāṣya* from the Tibetan in two volumes (1980); these also contain an edition of the Tibetan [15] text from the Derge Tanjur. Strangely enough, Rudoj does not even mention this translation. His own work is planned on a grand scale. The first volume contains a long introduction on Abhidharma philosophy, a translation of the first chapter, a detailed commentary, a reconstruction of the system, the Sanskrit, Tibetan, and Chinese texts of the *kārikās*, and a Sanskrit-Tibetan-Chinese index.

Prajñāpāramitā literature

In 1934 Nalinaksha Dutt published an edition of the first chapter of the recast version of the *Pañcaviṃśatisāhasrikā Prajñāpāramitā.* Takayasu Kimura undertook the laborious task of editing the other chapters (1986–). Kimura's edition is based upon four manuscripts, two from Tokyo and two from Cambridge. According to him the most correct manuscript is manuscript no. 234 from the Tokyo collection. It is to be hoped that Kimura will also be able to publish the remaining chapters.

In December 1982 seven gold plates were discovered in Anurādhapura. The text inscribed on the plates contains sections of the first chapter of the *Pañcaviṃśatisāhasrikā Prajñāpāramitā.* Oskar von Hinüber identified it as belonging to the recast version (1984), but Tsutomu Yamaguchi (1984) proved that it is a portion of the original text prior to its recasting. M. H. F. Jayasuriya also edited the same text, and translated it; his work appeared in 1988 but he does not refer to von Hinüber's edition. An urgent desideratum is an edition of the Gilgit manuscripts of the *Pañca-*

viṃśatisāhasrikā Prajñāpāramitā. A complete edition of the *Śatasāhasrikā Prajñāpāramitā,* of which P. Ghosha edited the first twelve chapters (1902–13), would also be very welcome.

The Gilgit manuscript of the *Vajracchedikā* has been edited twice, in 1956 by N. P. Chakravarti (Tucci 1956–71, pt. 1, 173–92) and in 1959 by Nalinaksha Dutt (1939–59, 4: 139–70). Gregory Schopen pub-[16]lished a transcription and translation of the Gilgit manuscript (1989), pointing out in the notes the errors and silent alterations that appear in Chakravarti's and Dutt's editions.

Hirofusa Amano, to whom we already owe a study of Haribhadra's "Small Commentary" (*'Grel-chuṅ*) on Maitreya's *Abhisamayālaṃkāra* (1975),[19] also edited the Sanskrit text on the basis of two Nepalese manuscripts (1983–89). In a separate article (1988) he shows that Haribhadra's Small Commentary is not an abridgment of his "Great Commentary" (*'Grel-chen; Ālokā*), as suggested by Obermiller.

Mahāyāna sūtras

One of the oldest Mahāyāna sūtras is the *Pratyutpanna-buddha-saṃmukhāvasthita-samādhi-sūtra.* Paul Harrison translated the Tibetan version that he had edited in 1978. His book consists of a long introduction, an appendix on the textual history of the sūtra in China, and a new edition of the Sanskrit fragment in the Hoernle collection.

Several scholars studied the *Samādhirājasūtra,* the Gilgit manuscript of which was published by Nalinaksha Dutt (1939–59, vol.2). The first four chapters were translated by a group of scholars at the University of Michigan from 1982 to 1983 (Gómez and Silk 1989, 3–88).[20] The translation is preceded by a lengthy introduction and a very useful bibliography. Christoph Cüppers published a study of the ninth chapter that consists of an edition based upon thirteen manuscripts, a translation of the version represented by the Nepalese tradition, and an edition and translation of the Tibetan version of Mañjuśrīkīrti's commentary: *Kīrtimālā* (1990). It is to be hoped that all chapters of the *Samādhirājasūtra* will be studied in the same exemplary way. Finally, mention must be made of a translation of the Gilgit text of the *Samādhirājasūtra* by the late Jean Filliozat that is being prepared for publication (Gómez and Silk 1989, 82, n. 39).

Jikidō Takasaki consulted seventeen manuscripts for a new edition

19. See my review in *IIJ* 20 (1978): 313–14.

20. For a reference to the existence of a manuscript translation by Jean Filliozat, see Gómez and Silk 1989, 82 n. 39.

(1981) of the Kṣaṇika chapter of the *Laṅkāvatārasūtra* that was edited in 1923 by Bunyiu Nanjio. A new edition of the entire text is an urgent desideratum. In a recent publication (1990) F. G. Sutton translates many passages [17] without even consulting the Tibetan translation, the use of which could have helped him to avoid misinterpretations.

Bhikkhu Pāsādika published the Tibetan version of Nāgārjuna's *Sūtrasamuccaya* (1989), which he had already translated in its entirety in the periodical *Linh-Son* (Pāsādika 1978–82). He plans a study of the text, a revision of the translation, and the publication of new Indo-Tibetan lexicographical material obtained through a comparative study of the Tibetan version and corresponding Sanskrit passages.

R. E. Emmerick published (1990) a revised edition of the translation of the *Suvarṇabhāsottamasūtra* that first appeared in 1970. In his preface Emmerick announces a new edition of the Sanskrit text by P. O. Skjærvø, for which the latter was able to use a Nepalese manuscript not available to Nobel.

Kōtatsu Fujita consulted no less than thirty-four manuscripts for a new edition (1988) of the vow section in the *Larger Sukhāvatīvyūha,* thus replacing his earlier edition of 1980. In his preface Fujita announces a romanized edition of the manuscripts of the entire text, to be followed later by a critical edition.

Several sections of Śāntideva's *Śikṣāsamuccaya* were translated in a rather unsatisfactory way by Jürg Hedinger (1984).[21]

Publications relating to the Sanskrit texts of the *Saddharmapuṇḍarīkasūtra* and the Mahāyāna *Mahāparinirvāṇasūtra* were mentioned above, in my discussion of facsimiles.

Madhyamaka

The Madhyamaka school continued to be widely studied. Mitsuyoshi Saigusa published the texts of the Sanskrit, Tibetan, and Chinese versions of the *Mūlamadhyamakakārikā*s together with Japanese renderings (1985). Akira Saitō examined the Sanskrit text of the *kārikā*s and the Tibetan translations (1985, 1986, 1987). A new English translation of the *kārikā*s by David J. Kalupahana (1986) found little favour with reviewers.[22] Claus Oetke studied the philosophical ideas of the *kārikā*s (1988b, 1989, 1990).

Fernando Tola and Carmen Dragonetti published the text and trans-[18]lation of the *Catustava* (1985), reproducing Tucci's edition of the

21. See my review in *IIJ* 30 (1987): 230–35.

22. See Eli Franco, "Mahāyāna Buddhism—an Unfortunate Misunderstanding?" *Berliner Indologische Studien* 4/5 (1989): 39–47, and Christian Lindtner, *JAOS* 108 (1988): 176–78.

Niraupamyastava and the *Paramārthastava* and Lindtner's edition of the *Lokātītastava* and the *Acintyastava.* The same scholars edited and translated the Tibetan text of the *Śūnyatāsaptati* (1987). The *Pratītyasamutpāda-kārikās* are attributed to Nāgārjuna. Lindtner accepts their authenticity (1982c), but this is disputed by Carmen Dragonetti, who assigns this work to Śuddhamati (1978, 1986).[23] Lindtner's *Nāgārjuniana* (1982a) was reviewed in detail by P. Williams (1984).

Karen Lang published the Sanskrit and Tibetan texts of Āryadeva's *Catuḥśataka,* together with an annotated translation (1986). The Sanskrit fragments comprise less than a third of the four hundred verses. A complete translation of Candrakīrti's commentary remains a desideratum.

Buddhapālita's commentary on the *Mūlamadhyamakakārikās* was analysed by William L. Ames (1986a). In his doctoral thesis, "A Study of the *Buddhapālita-Madhyamaka-vṛtti*" (Australian National University, 1984), Akira Saitō translated the entire commentary and edited the Tibetan text. The English translation is due to be eventually published in Delhi. M. D. Eckel translated chapters 18, 24, and 25 (1980) and W. Ames chapters 3–5, 23, and 26 (1986b) of Bhāvaviveka's *Prajñāpradīpa* in unpublished doctoral dissertations. A complete edition and English translation is being prepared by Eckel and Ames.

Raghunatha Pandeya published (1988–89) a Sanskrit "reconstruction" of the *Akutobhayā,* Buddhapālita's *Madhyamakavṛtti,* and Bhāvaviveka's *Prajñāpradīpavṛtti,* together with an edition of the *Prasannapadā* that is entirely based on La Vallée Poussin's edition.

Per K. Sørensen edited and translated the Tibetan text of Candrakīrti's *Triśaraṇasaptati* (1986; cf. de Jong 1988). Peter Fenner's work on the ontology of the Middle Way (1990) comprises a translation of the verses of the *Madhyamakāvatāra.* His book sets out to address two questions: What is the relationship between reason and insight? and How are the Mahāyāna religious doctrines of universal compassion and therapeutic skill related to the Mādhyamika concept of emptiness? An ex-[19]cellent translation of the difficult first chapter of the *Prasannapadā* was published by Teruyoshi Tanji (1988a), who also studied the commentaries on chapter 16 of the *kārikās* (1988b). Megumu Honda (1988) and Takeki Okuzumi (1988) published complete translations of the *Prasannapadā.*

V. V. Gokhale and S. S. Bahulkar published an English translation of chapter 1 of the Sanskrit text of the *Madhyamakahṛdayakārikās* and of the Tibetan version of the *Tarkajvālā* (1985). Both the *kārikās* and the *Tarkajvālā* are attributed by them to Bhavya or Bhāvaviveka, but this is not generally accepted. Further research is necessary, according to Seyfort

23. See also Scherrer-Staub 1987.

Ruegg in his article on the authorship of some works attributed to Bhavya/Bhāvaviveka (1990). Olle Qvarnström published a new edition of the *kārikās* of the eighth chapter: Vedāntatattvaviniścaya (1989). Qvarnström was able to make use of photographs of the manuscript copied by Rāhula Sāṅkṛtyāyana in 1936. Until recently editions of chapters of the *kārikās* were based upon this handwritten copy as, for instance, Shinjō Kawasaki's edition (1976–88) of the Mīmāṃsā and Sarvajña chapters (9 and 10). It is to be hoped that a critical edition of the entire text of the *kārikās* will be prepared, together with an English translation of the *Tarkajvālā*. Qvarnström's book consists of an English translation of chapter 8 and an edition of the Tibetan version of the same chapter by Per K. Sørensen.

M. D. Eckel edited and translated the Tibetan version of the *Satyadvayavibhaṅgavṛtti* by Jñānagarbha, one of the pioneers of the Yogācāra-Mādhyamika school, who lived probably in the eighth century (1987). Of fundamental importance for the study of Śāntarakṣita and Kamalaśīla is M. Ichigō's book on the *Madhyamakālaṁkāra* (1985). Volume 1 consists of a lengthy introduction on the Yogācāra-Mādhyamika school and the text and a translation of the *kārikās* of the *Madhyamakālaṁkāra*, and an edition of the Tibetan text of Śāntarakṣita's *vṛtti* and Kamalaśīla's *pañjikā*. Volume 2 is in Japanese and contains six essays relating to Śāntarakṣita and Kamalaśīla and a translation of [20] the *Madhyamakālaṁkāra* and its *vṛtti*. Ichigō later published a revised text of the introduction and of the translation of the *kārikās* (1989).[24]

Yogācāra and Tathāgatagarbha

Lambert Schmithausen finally published his great work on *ālayavijñāna* (1987); it contains a wealth of material both in the text volume and in the notes. Another important contribution to the study of the *Yogācārabhūmi* is H. S. Sakuma's book (1990), in which he traces the development of the *āśrayaparivṛtti* theory in the *Yogācārabhūmi*. Mark Tatz translated the chapter on ethics in the *Bodhisattvabhūmi*; his work includes a translation of Tsoṅ-kha-pa's commentary (1986).[25]

Gajin Nagao was engaged in the study of the *Mahāyānasaṃgraha* for

24. For a review of Eckel 1987 see my review in *IIJ* 33 (1990): 70–71. Ichigō's book was reviewed by David Jackson—see *Bukkyōgaku Seminā* 43 (1986): 1–12 and *Berliner Indologische Studien* 2 (1986): 13–22—and by Shirō Matsumoto in *Tōyō Gakujutsu Kenkyū* 25/2 (1986): 177–203.

25. Schmithausen 1987 was reviewed by Paul Griffiths in *JIABS* 12/1 (1989): 170–77; Tatz 1986 by me in *IIJ* 32 (1989): 215–19.

more than forty years. In 1987 he published the second volume of his translation (1982–87). His work includes an edition of the Tibetan text and a retranslation of chapters 1 and 2 into Sanskrit by Noritoshi Aramaki. In his book *On Being Mindless* (1986) Paul J. Griffiths makes much use of the *Mahāyānasaṃgraha* and the *Abhidharmasamuccaya*; these, in his view, represent the classical stage of the Yogācāra.[26] Later he published a long article on omniscience in the *Mahāyānasūtrālaṃkāra* and its commentaries (1990).

Many works of Vasubandhu were translated. Thomas A. Kochumuttom translated the *Madhyāntavibhāgabhāṣya*, chapter 1, the *Trisvabhāvanirdeśa*, the *Triṃśikākārikās*, and the *Viṃśatikākārikās* together with their *vṛtti* (1982). F. Tola and C. Dragonetti translated the *Trisvabhāvakārikās* of Vasubandhu (1983), and Stefan Anacker published a translation of seven works of Vasubandhu (1984): *Vādavidhi, Pañcaskandhaprakaraṇa, Karmasiddhiprakaraṇa, Viṃśatikākārikāvṛtti, Triṃśikākārikās, Madhyāntavibhāgabhāṣya,* and *Trisvabhāvanirdeśa.* Anacker is not much impressed by previous translations and remarks, for instance, that his translation of the *Karmasiddhiprakaraṇa* "can safely claim to be more accurate" than the one published by Lamotte. However, his own translation of the *Madhyāntavibhāgabhāṣya* is incredibly bad.[27] Finally, P. S. Jaini published Sanskrit fragments of Vinītadeva's *Triṃśikāṭīkā* (1985). [21]

In the field of *tathāgatagarbha* studies the most important publications come from Jikidō Takasaki, the leading Japanese specialist in this field. He published a Japanese translation of the *Ratnagotravibhāga* (1989), which he had previously rendered into English (1966). His collected articles on *tathāgatagarbha* were published in two volumes (1988–89). And Motilal Banarsidass announced the publication of a book by Brian E. Brown on *tathāgatagarbha* and *ālayavijñāna* (1990).

Epistemology

The epistemological school has been studied intensively in recent years by many scholars both in Japan and in the West. It is to be hoped that a specialist in this field will give a critical survey of the many publications that have appeared since Hajime Nakamura's *Indian Buddhism* (1980), which contains a chapter on logicians (pp. 294–312).

One of the most important publications on Dignāga is Richard Hayes's *Dignāga on the Interpretation of Signs* (1988), which contains a

26. See my review in *IIJ* 31 (1988): 160–63.
27. See Richard Stanley's review in *IIJ* 30 (1987): 57–60.

translation of the most important parts of chapters 2 and 5 of the *Pramāṇasamuccaya.* Shōryū Katsura studied the development of the concept of *vyāpti* (pervasion) that was established by Dignāga as the formal and structural basis of the inevitable relation. A brief summary of his long Japanese article (1986a) was published later the same year (1986b). Much bibliographical information is to be found in two articles that Katsura contributed to a collective work on Indian Buddhism: one on the logical school (1988b) and one on *apoha* (1989).

In June 1989 the second conference on Dharmakīrti was held in Vienna (the first had been held in Kyoto in July 1982). Hōjun Nagasaki published a report on the Vienna conference (1990), in which he mentions a rumour that Christian Lindtner and Hu Haiyan were preparing a critical edition of a Sanskrit manuscript of the *Pramāṇaviniścaya,* though neither of them seems to have seen the manuscript in Beijing.

Tilmann Vetter published a translation of verses 131cd–285 of the Pramāṇasiddhi chapter of the *Pramāṇavārttika* (1984). His work was discussed in a long review by Eli Franco (1989). Victor A. van [22] Bijlert's book (1989) includes an annotated translation of verses 1–7 of the same chapter. In 1985 Hiromasa Tosaki published the second volume of his translation of the Pratyakṣa chapter (1979–85). Both volumes were reviewed in the *Indo-Iranian Journal* by Masaaki Hattori.[28] Ramchandra Pandeya published a new edition of the *Pramāṇavārttika* with the *Svopajñavṛtti* and Manorathanandin's *vṛtti* (1989), but with no indication of the manuscripts he used.

Ernst Steinkellner edited and translated the Tibetan version of Dharmottara's *Paralokasiddhi* (1986). He also edited and translated another *Paralokasiddhi* text (1988), Prajñāsena's *'Jig rten pha rol sgrub pa,* composed by a Tibetan scholar and based upon tradition and upon a work composed by Śubhagupta (ca. 720–80).[29] Together with Helmut Krasser he edited and translated Dharmottara's digression on valid cognition in his *Pramāṇaviniścayaṭīkā* (1989).

Jñānaśrimitra's *apoha* doctrine was studied by Katsura (1988a). In 1984 Raghunath Pandey published an edition of the *Udayananirākaraṇa* that he attributed to Ratnakīrti. The manuscript has been described by Gudrun Bühnemann (1983), who pointed out in her review that the title is *Vādarahasya* (1984). Torsten Much remarked that the attribution to Ratnakīrti cannot be substantiated (1987).

28. *IIJ* 25 (1982): 58–61; 30 (1987): 309–10.

29. See my review in *IIJ* 33 (1990): 66–69. For more of his work on the *Paralokasiddhi,* see Steinkellner 1984 and 1985.

Tantrism

Two important tantras have been translated by Peter Gäng, the *Caṇḍamahāroṣaṇatantra* (1981) and the *Guhyasamājatantra* (1988). The translation of the first is based upon Christopher S. George's edition (1974) for chapters 1–8, whereas the translation of chapters 9–25 is based upon the Cambridge manuscripts Ad. 1319 and 1470. The translation of the *Guhyasamājatantra* is based upon Matsunaga's edition. It does not contain chapter 18. The translation is preceded by a long introduction dealing with the Buddha, aspects of Buddhist psychology, Buddhist yoga, the development of Buddhist yoga, aspects of Buddhist philosophy, the mysticism of tantric Buddhism, and the language and mysticism of the *Guhyasamāja*. Gäng is also the author of a book on problems of lan-[23]guage in the mysticism of tantric Buddhism (1987).

The *Kālacakra* has been studied by John R. Newman (1985), who contributed a brief history of the *Kālacakra* to a volume called *The Wheel of Time*. The same volume includes two articles by Roger Jackson (1985a, b) and two by Geshe Lhundub Sopa (1985a, b). In the first of the Kālacakra Research Publications David Reigle published a paper, "The Lost Kālacakra Mūla Tantra on the Kings of Śambhala" (1986). According to a prefatory note he is working on a critical edition of the *Vimalaprabhā*, the great *Kālacakra* commentary. The most important work on the *Kālacakra* is John Newman's Ph.D. thesis (1987), which consists of a long introduction including a history of the *Kālacakra* in India, a detailed survey of previous study of the *Kālacakra*, and a translation from the Sanskrit and the Tibetan of *Śrī Kālacakra* I. 1–27, 128–70 and *Vimalaprabhā* I. 1.1–9, 28, 10.128–49. Newman discusses in some detail Banerjee's edition (1985) of the *Śrī Kālacakra* (pp. 175–79) and briefly notes Jagannatha Upadhyaya's edition (1986) of the *Śrī Kālacakra* and the *Vimalaprabhā* (p. 211).

In 1927 Haraprasad Shastri published twenty-one works of Advayavajra under the title *Advayavajrasaṃgraha*. A group of scholars belonging to the Institute for Comprehensive Studies of Buddhism at Taishō University undertook a critical edition and Japanese translation of the *Advayavajrasaṃgraha* (Mikkyō Seiten Kenkyūkai 1988–91). The same group also published the Sanskrit text and a Japanese translation of the *Vajradhātumahāmaṇḍalopāyika-Sarvavajrodaya* (1986–87).

Hindu Śaktism has been incorporated into Buddhist Tantrism. Therefore it is probably useful to mention here Marion Meisig's critical edition, translation, and glossary of the *Mahācīnācāra-Tantra* (1988). Meisig has consulted no less than eighteen manuscripts. His work is a very important contribution to the study of Śaktism.

Dictionaries, catalogues, bibliographies

Fascicles 4 and 5 of the *Sanskrit-Wörterbuch der buddhisti-*[24]*schen Texte aus den Turfan-Funden* were published in 1984 and 1987. With the publication of the eighth fascicle the vowels will be complete. Heinz Bechert published a very useful list of abbreviations for Buddhist literature in India and Southeast Asia (1990) as a supplement to the Sanskrit dictionary of Buddhist texts from Turfan. Also, the vowel section of *A Critical Pāli Dictionary* approached completion, almost seventy years after the publication of the first fascicle. Four fascicles were published in 1985, 1987, 1988, and 1989.[30] Volume 2, part 6 of the *Pāli Tipiṭakaṁ Concordance* was published in 1984, but no new fascicles were announced during the years under review.

Three more fascicles of the *Encyclopaedia of Buddhism* were published.[31]

A Sanskrit-Tibetan-Chinese index of the *Saddharmapuṇḍarīkasūtra* was being published by the Reiyūkai (Ejima 1985–93). The first fascicle appeared in 1985, the seventh (puruṣottama—bauddha) in 1990. Takashi Maeda published a Tibetan-Sanskrit-Chinese index to the first chapter of the *Sarvatathāgatatattvasaṃgraha* (1985). Yumiko Ishihama and Yōichi Fukuda published a critical edition of the *Mahāvyutpatti* comprising the Sanskrit, Tibetan, and Mongolian terms (1989). The two Mongolian translations have been edited on the basis of the Leningrad manuscript and the Mongolian Tanjur. Mie Ishikawa edited the *sGra-sbyor bam-po gñis-pa* (1990).

Two comprehensive Tibetan dictionaries were published: George N. Roerich's Tibetan-Russian-English dictionary with Sanskrit equivalents (1983–93), and the Great Tibetan-Chinese dictionary published in Beijing in three volumes.[32]

T. C. H. Raper compiled a catalogue of the Pāli printed books in the India Office Library (1983),[33] and C. E. Godakumbura made a catalogue of Cambodian and Burmese Pāli manuscripts in the Copenhagen library (1983).[34] Heinz Braun and Daw Tin Tin Myint published the second volume of the catalogue of Burmese manuscripts in German collections

30. Vol. 2, fasc. 13 (1985): ulumpa—ekato; fasc. 14 (1987): ekato—ekâyana; fasc. 15 (1988): ekâyana—evam-adhippāya; fasc. 16 (1989): evam-adhimutti—odissaka.

31. Vol. 4, fasc. 2 (1984): Cittavisuddhippa-karaṇa—Democracy; fasc. 3 (1988): Demonology—Dhammadhātu; fasc. 4 (1989): Dhammadhātu—Dvesa.

32. For a review of all but the last part of Roerich's dictionary, see Brian Galloway, *IIJ* 32 (1989): 328–31; the title of the Great Tibetan-Chinese dictionary is: *Bod-rgya tshig-mdzod chen-mo.*

33. For reviews see K. R. Norman, *JRAS* 1984: 293–94 and de Jong, *IIJ* 30 (1987): 73–74.

34. See my review in *IIJ* 29 (1986): 324–25.

(1985).[35] Siegfried Lienhard published the first volume of the catalogue of Nepalese manuscripts in the State Library in Berlin (1988). [25]

Lewis Lancaster edited and revised a bibliography of Buddhist scriptures by Edward Conze (Conze 1982); this work was reviewed rather critically by Helmut Eimer (1987). Günther Grönbold compiled a bibliography of the Buddhist canon (1984),[36] and Peter Pfandt's bibliography of Mahāyāna texts translated into Western languages (1983) was revised in 1986.

Siglinde Dietz (1989b) reported on the bibliographical survey of Buddhist Sanskrit literature undertaken by the Academy of Sciences in Göttingen. Part 1 (*Vinaya-Texte*) was published by Akira Yuyama in 1979; Ernst Steinkellner and Torsten Much are preparing a volume on Pramāṇa literature.

In Japan Keishō Tsukamoto, Yūkei Matsunaga, and Hirofumi Isoda published two volumes of a comprehensive bibliography of Sanskrit Buddhist literature in five volumes (1989–). The first volume to appear is the fourth of the series and deals with Buddhist tantras. The second to appear is volume 3, which deals with Abhidharma, Madhyamaka, Yogācāra, and Buddhist epistemology and logic. Other volumes will describe early Buddhist texts, Mahāyāna texts, and śāstras. A fifth volume will deal with collections of manuscripts, writing material, scripts, languages, and catalogues, and will contain a detailed index.

Pāli studies

During the period under review the Pali Text Society continued to publish editions and translations of Pāli texts. K. R. Norman published a new translation of the *Suttanipāta* (1984a). His notes on the text will be published in a second volume. Padmanabh S. Jaini edited the *Lokaneyyappakaraṇa* (1986b), which contains 596 verses together with a prose narrative. According to Jaini, of the 596 verses only about 141 may be considered true *nīti* verses. Jaini also completed I. B. Horner's translation of volume 1 of the *Paññāsa Jātaka* (Horner and Jaini 1985) and translated volume 2 (1986a). A. A. Hazlewood translated the *Samantakūṭavaṇṇanā* (1986), written by Vedeha Thera in the thirteenth century. The first 717 verses describe the life of Siddhattha Gotama from his birth until the time when, after becoming the Buddha, he made his sacred footprint on Mount Samanta. The last 85 verses describe the beauties of the mountain and the making of [26] the footprint. Part 1 of Bhikkhu Ñāṇamoli's transla-

35. I reviewed this work in *IIJ* 30 (1987): 239–40.
36. Reviewed by me in *IIJ* 30 (1987): 76–78.

tion of the *Sammohavinodanī* (1987–91) was revised by L. S. Cousins, Nyanaponika Mahāthera, and C. M. M. Shaw. N. A. Jayawickrama made a new translation of the *Nidānakathā* of the *Jātakaṭṭhakathā* (1990). Peter Masefield translated the commentary on the Vimāna stories (1989). An index to the *Dhammasaṅgaṇi* was compiled by Tetsuya Tabata, Satoshi Nonome, and Shōkū Bandō (1987).

Very welcome is the revival of the *Journal of the Pali Text Society*, of which four volumes (10–13) appeared in the years 1985–1989. The *Journal* publishes texts, translations, studies, notes, etc.

Two scholars made important contributions to the study of Pāli commentaries. Friedgard Lottermoser wrote a dissertation entitled *Quoted Verse Passages in the Works of Buddhaghosa* (1982).[37] Sodō Mori published, in Japanese, a study of the Pāli commentaries (1984). Later he published a collection of twelve articles in English (1989) so as to make his views better known to non-Japanese scholars. Sodō Mori is also responsible for the publication of the journal *Bukkyō Kenkyū (Buddhist Studies)*, which is published principally for studies in Early and Pāli Buddhism. Volumes 14–19 were published during the period under review; they contain articles in both Japanese and English.

Japanese scholars have been active in translating Pāli texts. Volume 7 of a series of ten volumes of "Early Buddhist texts" (*Genshi butten*) contains a translation of the *Dhammapada* by Kōtatsu Fujita and a translation of the *Suttanipāta* by Noritoshi Aramaki, Fumio Enomoto, and Yoshifumi Honjō (see Kajiyama 1986). I have not seen other volumes and do not know if all ten volumes have appeared. Also translated into Japanese were the *jātaka*s in ten volumes, of which I have been able to consult volume 1, containing the translation of *jātaka*s 1–70 by Kōtatsu Fujita (1984), and volume 4, containing the translation of *jātaka*s 301–85 by Hisashi Matsumura and Shin'ya Matsuda (1988).

K. R. Norman and O. von Hinüber published numerous articles relating to Pāli studies (see Bibliography entries). Some of von Hinüber's selected papers have been published (1994). [27]

Monographs

David Snellgrove published a book entitled *Indo-Tibetan Buddhism* (1987); according to his preface, it represents an overall survey of all the work done throughout his university career. It consists of five long chapters: Origins in India; Later Developments in India; Tantric Buddhism;

37. For a lengthy review, see Sodō Mori, *Bukkyō Kenkyū* [*Buddhist Studies*] 15 (1985): 125–42.

Buddhist Communities in India and Beyond; The Conversion of Tibet. Everything Snellgrove writes deserves to be read by serious students of Buddhism. The most important chapters in his book are probably those dealing with Tantrism and the conversion of Tibet. Richard Gombrich published a book on Theravāda Buddhism (1988a) in which he does not hesitate to advance his personal and sometimes controversial views.[38] In the same series Paul Williams wrote on Mahāyāna Buddhism (1989). His book is less original but well informed.[39]

An English translation of Étienne Lamotte's *Histoire du Bouddhisme indien* (1958) was published in 1988.[40] The text has not been revised but the translation includes a bibliographical supplement that is not very satisfactory. The index of technical terms that includes Lamotte's French translation of each term and an English translation is, however, very welcome. It would be extremely useful to expand this index to include all Lamotte's publications.

The publication of a detailed study of Nāgārjuna and his doctrine by V. P. Androsov (1990) bears testimony to the revival of Buddhist studies in the U.S.S.R. Androsov introduces the concept of Nāgārjunism to denote the religio-philosophical trend in the evolution of Mahāyāna in the second to fourth centuries.

Heinz Bechert published two volumes (1985–87) containing the papers read in 1982 in Göttingen at a symposium on "Schulzugehörigkeit von Sanskrit-Werken der Hīnayāna-Literatur." This publication, which is provided with detailed indexes, is of great importance for the study of the Buddhist schools. In 1988 another symposium was held in Göttingen on the theme of "Das Datum des historischen Buddha und seine Bedeutung für die indische Geschichte und für die Weltgeschichte." The merit for this accrues to Heinz Bechert, who raised this prob-[28]lem in recent years (Bechert 1982, 1986, 1988; see also Bechert 1989), and it is to him that we owe the publication of the proceedings of the symposium, in which many prominent scholars took part (Bechert 1991–92). A third volume is still to be published. Jens-Uwe Hartmann earlier wrote an interesting report on the symposium (1988b).

POSTSCRIPT

In preparing this survey, which is limited to studies relating to Indian Buddhist texts, I was struck by the amount of work done in recent years.

38. For my review, see *IIJ* 32 (1989): 239–42.
39. Reviewed by me in *IIJ* 34 (1991): 306–7.
40. See my review in *IIJ* 34 (1991): 147–49.

Nevertheless, this survey is far from complete. Of the innumerable Japanese publications, I have mentioned only those very few that have come to my notice. A more complete survey can only be made by a Japanese scholar who is able to consult the many journals published in Japan. Whereas it may be possible for Japanese scholars to keep informed of the publications of their compatriots, this is practically impossible for non-Japanese scholars outside Japan. It would be extremely useful if a university or institute in Japan would take the initiative to publish regularly (preferably monthly) a bulletin in English that would list recent Japanese publications relating to Buddhism.

It is regrettable that the *Bibliographie bouddhique* has not been continued. Perhaps it is too difficult to organise such an international bibliography, but it ought to be possible to publish at regular intervals bibliographies that would cover one or more countries, languages, or language groups. European publications could be covered almost entirely by bibliographies of publications in (respectively) Germanic, Romance, Scandinavian, and Slavic languages. It would be necessary additionally to publish bibliographies for the United States and Canada, and for India and the Theravāda countries, and one for Chinese publications. This would amount to an annual or bi-annual publication of seven bibliographies, which would certainly be of immense benefit to all scholars working in the field of Buddhist studies. Perhaps it would also be possible to fill in, in the same way, the gap left since the cessation of the *Bibliographie bouddhique* in 1958.

In one of his publications Yūichi Kajiyama relates that he used to tell [29] his American students that for Buddhist studies it is necessary to know eight languages: Sanskrit, Pāli, Tibetan, Chinese, Japanese, English, French, and German (1983, 233). French and German publications are often not consulted at all, especially in South Asia and in the United States, as pointed out by Heinz Bechert (1979, 67). Japanese scholars are much better informed about publications in English, French, and German than Western scholars are about Japanese publications. One has only to consult a recent collective work such as the three volumes on Indian Buddhism (*Iwanami Kōza—Tōyō Shisō*, vols. 8–10 [Tokyo, 1988–89]) to become aware of the fact that knowledge of Japanese publications has become more and more important for specialists in Buddhism. Rare are scholars like Lambert Schmithausen who are able to make critical comments on Japanese publications (cf. Schmithausen 1987). Some progress is being made, but many scholars are not even aware, for instance, of the fact that the text they are translating has already been rendered into Japanese. To mention only one example, in 1979 Stefan Anacker published a translation of chapters 2 and 4 and a part of chapter 5 of the *Madhyānta-*

vibhāgabhāṣya (Kiyota 1978, 83–113). The complete translation appeared in his *Seven Works of Vasubandhu* (1984). In a review of Kiyota 1978 (*Eastern Buddhist* 12/2 [1979], 156–57) it was made abundantly clear with the help of a few examples that the translator was quite unprepared for his task. An excellent translation by Gajin Nagao (1976) was not even mentioned by Anacker.

Anacker's book was favourably reviewed. One reviewer speaks of "reliable and interesting [*sic*] translations" (*JAOS* 108 [1988], 181); another reviewer found the translations "most reliable" (*JIABS* 9/1 [1986], 137). Of the seven texts translated by Anacker the *Madhyāntavibhāgabhāṣya* is the only one not previously rendered in its entirety into a Western language. One would expect a reviewer to carefully [30] study Anacker's translation of this text, and, if possible, compare it with the translation published by Nagao, a renowned scholar in this field.

The problem may be that serious and critical reviews are not encouraged by editors of some journals. Let me illustrate this by the following anecdote. Once, I sent a rather critical review to a journal. I received an acknowledgment and a statement that, after it was circulated to the rest of the editorial team, I would be informed of the final decision as quickly as possible. Having waited seven months for a reply, I made an inquiry. According to the reply my review had been sent to the author, who had not yet replied. After waiting another three months I wrote again and suggested I might like to publish this review elsewhere. I then received a letter informing me that my review, together with the author's reply, would be published. I was asked to immediately forward a brief response! Finally the review was published together with the reply of the author and my own response. However, the matter did not end there. When the next issue of the journal appeared, my name was omitted from the Editorial Advisory Board without previous notice. With some difficulty I managed to obtain a reply to my enquiry about the removal of my name. The answer was that the names listed on the Editorial Advisory Board ought to reflect more accurately the people with whom the editors actually did consult, and that they were still in the process of revising the list entirely. Needless to say, several years have passed and no other names have been removed from that list. Sapienti sat!

Abbreviations

AMG, B.V.	*Annales du Musée Guimet, Bibliothèque de Vulgarisation*
BCL	*Bulletin de la Classe des Lettres de l'Académie royale de Belgique*
BEFEO	*Bulletin de l'École française d'Extrême-Orient*
BKI	*Bijdragen tot de Taal-, Land- en Volkenkunde (Koninklijk Instituut voor Taal-, Land- en Volkenkunde, Leiden)*
BMFJ	*Bulletin de la Maison Franco-Japonaise*
BSOAS	*Bulletin of the School of Oriental and African Studies*
BSOS	*Bulletin of the School of Oriental Studies*
CPD	*Critical Pāli Dictionary*
HJAS	*Harvard Journal of Asiatic Studies*
IIJ	*Indo-Iranian Journal*
IsMEO	Istituto Italiano per il Medio ed Estremo Oriente
JA	*Journal Asiatique*
JAOS	*Journal of the American Oriental Society*
JASB	*Journal of the Asiatic Society of Bengal*
J. Bombay Br. RAS	*Journal of the Bombay Branch of the Royal Asiatic Society*
JIABS	*Journal of the International Association of Buddhist Studies*
JOIB	*Journal of the Oriental Institute, Baroda*
JOR Madras	*Journal of Oriental Research, Madras*
JPTS	*Journal of the Pali Text Society*
JRAS	*Journal of the Royal Asiatic Society of Great Britain and Ireland*
KZ	Kuhn's *Zeitschrift für vergleichende Sprachforschung*
MCB	*Mélanges chinois et bouddhiques*
MSS	*Münchener Studien zur Sprachwissenschaft*
NAWG	*Nachrichten der Akademie der Wissenschaften in Göttingen, I, Phil.-hist. Kl.*
NGGW	*Nachrichten der Gesellschaft der Wissenschaften in Göttingen*
PEFEO	Publications de l'École française d'Extrême-Orient
RHR	*Revue de l'histoire des religions*
SPAW	*Sitzungsberichte der Preussischen Akademie der Wissenschaften*
StII	*Studien zur Indologie und Iranistik*

SWTF	*Sanskrit-Wörterbuch der buddhistischen Texte aus den Turfan-Funden*
WZKM	*Wiener Zeitschrift für die Kunde des Morgenlandes*
WZKS	*Wiener Zeitschrift für die Kunde Südasiens*
WZKSO	*Wiener Zeitschrift für die Kunde Süd- und Ostasiens*
ZDMG	*Zeitschrift der Deutschen Morgenländischen Gesellschaft*
ZII	*Zeitschrift für Indologie und Iranistik*
ZMR	*Zeitschrift für Missionswissenschaft und Religionswissenschaft*
ZVORAO	*Zapiski Vostočnogo Otdelenija Russkogo Arxeologičeskogo Obščestva*

Bibliography

Publications that I have not been able to consult are marked with an asterisk.

Akanuma, Chizen, ed. 1930–31. *Indo-Bukkyō Koyūmeishi Jiten* [Dictionary of Indian Buddhist Proper Names]. Nagoya: Hajinkaku Shobō.

Alabaster, Henry, tr. 1871. *The Wheel of the Law: Buddhism illustrated from Siamese sources.* London: Trübner & Co.

Alsdorf, Ludwig. 1957. Bemerkungen zum Vessantara-Jātaka. *WZKSO* 1:1–70.

———. 1959. Aśokas Schismen-Edikt und das Dritte Konzil. *IIJ* 3:161–74.

———. 1968a. Verkannte Mahāvastu-Strophen. *WZKSO* 12–13:13–22.

———. 1968b. *Die Āryā-Strophen des Pāli-Kanons.* Wiesbaden: Steiner.

———. 1971. Das Jātaka vom weisen Vidura. *WZKS* 15:23–56.

———. 1974. *Kleine Schriften.* Ed. Albrecht Wezler. Wiesbaden: Steiner.

———. 1977. Das Bhūridatta-jātaka. *WZKS* 21:25–55.

Amano, Hirofusa. 1975. *A study on the Abhisamaya-alaṃkāra-kārikā-śāstravṛtti.* Tokyo: Japan Science Press.

———. 1988. Genkanshōgonronshaku no chosaku mondai saikō [A reconsideration of the problem of the authorship of the *Abhisamayālaṃkāra-vṛtti*]. In *Naritasan Bukkyō Kenkyūjo Kiyō* [*Journal of Naritasan Institute for Buddhist Studies*] 11: *Bukkyō Shisōshi Ronshū,* 33–57. Naritasan Shinshōji.

Amano, H., ed. 1983–89. Genkanshōgonronshaku no bonbun shahon [Sanskrit manuscript of the *Abhisamayālaṃkāra-vṛtti*]. In 6 parts. *Hijiyama Joshi Tankidaigaku Kiyō* [*Bulletin of the Hijiyama Women's Junior College*] 17 (1983): 1–15; *Shimane Daigaku Kyōiku Gakubu Kiyō* [*Bulletin of the Faculty of Education of Shimane University*] 19 (1985): 124–38; 20:67–86; 21:39–51; 22:10–25; 23:1–7.

Ames, William L. 1986a. Buddhapālita's exposition of the Madhyamaka. *Journal of Indian Philosophy* 14:313–48.

———. 1986b. **Prajñāpradīpa* (tr. and ed. of chs. 3–5, 23, 26). Ph.D. dissertation, U. of Washington.

Anacker, Stefan, tr. 1984. *Seven works of Vasubandhu, the Buddhist psychological doctor.* Delhi: Motilal Banarsidass.

Andersen, Dines. 1897. *The Jātaka, together with its commentary.* Vol. 7 of V. Fausbøll's work by this title. London: Kegan Paul, Trench, Trübner.

Androsov, Valerij Pavlovič. 1990. *Nagardžuna i ego učenie.* Moscow: Nauka.

Aramaki, Noritoshi. 1980. A text-strata-analytical interpretation of the concept pañcaskandhas. *Jimbun* (*The Humanities*) [College of Liberal Arts, Kyoto University] 26:1–36.

———. 1983. *Suttanipāta Aṭṭhakavagga ni mirareru ronsō hihan ni tsuite. *Nakagawa Zenkyō Sensei shōtoku kinen ronshū,* 117–146. Kyoto: Dōhōsha.

———. 1984. *Genshi Bukkyō kyōten no seiritsu ni tsuite [The Buddha's teaching in its development: Verse sūtras precede prose sūtras]. *Tōyō Gakujutsu Kenkyū* 23/1:52–87.

———. 1985a. *Attadaṇḍasutta (Sm 035–954) wa "Shakuson no kotoba" de ariuru ka. *Nippon Bukkyō Gakkai Nenpō* 50:(1)–(18).

———. 1985b. *On the formation of a short prose Pratītyasamutpāda Sūtra. In *Buddhism and its relation to other religions: Essays in honour of Dr. Shōzen Kumoi on his seventieth birthday,* 87–121. Kyoto: Heirakuji Shoten.

Armelin, Indumati. 1978. *Le coeur de la loi suprême, traité de Fa-cheng:* Abhidharmahṛdayaśāstra *de Dharmaśrī.* Paris: P. Geuthner.

Babinger, Franz. 1920. Isaak Jakob Schmidt, 1779–1847. In *Festschrift für Friedrich Hirth zu seinem 75. Geburtstag 16. April 1920,* 7–21. Berlin: Oesterheld & Co.

Bailey, Harold Walter. 1946. Gāndhārī. *BSOAS* 11:764–97.

Bailey, David Roy Shackleton. 1948. A note on the titles of three Buddhist stotras. *JRAS:* 55–60.

———. 1952. Mecaka et le Sūtrālaṃkāra. *JA* 240-1: 71–73.

Bailey, D. R. Shackleton, tr. 1950–51. The Varṇāhavarṇa stotra of Mātṛceṭa. *BSOAS* 13:671–701, 809–810, 947–1003.

———. 1951. *The Śatapañcāśatka of Mātṛceṭa.* Cambridge: The University Press.

Balasooriya, Somaratna et al., eds. 1980. *Buddhist studies in honour of Walpola Rahula.* London: Gordon Fraser.

Balk, Michael. 1988. *Untersuchungen zum Udānavarga: unter Berücksichtigung mittelindischer Parallelen und eines tibetischen Kommentars.* Ph.D. dissertation, Bonn.

Balk, M., ed. 1984. *Prajñāvarman's Udānavargavivaraṇa.* Bonn: Indica et Tibetica Verlag.

Banerjee, Biswanath, ed. 1985. *A critical edition of Śrī Kālacakratantrarāja.* Calcutta: The Asiatic Society.

Barannikov, A. P. and O. F. Volkova, trs. 1962. *Girljanda džatak.* Moscow: Akademija Nauk SSSR.

Bareau, André. 1955a. *Les sectes bouddhiques du petit véhicule.* PEFEO 38. Saigon: École Française d'Extrême-Orient.

———. 1955b. *Les premiers conciles bouddhiques.* Paris: Presses Universitaires de France.

———. 1963–71. *Recherches sur la biographie du Buddha dans les Sūtrapiṭaka et les Vinayapiṭaka anciens.* 2 vols. (vol. 2 in 2 parts, each paginated separately [pub'd in 1970, 1971]). PEFEO 53 and 77. Paris: École Française d'Extrême-Orient.

———. 1974a. La jeunesse du Buddha dans les Sūtrapiṭaka et les Vinayapiṭaka anciens. *BEFEO* 61:199–274.

———. 1974b. Le Parinirvāṇa du Buddha et la naissance de la religion bouddhique. *BEFEO* 61:275–99.

———. 1975. Les récits canoniques des funérailles du Buddha et leurs anomalies: nouvel essai d'interprétation. *BEFEO* 62:151–89.

———. 1979. La composition et les étapes de la formation progressive du Mahāparinirvāṇasūtra ancien. *BEFEO* 66:45–103.

———. 1980a. The place of the Buddha Gautama in the Buddhist religion during the reign of Aśoka. In Balasooriya et al. 1980, 1–9.

———. 1980b. Le Buddha et Uruvilvā. In Institut Orientaliste 1980, 1–18.

———. 1981. Le massacre des Śākya: essai d'interprétation. *BEFEO* 69:45–73.

———. 1982a. Un personnage bien mystérieux: l'épouse du Buddha. In Hercus et al. 1982, 31–59.

———. 1987. Eugène Denis (1921–1986). *Buddhist Studies Review* 4:143–45.

Barr, Kaj. 1956. Poul Tuxen: 8. december 1880—29. maj 1955. *Oversigt over Det Kgl. Danske Videnskabernes Selskabs Virksomhed 1955–1956.* Copenhagen: Det Kgl. Danske Videnskabernes Selskabs.

Barth, Auguste. 1914–27. *Œuvres de Auguste Barth.* 5 vols. Vols. 1 and 2, 1914; vol. 3, 1917; vol. 4, 1918; vol. 5, 1927. Paris: E. Leroux.

Barthélemy-Saint-Hilaire, Jules. 1866. Du bouddhisme et de sa littérature à Ceylan: Collection de M. Grimblot, consul de France à Ceylan. *Journal des Savants:* 43–59, 100–116, 151–66.

Baruch, Willy. 1938. *Beiträge zum Saddharma-Puṇḍarīka-Sūtra.* Leiden: Brill.

Basham, Arthur L. 1982. The evolution of the concept of the boddhisattva. In Kawamura 1982, 19–59.

Basham, A. L., ed. 1980. *A corpus of Indian studies: Essays in honour of Professor Gaurinath Sastri.* Calcutta: Sanskrit Pustak Bhaudar.

Basu, Ratna, ed. 1989. *Eine literatur-kritische Studie zu Āryaśūras Jātakamālā zusammen mit einer kritischen Edition der anonymen Jātakamālāṭīkā und einer kritischen Edition der Jātakamālāpañjikā des Vīryasiṃha.* Ph.D. dissertation, Bonn.

Batchelor, Stephen, tr. 1979. *A guide to the Bodhisattva's way of life.* Dharamsala: Library of Tibetan Works and Archives.

Bechert, Heinz. 1961a. Aśokas "Schismen-Edikt" und der Begriff Sanghabheda. *WZKSO* 5:18–52.

———. 1961b. *Bruchstücke buddhistischer Verssammlungen aus zentralasiatischen Sanskrithandschriften.* Vol. 1. Berlin: Akademie-Verlag.

———. 1966. *Buddhismus, Staat und Gesellschaft in den Ländern des Theravāda-Buddhismus.* Vol. 1. Frankfurt am Main/Berlin: A. Metzner.

———. 1970. Some side-lights on the early history of Pāli lexicography. In *Añjali: Papers on Indology and Buddhism. A felicitation volume presented to Oliver Hector de Alwis Wijesekera on his sixtieth birthday,* edited by J. Tilakasiri, 1–3. Peradeniya: University of Ceylon.

———. 1972. *Über die "Marburger Fragmente" des Saddharmapuṇḍarīka.* Göttingen: Vandenhoeck & Ruprecht. (*NAWG* 1972, No. 1)

———. 1979. *Einführung in die Indologie.* Darmstadt: Wissenschaftliche Buchgesellschaft.

———. 1982. The date of the Buddha reconsidered. *Indologica Taurinensia* 10: 29–36.

———. 1986. *Die Lebenszeit des Buddha—das älteste feststehende Datum der indischen Geschichte? NAWG* 1986, No. 4.

———. 1988. Remarks on the date of the historical Buddha. *Bukkyō Kenkyū* 17: 97–117.

———. 1989. The problem of the determination of the date of the historical Buddha. *WZKS* 33:93–120.

Bechert, Heinz, ed. 1978. *Buddhism in Ceylon and studies on religious syncretism in Buddhist countries: Report on a symposium in Göttingen.* Symposien zur Buddhismusforschung 1. Göttingen: Vandenhoeck & Ruprecht.

———. 1980. *Die Sprache der ältesten buddhistischen Überlieferung.* Symposien zur Buddhismusforschung 2. Göttingen: Vandenhoeck & Ruprecht.

———. 1985–87. *Zur Schulzugehörigkeit von Werken der Hīnayāna-Literatur.* Symposien zur Buddhismusforschung 3. Pt. 1, 1985; pt. 2, 1987. Göttingen: Vandenhoeck & Ruprecht.

———. 1989–. *Sanskrithandschriften aus den Turfanfunden.* With Klaus Wille. Vols. 6 (1989) and 7 (1995) to date. Wiesbaden: Steiner.

———. 1989–96. *Sanskrit-Texte aus dem buddhistischen Kanon: Neuentdeckungen und Neueditionen.* Parts 1 (1989), 2 (1992), 3 (1996). Göttingen: Vandenhoeck & Ruprecht.

———. 1990. *Abkürzungsverzeichnis zur buddhistischen Literatur in Indien und Südostasien.* Göttingen: Vandenhoeck & Ruprecht.

———. 1991–92. *The dating of the historical Buddha.* Symposien zur Buddhismusforschung 4. Pt. 1, 1991; pt. 2, 1992. Göttingen: Vandenhoeck & Ruprecht.

Bechert, H., Daw Khin Khin Su, and Daw Tin Tin Myint, comps. 1978. *Burmese manuscripts,* Wiesbaden: Steiner.

Beckh, Hermann. 1916. *Buddhismus.* 2 vols. Berlin and Leipzig: G. J. Göschen.

———. 1958. *Buddha und seine Lehre.* 2 vols. in one. Rev. ed. of *Buddhismus.* Stuttgart: Freies Geistesleben.

Bendall, Cecil, ed. 1987–1902. *Çikshāsamuccaya: A compendium of Buddhistic teaching compiled by Çāntideva chiefly from earlier Mahāyāna-sūtras.* Bibliotheca Buddhica 1. St. Petersburg. Reprint, Osnabrück: Biblio Verlag, 1970.

Benedetto, Luigi Foscolo, ed. 1928. *Marco Polo: Il Milione.* Florence: L. S. Olschki.

Bergmann, Benjamin. 1804–5. *Nomadische Streifereien unter den Kalmüken in den Jahren 1802 und 1803.* Riga: Hartmann. Reprint, Oosterhout: Anthropological Publications, 1969.

Bernhard, Franz. 1965–68. *Udānavarga.* 2 vols. Göttingen: Vandenhoeck & Ruprecht.

Bhattacharya, Kamaleswar. 1973. *L'Ātman-Brahman dans le bouddhisme ancien.* Paris: A. Maisonneuve.

———. 1975. *On the Brahman in Buddhist literature. *Sri Venkateswara University Oriental Journal* 18:1ff.

———. 1979. *The ātman in two Prajñāpāramitā-Sūtras. *Our Heritage* (Special number; 150th anniversary volume; Calcutta Sanskrit College Research Series No. 119): 39–45.

———. 1980. Diṭṭhaṃ, Sutaṃ, Mutaṃ, Viññātaṃ. In Balasooriya 1980, 10–15.

———. 1988. Brahman in the Pali canon and in the Pali commentaries. In Maity 1988, 95–112.

———. 1989. Some thoughts on Ātman-Brahman in early Buddhism. In *Dr. B. M. Barua Birth Centenary Commemoration Volume 1989,* 63–83. Calcutta: Bauddha Dharmankur Sabha (Bengal Buddhist Association).

Bhattacharya, Kamaleswar, tr. 1972. The dialectical method of Nāgārjuna. *Journal of Indian Philosophy* 1:217–61. (Also in book form, same title, Delhi/Varanasi/Patna: Motilal Banarsidass, 1978, pp. 5–48)

Bhattacharya, Vidhushekara, ed. 1931. *The Catuḥśataka of Āryadeva: Part 2.* Calcutta: Visva-bharati Bookshop.

Bibliotheca Buddhica. 1970. 34 vols. Reprint of vols. orig. pub'd 1897–1962. Osnabrück: Biblio Verlag.

Bigandet, Paul Ambrose. 1858. *The life, or legend, of Gaudama.* Rangoon: T. S. Ranney. (2d enl. ed., Rangoon: C. Bennett, 1866; 3d ed., London: Trübner & Co., 1880; 4th ed., London: K. Paul, Trench, Trübner & Co., 1911)

Bishop, Arthur Stanley, ed. 1908. *Ceylon Buddhism: Being the collected writings of Daniel John Gogerly.* 2 vols., paged continuously. Colombo: The Wesleyan Methodist Book Room.

Bizot, François. 1976. *Le figuier à cinq branches: Recherches sur le bouddhisme khmer.* PEFEO 107. Paris: A. Maisonneuve.

———. 1980. La grotte de la naissance: Recherches sur le bouddhisme khmer II. *BEFEO* 67:221–73.

———. 1981. *Le don de soi-même: Recherches sur le bouddhisme khmer III.* PEFEO 130. Paris: A. Maisonneuve.

Böhtlingk, Otto von. 1844. Über eine Pali-Handschrift im Asiatischen Museum der Kaiserl. Akademie der Wissenschaften. *Bull. de la classe hist.-philol. de l'Acad. imp. des sciences de St.-Pétersbourg* 1, No. 22, 342–47.

Boin, Sara, tr. 1976. *The teaching of Vimalakīrti: From the French translation by Étienne Lamotte.* London/Boston: Routledge & K. Paul.

Bollée, W. B., ed. and tr. 1970. *Kuṇālajātaka.* London: Luzac.

Bongard-Levin, Grigorij Maksimovič, ed. 1986. *New Sanskrit fragments of the Mahāyāna Mahāparinirvāṇasūtra* (Central Asian Manuscript Collection at Leningrad). Tokyo: International Institute for Buddhist Studies.

Bongard-Levin, G. M. and M. I. Vorob'eva-Desjatovskaja, eds. 1985. *Pamjatniki indijskoj pis'mennosti iz Central'noj Azii.* Vol. 1. Bibliotheca Buddhica 33. Moscow: Nauka.

———. 1986. *Indian texts from Central Asia (Leningrad Manuscript Collection).* Tokyo: International Institute for Buddhist Studies.

Boyer, Auguste M., P. S. Noble, Edward James Rapson, and Émile Senart, eds. 1920–29. *Kharoṣṭhī inscriptions discovered by Sir Aurel Stein in Chinese Turkestan.* 3 vols. London: Clarendon Press.

Braun, Heinz and Daw Tin Tin Myint, comps. 1985. *Burmese manuscripts.* Pt. 2, with an introduction by Heinz Bechert. Stuttgart: Steiner. (cf. Bechert et al. 1978)

Bronkhorst, Johannes. 1986. *The two traditions of meditation in ancient India*. Stuttgart: F. Steiner.

Brough, John. 1954. The language of the Buddhist Sanskrit texts. *BSOAS* 16:351–75.

———. 1962. *The Gāndhārī Dharmapada*. London: Oxford University Press.

Brown, Brian E. 1990. *The Buddha nature: A study of Tathāgatagarbha and Ālaya-vijñāna*. Delhi: Motilal Banarsidass.

Bruhn, Klaus. 1979. Ludwig Alsdorf (1904–1978). *ZDMG* 129:1–7.

Bruhn, Klaus and Albrecht Wezler, eds. 1981. *Studien zum Jainismus und Buddhismus: Gedenkschrift für Ludwig Alsdorf*. Wiesbaden: Steiner.

Buchanan, Francis (aka Francis Hamilton, or Francis Hamilton Buchanan). 1799. On the religion and literature of the Burmas. *Asiatick Researches* 6:163–308.

Bugault, Guy. 1983. Logic and dialectics in the Madhyamakakārikās. *Journal of Indian Philosophy* 11:7–76.

Bühler, Georg, tr. 1887. *The Buddhist stupas of Amaravati and Jaggayyapeta in the Krishna district ... with translations of the Aśoka inscriptions at Jaugada and Dhauli*. Text by James Burgess, trans. by Bühler. London: Trübner & Co.

———. 1909. *Beiträge zur Erklärung der Aśoka-Inschriften*. Leipzig: F. A. Brockhaus.

Bühnemann, Gudrun. 1983. Tarkarahasya and Vādarahasya. *WZKS* 27:185–90.

———. 1984. Review of Ācāryaratnakīrtiviracitam Udayananirākaraṇam. *WZKS* 28:228–29.

Bühnemann, G., tr. 1980. *Der allwissende Buddha: ein Beweis und seine Probleme; Ratnakīrtis Sarvajñasiddhi*. Vienna: Arbeitskreis für Tibetische und Buddhistische Studien, Universität Wien.

Burjatskii Institut Obščestvennyx Nauk. 1968. *Materialy po istorii i filologii Central'noj Azii*. Ed. D. D. Lubsanov. Ulan-Ude: Akademija Nauk SSSR.

Burnouf, Eugène. 1827. *Observations grammaticales sur quelques passages de l'essai sur le Pali de MM. E. Burnouf et Ch. Lassen*. Paris: Dondey-Dupré.

———. 1844. *Introduction à l'histoire du Buddhisme indien*. Paris: Imprimerie Royale.

Burnouf, Eugène, tr. 1852. *Le Lotus de la Bonne Loi*. Paris: Imprimerie Nationale.

Burnouf, Eugène and Christian Lassen. 1826. *Essai sur le Pali, ou la langue sacrée de la presqu'île au-delà du Gange*. Paris: Dondey-Dupré.

Burton-Page, John. 1985. Obituary John Brough. *BSOAS* 48:333–39.

Caillat, Colette, ed. 1989. *Dialectes dans les littératures indo-aryennes*. Paris: Institut de Civilisation Indienne, Collège de France.

Caudharī, Sūryanārāyaṇ. 1951. *Āryaśūrakṛtā Jātakamālā*. Delhi. Reprint, 1971.

Chakravarti, Niranjan Prasad, ed. and tr. 1930. *L'Udānavarga sanskrit*. Vol. 1. Paris: Paul Geuthner.

Chambers, William. 1788. Some account of the sculptures and ruins at Mavalipuram. *Asiatick Researches* 1:145–70.

Chavannes, Édouard. 1914. Le Dr. Palmyr Cordier. *T'oung Pao* 15:551–53.

Chavannes, Édouard, tr. 1894. *Voyages des pèlerins bouddhistes: Mémoire composé à l'époque de la grande dynastie T'ang sur les religieux éminents qui allèrent chercher la loi dans les pays d'Occident par I-tsing*. Paris: E. Leroux.

———. 1910–11. *Cinq cents contes et apologues.* Vols. 1–3. Paris: E. Leroux.

———. 1934. *Cinq cents contes et apologues.* Vol. 4. Edited by P. Demiéville, with a preface by S. Lévi. Paris: E. Leroux.

Ch'en, Kenneth Kuan Shêng. 1964. *Buddhism in China: A historical survey.* Princeton: Princeton University Press.

Cheng, Hsueh-li, tr. 1982. *Nāgārjuna's "Twelve Gate Treatise."* Dordrecht: Reidel.

Childers, Robert Caesar. 1875. *A dictionary of the Pāli language.* London: Kegan Paul, Trench, Trübner & Co.

Childers, R. C., ed. and tr. 1870. Khuddaka-Pāṭha: A Pāli text, with a translation and notes. *JRAS,* new ser., 4:309–89.

———. 1875–76. The Pali text of the Mahāparinibbāna Sutta and Commentary. With a translation. *JRAS,* new ser., 7:49–80; 8:219–61.

Chopra, Tilak Raj. 1966. *The Kuśa-jātaka.* Hamburg: C. de Gruyter.

———. 1990. BHS triyantara and Hindi teṃtara. In *Frank-Richard Hamm Memorial Volume,* 28–46. Bonn: Indica et Tibetica Verlag.

Clough, Benjamin. 1824. *A compendious Pali grammar, with a copious vocabulary in the same language.* Colombo: Wesleyan Mission Press.

Clough, Benjamin, tr. 1834. *The ritual of the Buddhist priesthood, translated from the original Pāli work, entitled Karmawākya.* London: Oriental Translation Fund.

Collins, Steven. 1982a. Self and Non-Self in early Buddhism. *Numen* 29/2:250–71.

———. 1982b. *Selfless persons: Imagery and thought in Theravāda Buddhism.* Cambridge: Cambridge University Press.

Cone, Margaret, ed. 1989. Patna Dharmapada I. *JPTS* 13:101–217.

Cone, Margaret and Richard F. Gombrich, trs. 1977. *The perfect generosity of Prince Vessantara.* Oxford: Clarendon Press.

Conze, Edward. 1948. Text, sources, and bibliography of the Prajñāpāramitā-hṛdaya. *JRAS:* 33–51.

———. 1951. *Buddhism: Its essence and development.* Oxford: B. Cassirer. (Also New York: Harper, 1959)

———. 1960. *The Prajñāpāramitā literature.* The Hague: Mouton. (2d, rev. and enl., ed., Tokyo: The Reiyukai, 1978)

———. 1962b. *Buddhist thought in India.* London: Allen and Unwin.

———. 1967a. *Materials for a dictionary of the Prajñāpāramitā literature.* Tokyo: The Suzuki Research Foundation.

———. 1967b. *Thirty years of Buddhist studies.* Oxford: B. Cassirer.

———. 1975b. *Further Buddhist studies: Selected essays.* Oxford: B. Cassirer.

———. 1979. *The memoirs of a modern gnostic, part 1.* Sherborne: Samizdat Pub. Co.

———. 1982. *Buddhist scriptures: A bibliography.* Ed. and rev. Lewis Lancaster. New York/London: Garland Pub.

Conze, Edward, ed. and tr. 1957. *Vajracchedikā Prajñāpāramitā.* Rome: IsMEO.

———. 1962a. *The Gilgit manuscript of the Aṣṭādaśasāhasrikāprajñāpāramitā.* Part 1: chaps. 55 to 70, corresponding to 5th Abhisamaya. Rome: IsMEO.

———. 1974. *The Gilgit manuscript of the Aṣṭādaśasāhasrikāprajñāpāramitā.* Part 2: chaps. 70 to 82. Rome: IsMEO.

Conze, Edward, tr. 1954. *Abhisamayālaṅkāra.* Rome: IsMEO.

———. 1958a. *Aṣṭasāhasrikā Prajñāpāramitā.* Calcutta: The Asiatic Society.

———. 1958b. *Buddhist Wisdom Books: The Diamond Sutra and the Heart Sutra.* London: George Allen & Unwin.

———. 1961. *The Large Sutra on Perfect Wisdom with the Divisions of the Abhisamayālaṅkāra.* Part 1. London: Luzac.

———. 1964. *The Large Sutra on Perfect Wisdom with the Divisions of the Abhisamayālaṅkāra.* Parts 2 and 3. Madison: Department of Indian Studies, U. of Wisconsin.

———. 1973a. *The Perfection of Wisdom in Eight Thousand Lines & its verse summary.* Bolinas: Four Seasons Foundation. (New ed. of Conze 1958a, together with tr. of *Ratnaguṇasaṃcayagāthā*)

———. 1973b. *The short Prajñāpāramitā texts.* London: Luzac.

———. 1975a. *The Large Sutra on Perfect Wisdom: With the Divisions of the Abhisamayālaṅkāra.* New ed. in 1 vol. Berkeley: U. of California Press.

Cordier, Henri. 1915. Nécrologie William Woodville Rockhill. *T'oung Pao* 16:160–64.

———. 1918. Édouard Chavannes. *JA* 1918-1:197–248.

Cordier, Palmyr. 1909–15. *Catalogue du fonds tibétain de la Bibliothèque Nationale.* Parts 2 and 3. Paris: E. Leroux.

Cousins, Lance S. 1983. Pali oral literature. In Denwood and Piatigorsky 1983, 1–11.

Cousins, Lance S., A. Kunst, and K. R. Norman, eds. 1974. *Buddhist studies in honour of I. B. Horner.* Dordrecht/Boston: D. Reidel.

Cowell, Edward Byles, ed. 1893. *The Buddha-Karita of Asvaghosha.* Oxford: Clarendon Press.

Cowell, E. B. and Robert Alexander Neil, eds. 1886. *The Divyâvadâna: A collection of early Buddhist legends.* Cambridge: The University Press.

Cowell, E. B., F. Max Müller, and Junjirō Takakusu, eds. and trs. 1965. *Buddhist Mayāhāna texts.* 2 vols. in 1. Delhi: Motilal Banarsidass. (First pub'd 1894 by Oxford University Press, Sacred Books of the East 49, Parts 1, 2)

Creel, Herrlee Glessner. 1935. Obituary, Berthold Laufer: 1874–1934. *Monumenta Serica* 1:487–96.

Critical Pāli Dictionary, A. Copenhagen: Royal Danish Academy of Sciences and Letters. Vol. 1, 1924–48; vol. 2, 1960–90; vol. 3, 1992–.

Csoma de Körös, Alexander. 1836–39. Analysis of the Kah-gyur. *Asiatick Researches* 20:41–93, 393–552. (French translation: Feer 1881)

Culture Palace of the Nationalities, ed. 1984. **Lotus Sūtra.* Beijing: Culture Palace of the Nationalities.

Cumming, Sir John, ed. 1939. *Revealing India's Past: A co-operative record of archaeological conservation and exploration in India and beyond.* London: The India Society.

Cunningham, Sir Alexander. 1854. *The Bhilsa topes.* London: Smith, Elder and Co.

———. 1877. *Inscriptions of Asoka.* Corpus Inscriptionum Indicarum 1. Calcutta: Office of the Superintendent of Govt. Printing.

———. 1879. *The stûpa of Bharhut.* London: W. H. Allen and Co. (2d ed. [with an introduction by Vasudeva S. Agrawala], Varanasi: Indological Book House, 1962)

Cüppers, Christoph, ed. and tr. 1990. *The IXth chapter of the Samādhirājasūtra: A text-critical contribution to the study of Mahāyāna sūtras.* Stuttgart: Steiner.

Dabbs, Jack Autrey. 1963. *History of the discovery and exploration of Chinese Turkestan.* The Hague: Mouton.

Dahlmann, Joseph. 1896. *Nirvāṇa.* Berlin: F. L. Dames.

———. 1898. *Buddha.* Berlin: F. L. Dames.

———. 1902. *Die Sāṃkhya-Philosophie als Naturlehre und Erlösungslehre.* Berlin: F. L. Dames.

D'Alwis, James, ed. 1863. *An introduction to Kachchāyana's grammar of the Pāli language.* Colombo and London: Williams and Norgate.

Damsteegt, Theo. 1978. *Epigraphical Hybrid Sanskrit: Its rise, spread, characteristics and relationship with Buddhist Hybrid Sanskrit.* Leiden: Brill.

Das, Sarat Chandra and Hari Mohan Vīdyābhūśana, eds. 1888–1918. *Avadānakalpalatā: A collection of legendary stories about the bodhisattvas.* 2 vols. Calcutta: Asiatic Society of Bengal.

Dawson, Christopher Henry, ed. 1955. *The Mongol mission: Narratives and letters of the Franciscan missionaries in Mongolia and China in the thirteenth and fourteenth centuries.* Translated by a Nun of Stanbrook Abbey. London and New York: Sheed and Ward.

de Jong, Jan Willem. 1958. [Some observations on R. Loewenthal's *The Turkic languages and literatures of Central Asia*]. *IIJ* 2:81.

———. 1967. A propos du Varṇārhavarṇastotra de Mātṛceṭa. *IIJ* 10:181–83.

———. 1968a. *Buddha's word in China.* Canberra: Australian National University.

———. 1968b. Les Sūtrapiṭaka des Sarvāstivādin et des Mūlasarvāstivādin. In *Mélanges d'indianisme à la mémoire de Louis Renou*, 395–402. Paris: E. de Boccard.

———. 1971. Review of É. Lamotte, *Le Traité de la Grande Vertu de Sagesse de Nāgārjuna*, vol. 3. *Asia Major* 17:105–12.

———. 1972a. The problem of the Absolute in the Madhyamaka School. *Journal of Indian Philosophy* 2:1–6.

———. 1972b. Emptiness. *Journal of Indian Philosophy* 2:7–15.

———. 1973. Review of O. von Hinüber's *Studien zur Kasussyntax des Pāli. IIJ* 15:64–66.

———. 1974. Review of B. Jinananda's *Abhisamācārikā. IIJ* 16:150–52.

———. 1977b. The *Bodhisattvāvadānakalpalatā* and the *Ṣaḍdantāvadāna.* In Kawamura and Scott 1977, 27–38.

———. 1979. *Textcritical remarks on the Bodhisattvāvadānakalpalatā (pallavas 42–108).* Tokyo: Reiyukai Library.

———. 1980. Edward Conze 1904–1979. *IIJ* 22:143–46.

———. 1981. The Sanskrit text of the Ṣaḍdantāvadāna. *Indologica Taurinensia* 8:281–97.

———. 1987. Lamotte and the doctrine of non-self. *Cahiers d'Extrême-Asie* 3:151–53.

———. 1988. Review of P. K. Sørensen's *Candrakīrti: Triśaraṇasaptati. IIJ* 31: 41–42.

de Jong, J. W., ed. 1977a. *Nāgārjuna: Mūlamadhyamakakārikāḥ.* Madras: Adyar Library and Research Centre.

de Jong, J. W., tr. 1949. *Cinq chapitres de la Prasannapadā.* Buddhica 9. Paris: Geuthner.

Delbrueck, R. 1955–56. Südasiatische Seefahrt im Altertum. *Bonner Jahrbücher* 155:8–58; 156:229–308.

de Lubac, Henri. 1952. *La rencontre du bouddhisme et de l'Occident.* Paris: Aubier.

Demiéville, Paul. 1924. Les versions chinoises du Milindapañha. *BEFEO* 24: 1–258.

———. 1946. La carrière scientifique de Paul Pelliot, son œuvre relative à l'Extrême-Orient. In *Paul Pelliot,* edited by Georges Salles et al., 29–54. Paris.

———. 1950. Review of Lamotte 1944–80, vols. 1 and 2. *JA:* 375–95. (= *Choix d'études bouddhiques* 470–90)

———. 1951. A propos du concile de Vaiśālī. *T'oung Pao* 40:239–96.

———. 1952. *Le concile de Lhasa: Une controverse sur le quiétisme entre bouddhistes de l'Inde et de la Chine au VIIIe siècle de l'ère chrétienne.* Paris: Presses Universitaires de France.

———. 1954. Le *Yogācārabhūmi* of Saṅgharakṣa. *BEFEO* 44:339–436.

———. 1957b. Review of *Jōron kenkyū. T'oung Pao* 45:221–35.

———. 1970. Le bouddhisme chinois. In *Histoire des religions,* vol. 1 (Encyclopédie de la Pléiade 29), ed. Henri Charles Puech, 1249–319. Paris: Gallimard. (= *Choix d'études bouddhiques* 365–435)

Demiéville, Paul, ed. 1973a. *Choix d'études bouddhiques 1929–1970.* Leiden: Brill.

———. 1973b. *Choix d'études sinologiques 1921–1970.* Leiden: Brill.

Demiéville, Paul, ed. and tr. 1961. Un fragment sanskrit de l'Abhidharma des Sarvāstivādin. *JA* 249:461–75.

———. 1972. *Entretiens de Lin-tsi.* Paris: Fayard.

Demiéville, Paul, tr. 1957a. Le chapitre de la Bodhisattvabhūmi sur la perfection du Dhyāna. *Rocznik Orientalisticzny* 21:109–28. (= *Choix d'études bouddhiques,* 300–319)

Denis, Eugène, ed. 1977. *La Lokapaññatti et les idées cosmologiques du bouddhisme ancien.* 2 vols. Paris: Champion.

Denwood, Philip and Alexander Piatigorsky, eds. 1983. *Buddhist studies ancient and modern.* London: Curzon Press/Totowa, N.J.: Barnes & Noble.

de Rachewiltz, Igor. 1971. *Papal envoys to the Great Khans.* London: Faber and Faber.

Derrett, John Duncan Martin. 1969. Megasthenes. *Der kleine Pauly: Lexikon der Antike* 3, col. 1150–54.

Dhammapāla, Gatare, R. Gombrich, and K. R. Norman, eds. 1984. *Buddhist studies in honour of Hammalava Saddhātissa.* Nugegoda, Sri Lanka: Hammalava Saddhātissa Felicitation Volume Committee.

Dietz, Siglinde. 1984b. *Fragmente des Dharmaskandha.* Göttingen: Vandenhoeck & Ruprecht.

———. 1989a. A brief survey on the Sanskrit fragments of the Lokaprajñaptiśāstra. *Annual Memoirs of the Ōtani University Shin Buddhist Comprehensive Research Institute* 7:79–86.

———. 1989b. Investigation into Buddhist literature: A project of the Academy of

Sciences in Göttingen. *Annual Memoirs of the Ōtani University Shin Buddhist Comprehensive Research Institute* 7:71–77.

Dietz, S., ed. and tr. 1980. *Die buddhistische Briefliteratur Indiens: Nach dem tibetischen Tanjur herausgegeben, übersetzt und erläutert.* 3 parts. Inaugural-Dissertation, Bonn.

———. 1984a. *Die buddhistische Briefliteratur Indiens.* Wiesbaden: Harrassowitz.

Dihle, Alfred Charles. 1964. Indische Philosophen bei Clemens Alexandrinus. In *Mullus (Festschrift Theodor Klauser),* edited by Alfred Stuiber and Alfred Hermann, 60–70. Münster/Westf.: Aschendorff.

———. 1965. Buddha und Hieronymus. *Mittellateinisches Jahrbuch* 2:38–41.

Donnet, Daniel. 1980. [Bibliography of the works of Étienne Lamotte.] In Institut Orientaliste 1980, vii–xvi.

Dragonetti, Carmen. 1978. The Pratītyasamutpādahṛdayakārikā and the Pratītyasamutpādahṛdayavyākhyāna of Śuddhamati. *WZKS* 22:87–93.

———. 1986. On Śuddhamati's Pratītyasamutpādahṛdayakārikā and on Bodhicittavivaraṇa. *WZKS* 30:109–22.

Dresden, Mark Jan. 1942. Bibliographia Sogdica concisa. *Jaarbericht No. 8 van het Vooraziatisch-Egyptisch Gezelschap Ex Oriente Lux,* 729–34.

———. 1944. Introductio ad linguam hvatanicam. *Jaarbericht No. 9 van het ... Ex Oriente Lux,* 200–206.

Dschi, Hiän-lin. 1944. Die Umwandlung der Endung *-aṃ* in *-o* und *-u* im Mittelindischen. *NGGW:* 121–44.

———. 1949. Die Verwendung des Aorists als Kriterium für Alter und Ursprung buddhistischer Texte. *NGGW:* 245–301.

Duerlinger, James, tr. 1989. Vasubandhu's 'Refutation of the Theory of Selfhood' (*Âtmavâdapratiṣedha*). *Journal of Indian Philosophy* 17.2: 129–87.

Dutt, Nalinaksha, ed. 1934. *The Pañcaviṃśatisāhasrikā Prajñāpāramitā.* Calcutta Oriental Series 28. London: Luzac.

———. 1939–59. *Gilgit manuscripts.* 4 vols. (1, 1939; 2, 1941 [pt. 1], 1953 [pt. 2], 1954 [pt. 3]; 3, 1947 [pt. 1], 1942 [pt. 2], 1943 [pt. 3], 1950 [pt. 4]; 4, 1959). Srinagar-Kashmir/Calcutta: Calcutta Oriental Press. Reprint, Delhi: Sri Satguru, 1984.

———. 1966. *Bodhisattvabhūmiḥ, being the XVth section of Asaṅgapāda's Yogācārabhūmiḥ.* Tibetan Sanskrit Works 7. Patna: K. J. Jayaswal Research Institute. Reprint, 1978.

Eckel, Malcolm David. 1980. **A question of nihilism: Bhāvaviveka's response to the fundamental problems of Mādhyamika philosophy.* Ph.D. dissertation, Harvard University.

Eckel, M. D., ed. and tr. 1987. *Jñānagarbha's commentary on the distinction between the two truths: An eighth-century handbook of Madhyamaka philosophy.* Albany: SUNY Press.

Edgerton, Franklin. 1935. The meter of the Saddharmapuṇḍarīka. In *Mahamahopadhyaya Kuppuswami Sastri Commemoration Volume,* 39–45. Madras: G. S. Press.

———. 1936a. The Prakrit underlying Buddhist Hybrid Sanskrit. *BSOS* 8:501–16.

———. 1936b. Nouns of the *a*-declension in Buddhist Hybrid Sanskrit. *HJAS* 1:65–83.

———. 1937a. Gerunds in Buddhist Hybrid Sanskrit. *Language* 13:107–22.
———. 1937b. The aorist in Buddhist Hybrid Sanskrit. *JAOS* 57:16–34.
———. 1937c. Buddhist Hybrid Sanskrit *saṃdhā, saṃdhi-(nirmocana)*. *JAOS* 57:185–88.
———. 1946a. Meter, phonology, and orthography in Buddhist Hybrid Sanskrit. *JAOS* 66:197–206.
———. 1946b. Indic causatives in *-āpayati (-āpeti, -āvai)*. *Language* 22:94–102.
———. 1952. Review of E. Waldschmidt's *Mahāparinirvāṇa-sūtra*. *JAOS* 72:114–17.
———. 1953a. *Buddhist Hybrid Sanskrit grammar and dictionary*. 2 vols. New Haven: Yale University Press.
———. 1953b. Review of J. Ensink's *The question of Rāṣṭrapāla*. *JAOS* 73:169–70.
———. 1954a. *Buddhist Hybrid Sanskrit language and literature*. Benares: Benares Hindu University.
———. 1954b. Semantic notes on Buddhist Hybrid Sanskrit. In *Sprachgeschichte und Wortbedeutung (Festschrift Albert Debrunner)*, 129–34. Bern: Francke.
———. 1955. The nature of Buddhist Hybrid Sanskrit. *J. Gandanatha Jha Research Institute* 11/12.2:1–10.
———. 1957a. On editing Buddhist Hybrid Sanskrit. *JAOS* 77:184–92.
———. 1957b. Review of E. Waldschmidt's *Mahāvadāna-sūtra*. *JAOS* 77:227–32.
———. 1961. The Prajñāpāramitā-ratna-guṇa-saṃcaya-gāthā. *IIJ* 5:1–18.
———. 1963. Review of E. Waldschmidt's *Catuṣpariṣat-sūtra*. *Language* 39:489–93.
Edgerton, F., ed. 1953c. *Buddhist Hybrid Sanskrit reader*. New Haven: Yale University Press.
Edgerton, F., tr. 1965. *The beginnings of Indian philosophy*. Cambridge: Harvard University Press; London: G. Allen & Unwin.
Eimer, Helmut. 1987. Review of Conze 1982. *IIJ* 30: 60–64.
Eimer, Helmut, ed. 1983. Rab tu 'byuṅ ba'i gzi, *die tibetische Übersetzung des Pravrajyāvastu im Vinaya der Mūlasarvāstivādins*. Vol. 2: Text. Wiesbaden: Harrassowitz.
Ejima, Yasunori. 1987. Textcritical remarks on the ninth chapter of the Abhidharmakośabhāṣya. *Bukkyō Bunka* 20:2–40.
———. 1989. *Abhidharmakośabhāṣya of Vasubandhu. Chapter I: Dhātunirdeśa*. Tokyo: Sankibō Press.
Ejima, Y., ed. 1985–93. *Index to the Saddharmapuṇḍarīkasūtra: Sanskrit, Tibetan, Chinese*. Fascicles 1–11. Tokyo: Reiyukai.
Elisséef, S. 1938. Staël-Holstein's contribution to Asiatic Studies. *HJAS* 3:1–8.
Elizarenkova, Tat'jana Iakovlevna and Vladimir Nikolaevič Toporov. 1965. *Jazyk Pali*. Moscow: Nauka.
———. 1976. *The Pāli language*. Moscow: Nauka.
Emmerick, R. E., tr. 1990. *The Sūtra of Golden Light, being a translation of the Suvarṇabhāsottama-sūtra*. 2d rev. ed. Oxford: Oxford University Press.
Enomoto, Fumio. 1985. "Zōagongyō" kankei no bonbun danpen: "Turfan shutsudo bonbun shahon mokuroku" dai-gokan wo megutte. *Bukkyō Kenkyū* 15:81–93.
———. 1986. On the formation of the original texts of the Chinese Āgamas. *Buddhist Studies Review* 3/1:19–30.

———. 1989a. Sanskrit fragments from the Saṃyuktāgama discovered in Bamiyan and eastern Turkestan. In Bechert 1989–95, 1:7–16.

Enomoto, F., ed. 1989b. Śarīrārthagāthā: A collection of canonical verses in the *Yogācābhūmi*. Part 1: Text. In Bechert 1989–95, 1: 17–35.

Ensink, Jacob. 1952. *The question of Rāṣṭrapāla*. Zwolle: J. J. Tijl.

Esteves Pereira, Francisco Maria. 1921. *O Descobrimento do Tibet pelo P. António de Andrade*. Coimbra: Imprensa da Universidade.

Falk, Harry, ed. 1987. *Hinduismus und Buddhismus: Festschrift für Ulrich Schneider*. Freiburg: Hedwig Falk.

Fausbøll, Michael Viggo, ed. and tr. 1855. *Dhammapadam, ex tribus codicibus Hauniensibus...* . Copenhagen: C. A. Reitzel. (Eng. version: *The Dhammapada...* . London: Luzac, 1900)

———. 1861. *Five Jātakas*. Copenhagen: C. A. Reitzel.

———. 1871a. *The Dasaratha-Jātaka*. Copenhagen: Hagerup.

———. 1871b. Two Jatakas. *JRAS* 5:1–13.

———. 1872. *Ten Jātakas*. Copenhagen: H. Hagerup.

———. 1877–97. *The Jātaka, together with its commentary, being tales of the anterior births of Gotama Buddha*. 7 vols. London: Trübner & Co.

Fausbøll, Michael Viggo and Albrecht Friedrich Weber. 1862. Die Pāli-Legende von der Entstehung des Sâkya (Çâkya)- und Koliya-Geschlechtes. *Indische Studien* 5:412–37.

Feer, Léon, ed. 1899. *Papiers d'Eugène Burnouf conservés à la Bibliothèque Nationale*. Paris: H. Champion.

Feer, Léon, tr. 1881. Analyse du Kandjour, recueil des livres sacrés du Tibet. *Annales du Musée Guimet* 2:131–556.

Fenner, Peter. 1990. *The ontology of the Middle Way*. Dordrecht: Reidel.

Fergusson, James. 1868. *Tree and serpent worship*. London: W. H. Allen and Co.

Filippi, Filippo de. 1931. *An account of Tibet: The travels of Ippolito Desideri of Pistoia, S.J., 1712–1727*. London: G. Routledge & Sons. (Rev. ed. 1937)

Filliozat, Jean. 1949. Les échanges de l'Inde et de l'Empire romain aux premiers siècles de l'ère chrétienne. *Revue historique* 201:1–29.

———. 1974. *Laghu-prabandhāḥ: Choix d'articles d'Indologie*. Leiden: Brill.

Filliozat, Pierre. 1983. Bibliographie des travaux de Jean Filliozat. *JA* 271:5–24.

Finot, Louis. 1929. Nécrologie d'Émile Senart. *BEFEO* 28:335–47.

Finot, L., ed. 1898. *Rāṣṭrapālaparipṛcchā, Sūtra du Mahāyāna*. Bibliotheca Buddhica 2. St.-Pétersbourg: Commissionaires de l'Académie Impériale des Sciences.

Foucaux, Philippe Édouard, ed. and tr. 1847–48. *Rgya Tch'er rol pa; ou, Développement des Jeux*. Paris: Imprimerie Royale.

Foucher, Alfred Charles Auguste. 1916. Auguste Barth. *Bulletin de la commission archéologique de l'Indochine: Années 1914–1916*, 207–21. Paris: Imprimerie Nationale.

———. 1949. *La vie du Bouddha, d'après les textes et les monuments de l'Inde*. Paris: Payot.

Franco, Eli. 1989. Was the Buddha a Buddha? *Journal of Indian Philosophy* 17:81–99.

Franke, Rudolf Otto. 1929. Die Legende vom Mönche Abhiya. In *Königsberger*

Beiträge: Festgabe zur vierhundertjährigen Jubelfeier der Staats- und Universitätsbibliothek zu Königsberg, 115–24. Kaliningrad: Verlag Grafe & Unzer.

———. 1930. Maudgalyāyanas Wanderung durch die leidvollen Welten. *Zeitschrift für Missionskunde und Religionswissenschaft* 45:1–22.

———. 1978. *Kleine Schriften.* Ed. Oskar von Hinüber. Wiesbaden: Steiner.

Frauwallner, Erich. 1952. Die buddhistischen Konzile. *ZDMG* 102:240–61.

———. 1953. *Geschichte der indischen Philosophie.* Vol. 1. Salzburg: Otto Müller.

———. 1954. Die Reihenfolge und Entstehung der Werke Dharmakīrti's. In Schubert and Schneider 1954, 142–54.

———. 1956. *The earliest Vinaya and the beginnings of Buddhist literature.* Rome: IsMEO.

———. 1959. Dignāga, sein Werk und seine Entwicklung. *WZKSO* 3:83–164.

———. 1963. Abhidharma-Studien. I. Pañcaskandhakam und Pañcavastukam. *WZKSO* 7:20–36.

———. 1964. Abhidharma-Studien. II. Die kanonischen Abhidharma-Werke. *WZKSO* 8:59–99.

———. 1968. *Materialien zur ältesten Erkenntnislehre der Karmamīmāṃsā,* 62–106. Vienna: Böhlau.

———. 1971. Abhidharma-Studien. III. Der Abhisamayavādaḥ. IV. Der Abhidharma der anderen Schulen. *WZKS* 15:69–121.

———. 1972. Abhidharma-Studien. IV. Der Abhidharma der anderen Schulen (cont'd). *WZKS* 16:95–152.

———. 1973a. Abhidharma-Studien. V. Der Sarvāstivādaḥ: Eine entwicklungsgeschichtliche Studie. *WZKS* 17:97–121.

———. 1973b. *History of Indian philosophy.* 2 vols. Trans. V. M. Bedekar. Delhi: Motilal Banarsidass.

———. 1982. *Kleine Schriften.* Ed. Gerhard Oberhammer and Ernst Steinkellner. Wiesbaden: Steiner.

Frauwallner, E., ed. and tr. 1930. Dignāgas Ālambanaparīkṣā. *WZKM* 37: 174–94.

Friedmann, David Lasar, tr. 1937. *Sthiramati: Madhyāntavibhāgaṭīkā: Analysis of the Middle Path and the Extremes.* Ph.D. dissertation, Utrecht University. Reprinted 1984.

Fujita, Kōtatsu. 1984. *Kusharon shoin no Agongyō ichiran* [Āgamas cited in the *Abhidharmakośabhāṣya*]. Hokkaido University.

Fujita, K., ed. 1988. *The Vow in the Sanskrit manuscripts of the Larger Sukhāvatīvyūha.* Sapporo: Department of Indian Philosophy, Faculty of Letters, Hokkaido University.

Fujita, K., tr. 1984. *Jātakas 1–70.* Vol. 1 of *Jātaka zenshū* [Complete collection of Jātaka], ed. Hajime Nakamura. Tokyo: Shunjūsha.

Fujita Kōtatsu Hakushi Kanreki Kinen Ronshū Kankōkai, ed. 1989. *Indo tetsugaku to Bukkyō: Fujita Kōtatsu Hakushi kanreki kinen ronshū.* Kyoto: Heirakuji Shoten. (Eng. title: Indian Philosophy and Buddhism: Essays in honour of Professor Kotatsu Fujita on his sixtieth birthday)

Gäng, Peter. 1987. *Probleme der Sprache in der Mystik des tantrischen Buddhismus: ein Beitrag zur buddhistischen Hermeneutik.* Inaugural-Dissertation, Berlin.

Gäng, P., tr. 1981. *Das Tantra des Grausig-Gross-Schrecklichen.* Berlin: Stechapfel Verlag.

———. 1988. *Das Tantra der Verborgenen Vereinigung: Guhyasamāja-Tantra.* Munich: Eugen Diederichs Verlag.

Garbe, Richard. 1892. *Der Mondschein der Sâṃkhya-Wahrheit, Vâcaspatimiçra's Sâṃkhya-tattvakaumudî.* Munich: G. Franz Verlag.

———. 1894. *Die Sāṃkhya-Philosophie: Eine Darstellung des indischen Rationalismus.* Leipzig: H. Haessel.

———. 1896. *Sāṃkhya und Yoga.* Strassburg: K. J. Trübner.

———. 1917. *Die Sāṃkhya-Philosophie.* 2d ed. Leipzig: H. Haessel.

Geiger, Magdalene and Wilhelm Geiger. 1921. *Pāli Dhamma vornehmlich in der kanonischen Literatur.* Munich: Bayerischen Akademie der Wissenschaften.

Geiger, Wilhelm. 1916. *Pāli, Literatur und Sprache.* Strassburg: K. J. Trübner. (Eng. translation by Batakrishna Ghosh: *Pali literature and language* [Calcutta: University of Calcutta, 1943])

———. 1921. Dhamma und Brahman. *Zeitschrift für Buddhismus* 3:73–83.

———. 1973. *Kleine Schriften zur Indologie und Buddhismuskunde.* Ed. Heinz Bechert. Wiesbaden: F. Steiner.

Geiger, Wilhelm, tr. 1925–30. *Saṃyutta-nikāya.* 2 vols. (vol. 2, 1925; vol. 1, 1930). Munich-Neubiberg: Benares-Verlag.

Gelblum, Tuvia. 1985. David Friedmann (1903–1984). *JIABS* 8:149–50.

George, Christopher S., ed. and tr. 1974. *The Caṇḍamahārosaṇa Tantra: A critical edition and English translation, chapters 1–8.* New Haven: American Oriental Society.

Gernet, Jacques and Yves Hervouet. 1979. Paul Demiéville (1894–1979). *T'oung Pao* 65:1–12.

Gercenberg, Leonard Georgievič. 1965. *Khotano-Sakskij jazyk.* Moscow: Nauka.

Ghosha (Ghoṣa), Pratāpacandra, ed. 1902–13. *Śatasāhasrikā-Prajñā-Pāramitā: A theological and philosophical discourse of Buddha with his disciples...* . Bibliotheca Indica. Calcutta: Asiatic Society of Bengal.

Giorgi, Antonio Agostino. 1762. *Alphabetum Tibetanum Missionum Apostolicarum commodo editum.* Rome: Sacred Congregation for the Propagation of the Faith.

Glasenapp, Helmuth von. 1980. *Ausgewählte kleine Schriften.* Ed. Heinz Bechert and Volker Moeller. Wiesbaden: Steiner.

Gnoli, Gherardo. 1984. Giuseppe Tucci (1894–1984). *East and West* 34:11–21.

Gnoli, G. and L. Lanciotti, eds. 1985–88. *Orientalia Iosephi Tucci memoriae dicata.* Rome: IsMEO.

Gnoli, Raniero, ed. 1960. *The Pramāṇavārttikam of Dharmakīrti: The first chapter with the autocommentary.* Rome: IsMEO.

———. 1977–78. *The Gilgit manuscript of the Saṅghabhedavastu.* 2 vols. Rome: IsMEO.

———. 1978. *The Gilgit manuscript of the Śayanāsanavastu and the Adhikaraṇavastu.* Rome: IsMEO.

Gnoli, R., tr. 1961. *Nāgārjuna: Madhyamaka Kārikā: Le stanze del cammino di mezzo...* . Turin: Boringhieri.

———. 1964. *Storia della tigre, e altre storie delle vite anteriori del Buddha—Jatakamala.* Bari.

Godakumbura, C. E., comp. 1980. *Catalogue of Ceylonese manuscripts.* Copenhagen: The Royal Library.

———. 1983. *Catalogue of Cambodian and Burmese Pāli manuscripts.* Copenhagen: The Royal Library.

Gokhale, Vasudev Viśvanāth. 1947. Fragments from the Abhidharmasamuccaya of Asaṃga. *J. Bombay Br. RAS,* new ser., 23:13–38.

Gokhale, V. V. and S. S. Bahulkar, trs. 1985. Madhyamakahṛdayakārikā Tarkajvālā, Chapter I. In *Miscellanea Buddhica,* 25–75. Copenhagen: Akademisk Forlag.

Gombrich, Richard. 1984. Notes on the brahminical background to Buddhist ethics. In Dhammapāla et al. 1984, 91–101.

———. 1988a. *Theravāda Buddhism: A social history from ancient Benares to modern Colombo.* London: Routledge.

———. 1988b. How the Mahāyāna began. *Journal of Pali and Buddhist Studies* 1:29–46.

———. 1990. Recovering the Buddha's message. In Seyfort Ruegg and Schmithausen 1990, 5–23.

Gómez, Luis O., tr. 1972. Ultimo tratado de cultivo graduado (Uttarabhāvanākrama). *Diálogos* 8 (no. 23): 85–137.

———. 1977. Primer tratado de cultivo graduado (Pūrvabhāvanākrama)(Parte I). *Diálogos* 11 (nos. 29–30): 177–224.

———. 1979. El Bhāvanāyogāvatāra de Kamalaśīla. *Estudios de Asia y Africa* 14:110–37.

Gómez, Luis O. and Jonathan A. Silk, eds. 1989. *Studies in the literature of the Great Vehicle.* Ann Arbor: Center for South and Southeast Asian Studies, U. of Michigan.

Goudriaan, T. and Christiaan Hooykaas. 1971. *Stuti and Stava (Bauddha, Śaiva and Vaiṣṇava) of Balinese Brahman priests.* Amsterdam: North-Holland Pub. Co.

Griffiths, Paul. 1983. Review of S. Collins's *Selfless persons: Imagery and thought in Theravāda Buddhism. Philosophy East and West* 33:303–5.

———. 1986. *On being mindless: Buddhist meditation and the mind-body problem.* La Salle: Open Court.

———. 1990. Omniscience in the Mahāyānasūtralāṅkāra and its commentaries. *IIJ* 33: 85–120.

Grimblot, Paul. 1871. Extraits du Paritta. *JA* 1871-2:225–335.

Grönbold, Günter, comp. 1984. *Der buddhistische Kanon: eine Bibliographie.* Wiesbaden: Harrassowitz.

Guenther, Herbert V. 1963. *The life and teaching of Nāropa.* Oxford: Clarendon Press.

———. 1966. *Treasures on the Tibetan Middle Way.* Leiden: Brill.

———. 1972a. *Buddhist philosophy in theory and practice.* Berkeley: Penguin Books.

———. 1972b. *The tantric view of life.* Berkeley and London: Shambhala.

Guenther, Herbert V., tr. 1959. *The jewel ornament of liberation [by] sGam-po-pa.* London: Rider. (1971 ed., Berkeley: Shambhala)

———. 1969. *The royal song of Saraha: A study in the history of Buddhist thought.* Seattle: U. of Washington Press.

Guérinot, A. 1933. Bibliographie des travaux d'Émile Senart. *JA* 1933-2, suppl.: 1–75.

Hadano, Hakuyū. 1986–88. *Chibetto-Indogaku Shūsei.* 4 vols. Kyoto: Hōzōkan.

Hahn, Michael. 1974b. Der Autor Candragomin und sein Werk. *ZDMG,* Supplement II, XVIII. Deutscher Orientalistentag, 331–55. Wiesbaden: Steiner.

———. 1975a. Frank-Richard Hamm (1920–1973). *ZDMG* 125:6–10.

———. 1975b. Buddhacarita I, 1–7 und 25–40. *IIJ* 17:77–96.

———. 1977a. Strophen des Candragomin in der indischen Spruchliteratur. *IIJ* 19:21–30.

———. 1977b. *Haribhaṭṭa and Gopadatta: Two authors in the succession of Āryaśūra. On the rediscovery of parts of their Jātakamālās.* Studia Philologica Buddhica, Occasional Paper 1. Tokyo: Reiyukai. (2d, rev. and enl., ed., 1992, Tokyo: International Institute for Buddhist Studies)

———. 1981. Das Datum des Haribhaṭṭa. In Bruhn and Wezler 1981, 107–20. Wiesbaden: Steiner.

———. 1988. Indische und nepalesische Handschriften im Indologischen Seminar der Universität Bonn. In *Indology and Indo-Tibetology: Thirty years of Indian and Indo-Tibetan studies in Bonn,* ed. Helmut Eimer, 81–96. Bonn: Indica et Tibetica Verlag.

Hahn, M. ed. 1982a. *Nāgārjuna's Ratnāvalī.* Vol. 1, the basic texts (Sanskrit, Tibetan, Chinese). Bonn: Indica et Tibetica Verlag.

———. 1982b. *Die Subhāṣitaratnakaraṇḍakakathā: ein spätbuddhistischer Text zur Verdienstlehre. NAWG* 1982, No. 9. Göttingen: Vandenhoeck & Ruprecht.

———. 1985. *Der grosse Legendenkranz (Mahajjātakamāla).* Wiesbaden: Harrassowitz.

———. 1989. *Śivasvāmin's Kapphiṇābhyudaya or Exaltation of King Kapphiṇa.* With an introduction by Gauri Shankar. New Delhi: Aditya Prakashan.

———. 1990. Puṇyarāśyavadāna—another legend by Gopadatta? In *Frank-Richard Hamm Memorial Volume,* 103–32. Bonn: Indica et Tibetica Verlag.

Hahn, M. ed. and tr. 1973–80. Die Haribhaṭṭajātakamālā: (I) Das Ādarśamukhajātaka. *WZKS* 17:49–88; (II) Das Śyāmajātaka. *WZKS* 20:37–74; (III) Das Dardara-Jātaka. *WZKS* 22:75–108; (IV) Das Udayajātaka. *WZKS* 24:99–128.

———. 1974a. *Candragomins Lokānandanāṭaka: nach dem tibetischen Tanjur herausgegeben und übersetzt.* Wiesbaden: Harrassowitz.

Haldar, Aruna, ed. 1975. *Abhidharmakośabhāṣyam of Vasubandhu.* Ed. P. Pradhan. Rev. 2d ed. with introduction and indices, etc. Patna: K. P. Jayaswal Research Institute.

Handurukande, Ratna. 1987. Jātakamālās in Sanskrit. *The Sri Lanka Journal of the Humanities* 11/1–2 (1985): 91–109.

Handurukande, R., ed. and tr. 1884. *Five Buddhist legends in the campū style: From a collection named Avadānasārasamuccaya.* Bonn: Indica et Tibetica Verlag.

Hardy, Robert Spence. 1850. *Eastern monachism.* London: Partridge and Oakey.

———. 1853. *A manual of Buddhism in its modern development.* London: Partridge and Oakey.

———. 1866. *The legends and theories of the Buddhists.* London: Williams and Norgate.

Hare, Edward M., ed. 1952–. *Pāli Tipiṭakaṁ Concordance.* London: Luzac.

Harrison, Paul M. 1982. Sanskrit fragments of a Lokottaravādin tradition. In Hercus et al. 1982, 211–34.

Harrison, Paul M., ed. 1978. *The Tibetan text of the Pratyutpanna-buddha-saṃmukhāvasthita-samādhi-sūtra.* Tokyo: Reiyukai Library.

Harrison, P. M., tr. 1990. *The Samādhi of direct encounter with the buddhas of the present: An annotated English translation of the Tibetan version of the Pratyutpanna-Buddha-Saṃmukhāvasthita-Samādhi-Sūtra.* Tokyo: International Institute for Buddhist Studies.

Härtel, Herbert. 1985a. Laudatio auf Herrn Professor Dr. Ernst Waldschmidt anlässlich seines 85. Geburtstages. In Bechert 1985–87, 1:11–19.

———. 1985b. Ernst Waldschmidt (1897–1985). *ZDMG* 137:5–11.

Hartmann, Jens-Uwe. 1988a. *Neue Aśvaghoṣa- und Mātṛceṭa-Fragmente aus Ostturkistan. NAWG* 1988, No. 2. Göttingen: Vandenhoeck & Ruprecht.

———. 1988b. Das Datum des historischen Buddha: Göttingen, 11–18. 4. 1988. *Internationales Asienforum* 19:391–403.

———. 1989. Fragmente aus dem Dīrghāgama der Sarvāstivādins. In Bechert 1989–95, 1:37–67.

Hartmann, J.-U., ed. and tr. 1987. *Das Varṇārhavarṇastotra des Mātṛceṭa.* Göttingen: Vandenhoeck & Ruprecht.

Hattori, Masaaki, tr. 1968. *Dignāga on perception: Being the Pratyakṣapariccheda of Dignāga's Pramāṇasamuccaya.* Harvard Oriental Series 47. Cambridge: Harvard University Press.

Hayes, Richard P. 1988. *Dignāga on the interpretation of signs.* Dordrecht: D. Reidel.

Hazlewood, Ann Appleby, tr. 1986. *In praise of Mount Samanta (Samanta-kūṭavaṇṇanā).* London: Pali Text Society.

Hedinger, Jürg, tr. 1984. *Aspekte der Schulung in der Laufbahn eines Bodhisattva: Dargestellt nach dem Śikṣāsamuccaya des Śāntideva.* Wiesbaden: Harrassowitz.

Heesterman, J. C., G. H. Schokker, and V. I. Subramoniam, eds. 1968. *Pratidānam: Indian, Iranian, and Indo-European studies presented to Franciscus Bernardus Jacobus Kuiper on his sixtieth birthday.* The Hague/Paris: Mouton.

Hendriksen, Hans. 1944. *Syntax of the infinite verb-forms of Pāli.* Trans. Annie I. Fausbøll. Copenhagen: E. Munksgaard.

Hercus, Luise Anna, F. B. J. Kuiper, Tissa Rajapatirana, and Edmund R. Skrzypczak, eds. 1982. *Indological and Buddhist Studies: Volume in honour of Professor J. W. de Jong on his sixtieth birthday.* Canberra: Faculty of Asian Studies, The Australian National University.

Hervouet, Yves. 1981. Paul Demiéville et l'École française d'Extrême-Orient. *BEFEO* 69:1–29.

Hikata, Ryūshō and Shin'ichi Takahara, trs. 1990. *Jātaka-mālā.* Tokyo: Kōdansha.

Hinüber, Oskar von. 1968. *Studien zur Kasussyntax des Pāli, besonders des Vinaya-piṭaka.* Munich: Kitzinger in Kommission.

———. 1974. Reste des reduplizierten Aorists im Pāli. *MSS* 32:65–72.

———. 1975. Kulturgeschichtliches aus dem *Bhikṣuṇī-Vinaya:* die *saṃkakṣikā. ZDMG* 125:133–39.

———. 1976. Sprachliche Beobachtungen zum Aufbau des Pāli-Kanons. *StII* 2:27–40.

———. 1977a. Zur Geschichte des Sprachnamens Pāli. In Museum für Indische Kunst 1977, 237–46.

———. 1977b. Notes on the e-preterite in Middle Indo-Aryan. *MSS* 36:39–48.

———. 1978a. *Gotrabhū:* Die sprachliche Vorgeschichte eines philosophischen Terminus. *ZDMG* 128:326–32.

———. 1978b. On the tradition of Pāli texts in India, Ceylon and Burma. In Bechert 1978, 48–57.

———. 1979a. *Die Erforschung der Gilgit-Handschriften. NAWG* 1979, no. 12:327–60.

———. 1979b. Pāli kaṭhati: ein Beitrag zur Überlieferungsgeschichte des Theravāda-Kanons. *IIJ* 21:21–26.

———. 1980a. Die Kolophone der Gilgit-Handschriften. *StII* 5/6:49–82.

———. 1980b. Über drei Begriffe der buddhistischen Rechtssprache: *issaravatā, gīvā* und *bhaṇḍadeyya. Indologica Taurinensia* 7:275–79.

———. 1981a. Die Entwicklung der Lautgruppen *-tm-, -dm-* und *-sm-* im Mittel- und Neuindischen. *MSS* 40:61–71.

———. 1981b. A Vedic verb in Pāli: *udājita.* In *Abhinandana-grantha: Dr Ludwik Sternbach felicitation volume,* 819–22. Lucknow: Akhila Bharatiya Sanskrit Parishad.

———. 1981c. Namen in Schutzzaubern aus Gilgit. *StII* 7:163–71.

———. 1982a. Upāli's verses in the Majjhimanikāya and the Madhyamāgama. In Hercus et al. 1982, 243–51.

———. 1982b. Die Bedeutung des Handschriftenfundes bei Gilgit. *ZDMG* Suppl. V, XXXI. Deutscher Orientalistentag, 47–66. Wiesbaden: Steiner.

———. 1982d. Pāli as an artificial language. *Indologica Taurinensia* 10:133–40.

———. 1982–83. Zum Perfekt im Pāli. *KZ* 96:29–32.

———. 1983a. *Notes on the Pāli tradition in Burma. NAWG* 1983, No. 3. Göttingen: Vandenhoeck & Ruprecht.

———. 1983b. Die älteste Literatursprache des Buddhismus. *Saeculum* 34/1:1–9.

———. 1983c. Pāli manuscripts of canonical texts from North Thailand. *Journal of the Siam Society* 71:75–88.

———. 1985. Two Jātaka manuscripts from the National Library in Bangkok. *JPTS* 10:1–22.

———. 1987a. The Pāli manuscripts kept at the Siam Society, Bangkok: A short catalogue. *Journal of the Siam Society* 75:9–74.

———. 1987b. Das buddhistische Recht und die Phonetik des Pāli. *StII* 13/14:101–27.

———. 1987–88. The oldest dated manuscript of the Milindapañha. *JPTS* 11:111–19, 12:173–74.

———. 1988. *Die Sprachgeschichte des Pāli im Spiegel der südostasiatischen Handschriftenüberlieferung.* Mainz: F. Steiner.

———. 1994. *Selected papers on Pāli studies.* Oxford: Pali Text Society.

Hinüber, Oskar von, ed. 1982c. *A new fragmentary Gilgit manuscript of the Saddharma-puṇḍarīkasūtra.* Tokyo: Reiyukai.

———. 1984. *Sieben Goldblätter einer Pañacaviṃśatisāhasrikā Prajñāpāramitā aus Anurādhapura. NAWG* 1983, No. 7.

Hoernle, August Friedrich Rudolf. 1893. The Weber manuscripts. *JASB* 62, pt. 1: 1–40.

———. 1897. Three further collections of ancient manuscripts from Central Asia. *JASB* 66, pt. 1: 213–60.

———. 1899–1901. A report on the British Collection of Antiquities from Central Asia. *JASB* 68, pt. 1, extra no. 1; and 70, pt. 1, extra no. 1.

Hoernle, A. F. R., ed. 1893–1912. *The Bower Manuscript.* Calcutta: Superintendent of Govt. Printing.

Hofinger, Marcel. 1946. *Étude sur le concile de Vaiśālī.* Louvain: Bureaux du Muséon.

Honda, Megumu, tr. 1988. **Chandorakīrti* Chūronchū *wayaku* [Japanese translation of Candrakīrti's Prasannapadā]. Tokyo: Kokusho Kankōkai.

Honjō, Yoshifumi. 1984. **Kusharon shoe Agon zenpyō* [A table of Āgama citations in the Abhidharmakośabhāṣya and the Abhidharmakośopāyikā]. Part 1. Kyoto: privately published.

Hooykaas, Christiaan. 1973. *Balinese Bauddha brahmans.* Amsterdam: North-Holland Pub. Co.

Horiuchi, Kanjin, ed. 1974–83. *The Sarvatathāgatatattvasaṃgraha.* Vol. 1, 1983; vol. 2, 1974. Kōyasan.

Horner, Isaline Blew, tr. 1938–66. *The Book of the Discipline (Vinaya-Piṭaka).* 6 vols. Sacred Books of the Buddhists 10, 11, 13, 14, 20 and 25. London: Luzac.

———. 1954–59. *The Middle Length Sayings.* 3 vols. Pali Text Society Translation Series 29, 30, and 31. London: Luzac.

———. 1974. *The minor anthologies of the Pali Canon. Part IV.* Vimānavatthu: *Stories of the Mansions.* Sacred Books of the Buddhists 30. London: Pali Text Society.

———. 1975. *The minor anthologies of the Pali Canon. Part III. Chronicle of Buddhas* (Buddhavaṃsa) *and Basket of Conduct* (Cariyāpiṭaka). Sacred Books of the Buddhists 31. London: Pali Text Society.

———. 1978. *The Clarifier of the Sweet Meaning* (Madhuratthavilāsinī): *Commentary on the Chronicle of the Buddhas by Buddhadatta Thera.* Sacred Books of the Buddhists 33. London: Pali Text Society.

Horner, I. B. and Padmanabh S. Jaini, trs. 1985. *Apocryphal birth-stories* (Paññāsa-Jātaka). Vol. 1. London: Pali Text Society.

Horsch, Paul. 1968. Buddhismus und Upaniṣaden. In Heesterman et al. 1968, 462–77.

Huber, Édouard. 1904. Trois contes du Sūtrālaṃkāra d'Açvaghoṣa conservés dans le Divyāvadāna. *BEFEO* 4:709–26.

———. 1906. Les sources du Divyāvadāna. *BEFEO* 6:1–43.

Huber, Édouard, tr. 1908. *Sûtrâlaṃkâra, traduit en français sur la version chinoise de Kumârajîva.* Paris: E. Leroux.

Hultzsch, Eugen, ed. 1925. *The inscriptions of Asoka.* New ed. Oxford: Clarendon Press.

Hurvitz, Leon. 1977. The Abhidharma on the "four aids to penetration." In Kawamura and Scott 1977, 59–104.

———. 1978. Fa-sheng's observations on the four stations of mindfulness. In Kiyota 1978, 207–48.

———. 1979. Dharmaśrī on the sixteen degrees of comprehension. *JIABS* 2:7–30.

Huth, George, ed. and tr. 1892–96. *Geschichte des Buddhismus in der Mongolei.* 2 vols. Strassburg: K. B. Trübner.

Ichigō, Masamichi, ed. and tr. 1985. *Chūgan Shōgonron no kenkyū: Śāntarakṣita no shisō.* 2 vols. Kyoto: Bun'eidō.

———. 1989. Śāntarakṣita's Madhyamakālaṁkāra: Introduction, edition and translation. In Gómez and Silk 1989, 141–240.

Iggleden, R. E. W. and C. W. Iggleden. 1974. Isaline Blew Horner: A biographical sketch. In Cousins et al. 1974, 1–8.

Imanishi, J., ed. and tr. 1975. *Fragmente des Abhidharmaprakaraṇabhāṣyam in Text und Übersetzung. NAWG* 1975 No. 1. Göttingen: Vandenhoeck & Ruprecht.

Inada, Kenneth K., tr. 1970. *Nāgārjuna: A translation of his Mūlamadhyamakakārikā with an introductory essay.* Tokyo: Hokuseido.

Institut Orientaliste, ed. 1980. *Indianisme et Bouddhisme: Mélanges offerts à Mgr. Étienne Lamotte.* Louvain-la-Neuve: Université Catholique de Louvain.

Institute for the Comprehensive Study of the Lotus Sūtra, Risshō University, comp. 1986–. *Sanskrit manuscripts of Saddharmapuṇḍarīka, collected from Nepal, Kashmir and Central Asia: Romanized text and index.* Vol. 1, 1986; vol. 2, 1988. Tokyo: Publishing Association of Saddharmapuṇḍarīka Manuscripts.

Ishihama, J., A. Sanada, and T. Inokuchi, comps. 1958. Bibliography of the Central Asiatic Studies. In *Introduction and explanatory remarks of the Chinese Buddhist texts from Tunhuang in eastern Turkestan,* ed. The Research Society of Central Asian Culture, 53–87. Monumenta Serindica 1 (Japanese title: Saiiki Bunka Kenkyū I). Kyoto: Hōzōkan.

Ishihama, Yumiko and Yōichi Fukuda, eds. 1989. *A new critical edition of the Mahāvyutpatti: Sanskrit-Tibetan-Mongolian dictionary of Buddhist terminology.* Studia Tibetica 16. Tokyo: The Toyo Bunko. (= vol. 1 of *Materials for Tibetan-Mongolian Dictionaries*)

Ishikawa, Mie, ed. 1990. *A critical edition of the* Sgra sbyor bam po gnyis pa, *an old and basic commentary on the Mahāvyutpatti.* Studia Tibetica 18. Tokyo: The Toyo Bunko. (= vol. 2 of *Materials for Tibetan-Mongolian Dictionaries*)

Iwano, Shinyū, comp. 1924-88. *Kokuyaku Issaikyō.* 155 vols. (Indian texts) and 100 vols. (Chinese and Japanese texts). Tokyo: Daitō Shuppan-sha.

Jackson, Roger. 1985a. The Kalachakra in context. In Sopa and Jackson 1985, 1–49.

———. 1985b. The Kalachakra generation-stage Sadhana. In Sopa and Jackson 1985, 119–38.

Jacobi, Hermann Georg. 1896. Der Ursprung des Buddhismus aus dem Sānkhya-Yoga. *NGGW:* 43–58. (= *Kleine Schriften* 2:646–61)

———. 1898. Über das Verhältnis der buddhistischen Philosophie zu Sāṃkhya-Yoga und die Bedeutung der Nidānas. *ZDMG* 52:1–15. (= *Kleine Schriften* 2: 662–76)

———. 1970. *Kleine Schriften.* 2 vols. Edited by Bernhard Kölver. Wiesbaden: F. Steiner.

Jaini, Padmanabh S. 1985. The Sanskrit fragments of Vinītadeva's Triṃśikāṭīkā. *BSOAS* 48:470–92.

Jaini, P. S., ed. 1959. *Abhidharmadīpa with Vibhāṣāprabhāvṛtti.* Tibetan Sanskrit Works 4. Patna: K. P. Jayaswal Research Institute.

———. 1979. *Sāratamā: A pañjikā on the Aṣṭasāhasrikā Prajñāpāramitā sūtra.* Tibetan Sanskrit Works 18. Patna: K. P. Jayaswal Research Institute.

———. 1981–83. Paññāsa-jātaka *or* Zimme Paṇṇasa *(in the Burmese recension).* 2 vols. London: Pali Text Society.

———. 1986b. *Lokaneyyappakaraṇaṃ.* London: Pali Text Society.

Jaini, P. S., tr. 1986a. *Apocryphal birth-stories* (Paññāsa-Jātaka). Vol. 2. London: Pali Text Society.

Jamspal, Ven. Lozang, Ven. Ngawang Samten Chophel, and Peter Della Santina, trs. 1978. *Nāgārjuna's letter to King Gautamīputra.* Delhi: Motilal Banarsidass.

Jayasuriya, M. H. F., ed. and tr. 1988. *Jetavanārāma gold plates.* Kelaniya: U. of Kelaniya.

Jayawickrama, N. A., tr. 1990. *The story of Gotama Buddha (Jātaka-nidāna).* Oxford: Pali Text Society.

Jha, Subhadra, tr. 1983. *The Abhidharmakośa of Vasubandhu, with the Commentary.* Vol. 1. Patna: K. P. Jayaswal Research Institute.

Jiang, Zhingyin, ed. 1988. **A Sanskrit manuscript of Saddharmapuṇḍarīka, kept in the Library of the Nationalities, Beijing.* Romanized text ... with a preface by Ji Xianlin. Beijing: China Social Sciences Publishing House.

Jinananda, B. 1969. *Abhisamācārikā.* Tibetan Sanskrit Works 9. Patna: K. P. Jayaswal Research Institute.

Johnston, Edward Hamilton, ed. 1928. *The Saundaranda of Aśvaghoṣa.* London: Oxford University Press.

———. 1950. *The Ratnagotravibhāga Mahāyanottaratantraśāstra.* Patna: Bihar Research Society.

Johnston, E. H., ed. and tr. 1936, *The Buddhacarita or Acts of the Buddha.* 2 vols. Calcutta: Baptist Mission Press.

Johnston, E. H., tr. 1932. *The Saundaranda; or, Nanda the Fair.* London: Oxford University Press.

———. 1937. The Buddha's Mission and Last Journey. *Acta Orientalia* 15:1–128, 231–92. (Includes trans. of *Buddhacarita* chaps. 15 to 28)

Johnston, E. H. and Arnold Kunst, eds. 1951. The Vigrahavyāvartanī of Nāgārjuna. *MCB* 9 (1948–51): 99–152.

Jones, J. J., tr. 1949–56. *The Mahāvastu.* 3 vols. Sacred Books of the Buddhists 16 (1949), 18 (1952), 19 (1956). London: Luzac.

Julien, Stanislas, tr. 1853. *Histoire de la vie de Hiouen-thsang et de ses voyages dans l'Inde.* Paris: Imprimerie Impériale.

———. 1857–58. *Mémoires sur les Contrées occidentales de Hiouen-thsang.* Paris: Imprimerie Impériale.

Kahrs, Eivind, ed. 1986. *Kalyāṇamitrārāgaṇam: Essays in honour of Nils Simonsson.* Oslo: Oxford University Press.

Kajiyama, Yūichi. 1989. *Studies in Buddhist philosophy (selected papers).* Kyoto: Rinsen Book Co.

Kajiyama, Y., ed. 1986. *Genshi butten* [Early Buddhist classics]. Vol. 7: *Buddha no shi* [Buddha's poems] (*Dhammapada,* tr. Kōtatsu Fujita; *Suttanipāta,* tr. Noritoshi Aramaki and Yoshifumi Honjō). Tokyo: Kōdansha.

Kalupahana, David. J., tr. 1986. *Nāgārjuna: The philosophy of the Middle Way.* Albany: SUNY Press.

Katsura, Shōryū. 1986a. The origin and development of the concept of *vyāpti* in Indian logic—from the *Carakasaṃhitā* up to Dharmakīrti [in Japanese]. *Hiroshima Daigaku Bungaku-bu Kiyō* 45, spec. issue no. 1:1–122.

———. 1986b. On the origin and development of the concept of *vyāpti* in Indian logic. *Tetsugaku* 38 :1–16.

———. 1988a. Jñānaśrimitra no apoharon. *Bukkyōgaku Seminā* 48:70ff.

———. 1988b. Ronrigakuha. In *Indo Bukkyō 1,* 314–42 (vol. 8 of Iwanami Kōza: Tōyō Shisō). Tokyo: Iwanami Shoten.

———. 1989. Gainen—apoharon wo chūshin ni. In *Indo Bukkyō 3,* 135–59 (vol. 8 of Iwanami Kōza: Tōyō Shisō). Tokyo: Iwanami Shoten.

Kawaguchi, Ekai. 1956. *Saddharmapuṇḍarīkanā[ma]mahāyānasūtram.* Reprint of 1926 ed. Tokyo: Bonbun Hokkekyō Hanpukai.

Kawamura, Leslie S., ed. 1982. *The bodhisattva doctrine in Buddhism.* Waterloo, Ont.: Wilfred Laurier University Press.

Kawamura, L. S., tr. 1975. *Golden zephyr: Instructions from a spiritual friend.* Emeryville: Dharma Publishing.

Kawamura, L. S. and Keith Scott, eds. 1977. *Buddhist thought and Asian civilization: Essays in honor of Herbert V. Guenther on his sixtieth birthday.* Emeryville, Cal.: Dharma.

Kawasaki, Shinjō, ed. 1976–88. *The Mīmāṃsā chapter of Bhavya's Madhyamakahṛdaya-kārikā ... Sanskrit and Tibetan texts—with the Sarvajña chapter.* Studies nos. 2, 12, and 13 (1976, 1986, 1987). Tsukuba: Institute of Philosophy, U. of Tsukuba.

Kaye, George Rusby. 1927–33. *The Bakshālī Manuscript and a study in mediaeval mathematics.* 3 vols. in 2. Calcutta: Govt. of India Central Publication Branch.

Keith, Arthur Berriedale. 1918. *The Sāṃkhya system.* London: Oxford University Press. (2d ed, 1924)

———. 1923. *Buddhist philosophy in India and Ceylon.* Oxford: Clarendon Press.

Kern, Hendrik. 1873. *Over de Jaartelling der Zuidelijke Buddhisten en de Gedenkstukken van Açoka den Buddhist* [Chronology of the Southern Buddhists and the monuments of Aśoka the Buddhist]. Amsterdam: C. G. van der Post.

———. 1882. *Geschiedenis van het Buddhisme in Indië.* Vol. 1. Haarlem: Tjeenk Willink.

———. 1882–84. *Der Buddhismus und seine Geschichte in Indien.* Trans. from the Dutch by Hermann Jacobi. Leipzig: O. Schulze.

———. 1884a. *Geschiedenis van het Buddhisme in Indië.* Vol. 2. Haarlem: Tjeenk Willink.

———. 1897. Een Russisch Geleerde over de beeldhouwwerken van de Boro Boedoer. *Bijdragen tot de Taal-, Land- en Volkenkunde van Nederl. Indië* 47:49–56. (= *Verspreide geschriften* 4 [1916]: 209–31)

———. 1901–3. *Histoire du Bouddhisme dans l'Inde.* Trans. from the Dutch by Gédéon Huet. Paris: E. Leroux.

———. 1929. *Verspreide Geschriften: Register en Bibliografie.* The Hague: M. Nijhoff.

Kern, H., ed. 1891. *The Jātaka-mālā; or, Bodhisattvāvadāna-mālā, by Ārya-Çūra.* Harvard Oriental Series 1. Boston: Ginn.

Kern, H., tr. 1884b. *The Saddharmapuṇḍarīka, or The Lotus of the True Law.* Sacred Books of the East 21. Oxford: Clarendon Press. Reprint, Delhi: Motilal Banarsidass, 1965.

Kern, H. and Bunyiu Nanjio, eds. 1908–12. *Saddharmapuṇḍarīka.* Bibliotheca Buddhica 10. St. Petersburg. Reprint, Osnabrück: Biblio Verlag, 1970.

Khoroche, Peter, tr. 1989. *Once the Buddha was a monkey: Ārya Śūra's Jātakamālā.* Chicago: U. of Chicago Press.

Kimura, Takayasu, ed. 1986–. *Pancaviṃśatisāhasrikā Prajñāpāramitā.* Chapters 2–3, 1986; chap. 4, 1990; chap. 5, 1992. Tokyo: Sankibō Busshorin.

Kircher, Athanasius, S.J. 1667. *China monumentis, qua sacris qua profanis, necnon variis naturae et artis spectaculis, aliarumque rerum memorabilium argumentis illustrata.* Amsterdam: J. Jansson a' Waesberge & Elizeum Weyerstraet.

Kirfel, Willibald, ed. 1914. *Briefwechsel A. W. von Schlegel—Christian Lassen.* Bonn: F. Cohen.

Kiyota, Minoru, ed. 1978. *Mahāyāna Buddhist meditation: Theory and practice.* Honolulu: University Press of Hawaii.

Kochumuttom, Thomas A., tr. 1982. *A Buddhist doctrine of experience: A new translation and interpretation of the works of Vasubandhu the Yogācārin.* Delhi: Motilal Banarsidass.

Konow, Sten, ed. and tr. 1929. *Kharoṣṭhī inscriptions (with the exception of those of Aśoka).* Corpus Inscriptionum Indicarum 2, pt. 1. Calcutta: Govt. of India Central Publication Branch.

Kotschetow, A. N. 1967. Die buddhistische Forschung in der UdSSR. In *Buddhist Yearly 1967*: 86–118.

Krom, Nicolaas Johannes. 1933. Het Karmawibhangga op Barabuḍur. *Mededeelingen der Koninklijke Akademie van Wetenschappen, Afdeling Letterkunde.* Vol. 76, ser. B, no. 8, pp. 215–83. Amsterdam: Noord-Hollandsche Uitgeversmaatschappij.

Kuhn, Adalbert. 1859. *Die Herabkunft des Feuers und des Göttertranks.* Berlin: F. Dummler.

Kuhn, Ernst. 1894. *Barlaam und Joasaph: Eine bibliographisch-literaturgeschichtliche Studie.* Munich: G. Franz in Comm.

Kunst, Arnold, ed. 1946–47. Kamalaśīla's commentary on Śāntarakṣita's Anumānaparīkṣā of the Tattvasaṃgraha. *MCB* 8:106–216.

Kunst, Arnold, tr. 1939. *Probleme der buddhistischen Logik in der Darstellung des Tattvasaṅgraha.* Cracow: Académie Polonaise des Sciences et des Lettres.

Kværne, Per. 1975. On the concept of *sahaja* in Indian Buddhist Tantric literature. *Temenos* 11:88–135.

———. 1977. *An anthology of Buddhist Tantric songs: A study of the Caryāgīti.* Oslo: Universitetsforlaget; Irvington-on-Hudson: Columbia University Press.

Laboulaye, Édouard. 1859. *Journal des Débats* 26 July 1859.
Lacôte, Félix, ed. and tr. 1908–29. *Bṛhat-kathā-çlokasaṃgraha.* 4 vols. Paris: Imprimerie Nationale.
Lalou, Marcelle. 1939–61. *Inventaire des manuscrits tibétains de Touen-houang.* 3 vols. (vol. 1, 1939; vol. 2, 1950; vol. 3, 1961). Paris: Bibliothèque Nationale.
Lalou, Marcelle, ed. (with Jean Przyluski). 1930–67. *Bibliographie bouddhique.*
La Loubère, Simon de. 1691. *Description du royaume de Siam.* 2 vols. Paris: Jean Baptiste Coignard/Amsterdam: A. Wolfgang.
Lamotte, Étienne. 1953. Les premières relations entre l'Inde et l'Occident. *La Nouvelle Clio:* 83–118.
———. 1958. *Histoire du bouddhisme indien des origines à l'ère Saka.* Bibliothèque du Muséon 43. Louvain: Publications Universitaires. (Eng. trans. by S. Webb-Boin: *History of Indian Buddhism from the origins to the Śaka era* [Leuven: Peters Press; Louvain-la-Neuve, Institut Orientaliste, 1988])
———. 1965a. Notice sur Louis de La Vallée Poussin. *Académie royale de Belgique – Annuaire pour 1965.* Brussels: Palais des Académies.
Lamotte, É., ed. and tr. 1935. *Saṃdhinirmocana sūtra, l'explication des mystères.* Louvain: Bibliothèque de l'Université.
———. 1938–39. *La somme du Grand Véhicule d'Asaṅga (Mahāyānasaṃgraha).* 2 vols. Louvain: Bureaux du Muséon; Paris: A. Maisonneuve.
Lamotte, É., tr. 1935–36a. Le traité de l'acte de Vasubandhu: Karmasiddhiprakaraṇa. *MCB* 4:151–263. (Eng. trans. by Leo M. Pruden [Berkeley: Asian Humanities Press], 1988)
———. 1935–36b. Madhyamakavṛtti—XVIIe chapitre: Examen de l'acte et du fruit. *MCB* 4:265–288.
———. 1944–80. *Le traité de la Grande Vertu de Sagesse de Nagarjuna, Mahāprajñāpāramitāśāstra.* 5 vols. Vols. 1, 2, Louvain: Bureaux du Muséon (1944, 1949); vols. 3, 4, 5, Louvain: Université de Louvain, Institut Orientaliste (1970, 1976, 1980).
———. 1962. *L'enseignement de Vimalakīrti.* Bibliothèque du Muséon 51. Louvain: Publications Universitaires.
———. 1965b. *La concentration de la marche héroïque.* Brussels: Institut Belge des Hautes Études Chinoises. (= *MCB* 13:1–308)
Lancaster, Lewis R., comp. 1979. *The Korean Buddhist canon: A descriptive catalogue.* In collaboration with Sung-bae Park. Berkeley: U. of California Press.
Lancaster, Lewis R., ed. 1977 [1979]. *Prajñāpāramitā and related systems: Studies in honor of Edward Conze.* Berkeley Buddhist Studies 1. Berkeley: U. of California Press.
Lang, David M. 1957. *The wisdom of Balahvar.* London: Allen and Unwin.
Lang, D. M., tr. 1966. *The Balavariani (Barlaam and Josaphat).* London: Allen and Unwin.
Lang, Karen, ed. and tr. 1986. *Āryadeva's Catuḥśataka: On the Buddha's cultivation of merit and knowledge.* Copenhagen: Akademisk Forlag.
Latham, Ronald, tr. 1958. *The travels of Marco Polo.* Harmondsworth, Middlesex: Penguin Books.
Laufer, Berthold. 1906. Nécrologie Dr. Georg Huth. *T'oung Pao* 7:702–6.

———. 1915. Nécrologie William Woodville Rockhill. *T'oung Pao* 16:289–90.

La Vallée Poussin, Louis de. 1896b. Caturāryasatyaparīkṣā. In *Mélanges Charles de Harlez,* 313–20. Leyden: E. J. Brill.

———. 1898. *Bouddhisme: Études et Matériaux.* London: Luzac & Co.

———. 1902–3. Dogmatique bouddhique. *JA* 1902-2:237–306; 1903-2:357–450.

———. 1905a. Les deux premiers conciles. *Muséon* 6:213–323. (Eng. tr.: The Buddhist Councils. *Indian Antiquary* 37 [1908]: 1–18, 81–106)

———. 1905b. Dogmatique bouddhique: Les soixante-quinze et les cent dharmas. *Muséon* 6:178–94. (With the collaboration of T. Suzuki and P. Cordier)

———. 1906. Studies in Buddhist dogma: The three bodies of a Buddha (Trikāya). *JRAS:* 943–77.

———. 1909. *Bouddhisme: Opinions sur l'histoire de la dogmatique.* Paris: G. Beauchesne. (Rev. ed., 1925)

———. 1910. The "Five Points" of Mahādeva and the Kathāvatthu. *JRAS:* 413–23.

———. 1911. Councils (Buddhist). *Encyclopaedia of Religion and Ethics* 4:179–85.

———. 1913a. Note sur les Corps du Bouddha. *Muséon* 14:257–90.

———. 1913b. *Bouddhisme: Études et matériaux—Théorie des douze causes.* Ghent: E. van Goethem; London: Luzac & Co.

———. 1917. *The way to Nirvāṇa.* Cambridge: The University Press.

———. 1924. *Indo-Européens et Indo-Iraniens: L'Inde jusque vers 300 av. J.-C.* Paris: E. de Boccard. (Rev. and enlarged ed., 1936)

———. 1925. *Nirvāṇa.* Paris: G. Beauchesne.

———. 1927. *La Morale bouddhique.* Paris: Nouvelle Librairie Nationale.

———. 1930a. *Le dogme et la philosophie du bouddhisme.* Paris: Gabriel Beauchesne.

———. 1930b. *L'Inde au temps des Mauryas et des Barbares...* . Paris: E. de Boccard.

———. 1933. Réflexions sur le Madhyamaka. *MCB* 2:1–59.

———. 1935. *Dynasties et histoire de l'Inde depuis Kanishka jusqu'aux invasions musulmanes.* Paris: E. de Boccard.

———. 1937a. Le bouddhisme et le yoga de Patañjali. *MCB* 5:223–42.

———. 1937b. Bibliographie d'Eugène Obermiller. *MCB* 5: 244.

———. 1938. Buddhica. *HJAS* 3:137–60.

———. 1962. *Catalogue of the Tibetan manuscripts from Tun-huang in the India Office Library.* London: Oxford University Press.

La Vallée Poussin, L. de, ed. 1896a. *Pañcakrama.* Études et textes tantriques 1. Ghent: U. of Ghent.

———. 1901–14. *Prajñākaramati's commentary to the Bodhicaryāvatāra of Çāntideva.* Bibliotheca Indica. Calcutta: Asiatic Society of Bengal.

———. 1903–13. Madhyamakavṛttiḥ: *Mūlamadhyamakakārikās (Mādhyamikasūtras) de Nāgārjuna avec la Prasannapadā, commentaire de Candrakīrti.* Bibliotheca Buddhica 4. St.-Pétersbourg: Académie Impériale des Sciences. Reprint, Osnabrück: Biblio Verlag, 1970.

———. 1907–12. *Madhyamakāvatāra par Candrakīrti: Traduction tibétaine.* Bibliotheca Buddhica 9. St.-Pétersbourg: Acad. Imp. des Sciences. Reprint, Osnabrück: Biblio Verlag, 1970.

———. 1907–13. *Nyāyabindu: Tibetan translation, with the commentary of Vinītadeva.* Bibliotheca Indica. Calcutta: Asiatic Society of Bengal.

La Vallée Poussin, L. de, tr. 1907. *Bodhicaryāvatāra: Introduction à la pratique des futurs Bouddhas.* Paris: Bloud & Co.

———. 1907–11. Madhyamakāvatāra ... traduit d'après la version tibétaine. *Muséon* 8:249–317; 11:271–358; 12:235–328.

———. 1923–31. *L'Abhidharmakośa de Vasubandhu.* 6 vols. Paris and Louvain: P. Geuthner. (for Eng. tr., see Pruden 1988–90)

———. 1928–29. *Vijñaptimātratāsiddhi: La Siddhi de Hiuan-tsang.* 2 vols., paged consecutively. Paris: P. Geuthner.

Lefmann, Salomon, ed. 1902. *Lalitavistara: Leben und Lehre des Çâkya-Buddha.* Vol. 1. Halle a S.: Buchhandlung des Waisenhauses.

———. 1908. (Vol. 2 of the above)

Lessing, Ferdinand D. and Alex Wayman, trs. 1968. *Mkhas-Grub rje's Fundamentals of the Buddhist Tantras.* Indo-Iranian Monographs 8. The Hague: Mouton.

Letts, Malcolm. 1949. *Sir John Mandeville: The man and his book.* London: Patchwork Press.

Letts, M., ed. 1953. *Mandeville's Travels.* Texts and translations. 2 vols. London: Hakluyt Society.

Leumann, Ernst. 1900. *Über eine von den unbekannten Literatursprachen Mittelasiens.* Mémoires de l'Acad. imp. des sc. de St.-Pétersbourg, 8th ser., vol. 4, no. 8. St. Petersburg.

Leumann, E., tr. 1952–62. Mahāvastu I. Trans. of 1:1–193.12. *Proceedings of the Faculty of Liberal Arts & Education* (Yamanashi University)1 (1952), 2 (1957), 3 (1962).

Leumann, E. and Watanabe Shōkō, trs. 1970. Mahāvastu II. pp. 83–121. Trans. of 2:83.13–121.14. *Indo Koten Kenkyū (Acta Indologica)* 1:63–108.

Lévi, Sylvain. 1892. Le Buddhacarita d'Açvaghoṣa. *JA* 1892-1:201–36.

———. 1896–97. Notes sur les Indo-Scythes. *JA* 1896-2:444–84; 1897-1:5–42, 1897-2:526–31.

———. 1904. Le Samyuktāgama sanscrit et les feuillets Grünwedel. *T'oung Pao,* 2d ser., 5:297–309.

———. 1907. Les éléments de formation du Divyāvadāna. *T'oung Pao,* 2d ser., 8:105–22.

———. 1908. Açvaghoṣa: Le Sūtrālaṃkāra et ses sources. *JA* 1908-2:57–184.

———. 1909. Les Saintes Écritures du Bouddhisme: Comment s'est constitué le canon sacré. *AMG, B.V.* 31:105–29. (= *Mémorial Sylvain Lévi,* 75–84)

———. 1912. Observations sur une langue précanonique du Bouddhisme. *JA* 1912-2:495–514.

———. 1915. Sur la récitation primitive des textes bouddhiques. *JA* 1915-1:401–47.

———. 1918. Pour l'histoire du Rāmāyaṇa. *JA* 1918-1:5–161.

———. 1925a. Notes indiennes. *JA* 1925-1:17–69.

———. 1927a. Matériaux japonais pour l'étude du bouddhisme. *BMFJ* 1:1–63.

———. 1927b. La Dṛṣṭānta-pankti et son auteur. *JA* 1927-2:95–127.

———. 1928. Encore Aśvaghoṣa. *JA* 1928-2:193–216.

———. 1929. Autour d'Aśvaghoṣa. *JA* 1929-2:255–85.

———. 1932a. *Un système de philosophie bouddhique: Matériaux pour l'étude du système Vijñaptimātra.* Paris: H. Champion.

———. 1932c. Notes sur des manuscrits sanscrits provenant de Bamiyan (Afghanistan), et de Gilgit (Cachemire). *JA* 1932-1:1–45.

———. 1936. Kaniṣka et Śātavāhana. *JA* 1936-1:61–121.

———. 1937. Rétrospective: L'œuvre complet de Sylvain Lévi. *Bibliographie bouddhique.* Vols. 7–8: 1–64. Paris: Librairie d'Amérique et d'Orient.

Lévi, S., ed. 1925b. *Vijñaptimātratāsiddhi; deux traités de Vasubandhu: Viṃśatikā ... et Triṃśikā...* . Paris: H. Champion.

———. 1933. *Sanskrit texts from Bāli.* Gaekwad's Oriental Series 67. Baroda: Oriental Institute.

Lévi, S., ed. and tr. 1907–11. *Mahāyāna-sūtrālaṃkāra.* 2 vols. Paris: H. Champion. Reprint, Kyoto: Rinsen Book Co., 1983.

———. 1932b. *Mahākarmavibhaṅga et Karmavibhaṅgopadeśa.* Paris: E. Leroux.

Lévi, S. and Édouard Chavannes. 1915. Quelques titres énigmatiques dans la hiérarchie ecclésiastique du Bouddhisme indien. *JA* 1915-1:193–223; 1915-2:307–10.

———. 1916. Les seize Arhats protecteurs de la Loi. *JA* 1916-2:5–50, 189–304.

Liebenthal, Walter, tr. 1948. *The Book of Chao.* Monumenta Serica Monograph 13. Peking: Catholic University of Peking.

Liebrecht, Felix. 1860. *Jahrbuch für romanische und englische Literatur* 2:314–34.

Lienhard, Siegfried. 1988. *Nepalese manuscripts.* Part 1: Nevārī and Sanskrit, Staatsbibliothek Preussischer Kulturbesitz, Berlin. With the collaboration of Thakur Lal Manandhar. Stuttgart: F. Steiner.

Lin, Li-kouang. 1949. *L'aide-mémoire de la Vraie Loi.* Paris: A. Maisonneuve.

Lin, Li-kouang, tr. 1946–73. *Dharmasamuccaya: Compendium de la Loi.* 3 vols. Annales de Musée Guimet, Bibliothèque d'Études 53. Paris: A. Maisonneuve. (Vols. 2 and 3 ed. and rev. by A. Bareau, J. W. de Jong, and P. Demiéville)

Lindtner, Christian. 1980. *Nāgārjuna: Juvelkæden og andre skrifter.* Copenhagen: Sankt Ansgars Forlag.

———. 1982a. *Nagarjuniana: Studies in the writings and philosophy of Nāgārjuna.* Indisker Studier 4. Copenhagen: Akademisk Forlag. Reprint, Delhi: Motilal Banarsidass, 1987.

———. 1982c. Adversaria buddhica. *WZKS* 26:167–72.

Lindtner, C., ed. 1982b. *Nāgārjunas filosofiske værker.* Indisker Studier 2. Copenhagen: Akademisk Forlag.

———. 1979. Candrakīrti's Pañcaskandhaprakaraṇa. I. Tibetan text. *Acta Orientalia* 40:87–145.

Lindtner, C., tr. 1981a. Buddhapālita on Emptiness (Buddhapālita-mūlamadhyamakavṛtti XVIII). *IIJ* 23:187–217.

———. 1981b. *To buddhistiske læredigte.* Copenhagen: Akademisk Forlag.

Loewenthal, Rudolf. 1957. *The Turkic languages and literatures of Central Asia: A bibliography.* The Hague: Mouton.

Lokesh Chandra, ed. 1976. *Saddharma-Puṇḍarīka-Sūtra: Kashgar manuscript.* New Delhi: International Academy of Indian Culture. (2d ed., Tokyo, 1977)

Lottermoser, Friedgard. 1982. *Quoted verse passages in the works of Buddhaghosa: Contribution towards the study of the lost Sīhaḷaṭṭhakathā literature.* Ph.D. dissertation, U. of Göttingen.

Lüders, Heinrich. 1911b. Das Śāriputraprakaraṇa, ein Drama des Aśvaghoṣa. *SPAW:* 388–411. (= Lüders 1940, 190–213)

———. 1940. *Philologica Indica: Ausgewählte kleine Schriften von Heinrich Lüders.* Göttingen: Vandenhoeck & Ruprecht.

———. 1973. *Kleine Schriften.* Ed. Oskar von Hinüber. Wiesbaden: F. Steiner.

Lüders, Heinrich, ed. 1911a. *Bruchstücke buddhistischer Dramen.* Berlin: G. Reimer.

———. 1926. *Bruchstücke der Kalpanāmaṇḍitikā des Kumāralāta.* Leipzig: Deutsche Morgenländische Gesellschaft.

Lüders, H. and Ernst Waldschmidt, eds. 1954. *Beobachtungen über die Sprache des buddhistischen Urkanons.* Berlin: Akademie-Verlag.

Macdonald, Ariane W. 1962. *Le Maṇḍala du Mañjuśrīmūlakalpa.* Collection Jean Przyluski 3. Paris: A. Maisonneuve.

Macdonald, Ariane W. and Marcelle Lalou, eds. 1970. *L'œuvre de Jean Przyluski.* Paris: A. Maisonneuve.

MacQueen, Graeme. 1984. The doctrines of the six heretics according to the Śrāmaṇyaphala Sūtra. *IIJ* 27:291–307.

———. 1988. *A study of the Śrāmaṇyaphala-sūtra.* Wiesbaden: Harrassowitz.

Maeda, Takashi. 1985. *Tibetan-Sanskrit-Chinese index to the Sarvatathāgatatattva-saṅgraha nāma Mahāyāna sūtra* (for the 1st chapter). Tokyo: Kokusho Kankōkai.

Maisey, Frederick Charles. 1892. *Sanchi and its remains.* London: K. Paul, Trench, Trübner & Co.

Maity, S. K. 1988. *Studies in Orientology: Essays in memory of Prof. A. L. Basham.* Agra: Y. K. Publishers.

Marshall, Sir John. 1918. *A guide to Sanchi.* Delhi: Superintendent, Govt. Printing. (2d ed., 1936; 3d ed., 1955)

———. 1940. *The monuments of Sāñchī.* With Alfred Foucher and Nani Gopal Majumdar. London: Probsthain.

Masefield, Peter, tr. 1989. *Elucidation of the intrinsic meaning: So named the commentary on the Vimāna stories.* Sacred Books of the Buddhists 35. London: Pali Text Society.

Matsuda, Kazunobu. 1982. Bonbun danpen Loka-prajñapti ni tsuite. *Bukkyōgaku* 14:1–21.

———. 1986. *Newly identified Sanskrit fragments of the Dharmaskandha in the Gilgit manuscripts.* Kyoto: Bun'eidō.

———. 1987. New Sanskrit fragments of the Mahāyāna Mahāparinirvāṇasūtra in the Stein/Hoernle Collection: A preliminary report. *The Eastern Buddhist* 20/2:105–14.

———. 1988. *Sanskrit fragments of the Mahāyāna Mahāparinirvāṇasūtra.* Tokyo: Toyo Bunko.

Matsumura, Hisashi, ed. 1989. Āyuḥparyantasūtra: Das Sūtra von der Lebensdauer in den verschiedenen Welten. In Bechert 1989–96, 1: 69–100.

Matsumura, Hisashi and Shin'ya Matsuda, trs. 1988. *Jātakas 301–85.* Vol. 4 of *Jātaka zenshū,* ed. Hajime Nakamura. Tokyo: Shunjūsha.

May, Jacques. 1959a. Kant et le Mādhyamika. *IIJ* 2:102–11.
———. 1971. La philosophie bouddhique idéaliste. *Asiatische Studien* 25:265–323.
———. 1979. Chūgan. *Hōbōgirin*, fasc. 5:470–93.
May, J., tr. 1959b. *Candrakīrti, Prasannapadā Madhyamakavṛtti: Douze chapitres traduits du sanscrit et du tibétain, accompagnés d'une introduction, de notes et d'une édition critique de la version tibétaine.* Collection Jean Przyluski 2. Paris: A. Maisonneuve.
———. 1980. Āryadeva et Candrakīrti sur la permanence. In Institut Orientaliste 1980, 215–32.
———. 1981a. Āryadeva et Candrakīrti sur la permanence (II). *BEFEO* 69:75–96.
———. 1981b. Āryadeva et Candrakīrti sur la permanence (III). *Asiatische Studien* 35/2:47–76.
Meadows, Carol. 1986. *Ārya-Śūra's compendium of the perfections.* Bonn: Indica et Tibetica Verlag.
Mehendale, Madhukar Anant. 1948. *Aśokan inscriptions in India: A linguistic study, together with an exhaustive bibliography.* Bombay: U. of Bombay.
Meisig, Konrad. 1987. *Das Śrāmaṇyaphala-sūtra: Synoptische Übersetzungen und Glossar der chinesischen Fassungen verglichen mit dem Sanskrit und Pāli.* Wiesbaden: O. Harrassowitz.
———. 1988. *Das Sūtra von den vier Ständen: Das Aggañña-Sutta im Licht seiner chinesischen Parallelen.* Wiesbaden: O. Harrassowitz.
Meisig, Marion, ed. and tr. 1988. *Die "China-Lehre" des Śaktismus: Mahācīnācāra-Tantra kritisch ediert nebst Übersetzung und Glossar.* Wiesbaden: O. Harrassowitz.
Mémorial Sylvain Lévi. See Renou 1937.
Mikkyō Seiten Kenkyūkai, eds. and trs. 1986–87. Vajradhātumahāmaṇḍalopāyika-Sarvavajrodaya. *Taishō Daigaku Sōgō Bukkyō Kenkyūjo Nenpō* 8: 258(23)–224(57); 9: 294(13)–222(85).
———. 1988–91. *Advayavajrasaṃgraha*: New critical edition with Japanese translation. *Taishō Daigaku Sōgō Bukkyō Kenkyūjo Nenpō* 10: 234(1)–178(57); 11: 259(86)–200(145); 12: 316(49)–282(83); 13: 291(46)–242(95).
Mimaki, Katsumi, Musashi Tachikawa, and Akira Yuyama, eds. 1989. *Three works of Vasubandhu in Sanskrit manuscript: The* Trisvabhāvanirdeśa, *the* Viṃśatikā *with its* vṛtti, *and the* Triṃśikā *with Sthiramati's commentary.* Bibliotheca Codicum Asiaticorum 1. Tokyo: The Centre for East Asian Cultural Studies.
Minaev, Ivan Pavlovič. 1872. *Očerk fonetiki i morfologii jazyka pali.* St. Petersburg: Demakova.
———. 1874. *Grammaire Pālie.* Trans. S. Guyard. Paris: E. Leroux.
———. 1883. *Pāli grammar.* Trans. Charles G. Adams from the French of S. Guyard. Maulmain, British Burma.
Minaev, I. P., ed. and tr. 1869. *Pratimokša-sutra: Buddijskij služebnik.* St. Petersburg.
———. 1890. Çāntideva: Bodhicaryāvatāra. *ZVORAO* 4:153–228.
Mitra, Rajendralal. 1853–77. *Lalita Vistara, or, Memoirs of the early life of Śākya Siñha.* Bibliotheca Indica 15. Calcutta: Asiatic Society of Bengal.
Miyamoto, Shōson, et al., eds. 1962-90. *Taishō Shinshū Daizōkyō Sakuin* [Index of the *Taishō Shinshū Daizōkyō*]. 45 vols. Tokyo: Daizō Shuppan.

Mizuno, Kōgen. 1981. *Hokkukyō no Kenkyū*. Tokyo: Shunjūsha.

Mochizuki, Shinkō, ed. 1932–36. *Bukkyō Daijiten*. 7 vols., including an index and supplements. Tokyo: Sekai Seiten Kankō Kyōkai. (Second edition in 8 vols. Tokyo, 1954–8; Third edition in 10 vols. Tokyo, 1958–63)

Mori, Sodō. 1984. *A study of the Pāli commentaries: Theravādic aspects of the Aṭṭhakathās*. Tokyo: Sankibō Busshorin.

———. 1989. *Studies of the Pāli commentaries: A provisional collection of articles*. Private publication not for sale.

Moule, Arthur Christopher and Paul Pelliot. 1938. *Marco Polo: The description of the world*. Vol. 1. London: Routledge.

Much, M. T. 1987. Review of *Ācāryaratnakīrtiviracitam Udayananirākaraṇam*. *Buddhist Studies Review* 4/1:88–90.

Mukherjee, S. N. 1982. Publications of A. L. Basham. In Mukherjee 1982, 326–31.

Mukherjee, S. N., ed. 1982. *India: History and thought. Essays in honour of A. L. Basham*. Calcutta: Subarnarekha.

Müller, Friedrich Max. 1856. Comparative mythology. In *Oxford Essays*, vol. 2. London: J. W. Parker and Son.

———. 1861–64. *Lectures on the science of language*. London: Longman, Green, Longman, and Roberts.

———. 1867. *Chips from a German workshop*. Vol. 1. London: Longmans, Green, and Co.

Müller, F. M., ed. 1881. *Vajracchedikā*. Part 1 of *Buddhist texts from Japan*. Oxford: Clarendon Press.

Müller, F. M. and Bunyiu Nanjio, eds. 1883. *Sukhâvatî-vyûha: Description of Sukhavati, the land of bliss*. Oxford: Clarendon Press.

Murakami, Shinkan. 1979. Muyoku to mushou: Mahābhārata to Bukkyō (1). *Tōhoku Daigaku Bungaku-bu Kenkyū Nenpō* 29:140–213. English abstract on pp. 248–244.

Murti, Tirupattur Ramaseshayyer Vankatachala. 1955. *The central philosophy of Buddhism: A study of the Madhyamika system*. London: G. Allen & Unwin.

Museum für Indische Kunst, ed. 1977. *Beiträge zur Indien-Forschung: Ernst Waldschmidt zum 80. Geburtstag gewidmet*. Berlin: Museum für Indische Kunst.

Nagao, Gajin. 1982–87. *Shōdaijōron: wayaku to chūkai* [Mahāyānasaṅgraha: A Japanese translation and commentary]. 2 vols. Tokyo: Kōdansha.

Nagao, G., tr. 1976. *Seshin ronshū*. Vol. 15 of *Daijō butten*. Tokyo: Chūō Kōronsha.

Nagasaki, Hōjun. 1990. Dai-nikai kokusai Dharmakīrti gakkai ni shusseki shite. *Ōtani Daigaku Shinshū Sōgō Kenkyūjo Kenkyū Jōhō* 23:12–15.

Nakamura, Hajime. 1970–71. *Genshi Bukkyō no shisō* [The thought of early Buddhism]. 2 vols. Tokyo: Shunjūsha.

———. 1980. *Indian Buddhism: A survey with bibliographical notes*. Intercultural Research Institute Monograph 9. Hirakata (Osaka): Kansai University of Foreign Studies.

Nakatani, H., ed. 1987. *Udānavarga de Subasi*. 2 vols. Paris: Collège de France.

Ñāṇamoli, Bhikkhu, tr. 1982. *The path of discrimination* (Paṭisambhidāmagga). London: Pali Text Society.

———. 1987–91. *The dispeller of delusion (Sammohavinodanī)*. 2 parts. Rev. for publication by L. S. Cousins, Nyanaponika Mahāthera, and C. M. M. Shaw. Oxford: Pali Text Society.

Narain, A. K., ed. 1979. *Studies in Pāli and Buddhism: A memorial volume in honor of Bhikkhu Jagdish Kashyap*. Delhi: B. R. Pub. Corp.

Newman, John Ronald. 1985. A brief history of the Kalachakra. In Sopa and Jackson 1985, 51–90.

———. 1987. *The outer Wheel of Time: Vajrayāna Buddhist cosmology in the Kalacakra.* Ph.D. dissertation. U. of Wisconsin.

Nobel, Johannes. 1928. Kumāralāta und sein Werk. *NGGW:* 295–304.

———. 1931. Um Aśvaghoṣa. *NGGW:* 330–36.

———. 1955a. Besprechung Edgerton, Buddhist Hybrid Sanscrit Grammar and Dictionary. *Deutsche Literaturzeitung* 76, cols. 256–60.

Nobel, J., ed. 1937. *Suvarṇabhāsottamasūtra.* Leiden: Harrassowitz.

Nobel, J., ed. and tr. 1944–50. *Suvarṇaprabhāsottamasūtra.* Vol. 1: *Die tibetischen Übersetzungen.* Vol. 2: *Wörterbuch Tibetisch-Deutsch-Sanskrit.* Leiden: Brill.

———. 1955b. *Udrāyaṇa, König von Roruka.* 2 vols. (vol. 2 = a dictionary). Wiesbaden: Harrassowitz.

———. 1958. *Suvarṇaprabhāsottamasūtra: Das Goldglanz-Sūtra. I-tsing's chinesische Version und ihre tibetische Übersetzung.* 2 vols. Leiden: Brill.

Norman, Kenneth Roy. 1971a. Notes on the Gāndhārī Dharmapada. *Indian Linguistics* 32:213–220.

———. 1976a. Pāli and the language of the heretics. *Acta Orientalia* 37:117–25.

———. 1976b. Middle Indo-Aryan studies XIII: The palatalization of vowels in Middle Indo-Aryan. *JOIB* 25:328–42.

———. 1976c. The labalisation of vowels in Middle Indo-Aryan. *StII* 2:41–58.

———. 1976d. Notes on the so-called "Queen's edict" of Aśoka. *Studies in Indian Epigraphy* 3:35–42.

———. 1977. The Buddha's view of devas. In Museum für Indische Kunst 1977, 329–36.

———. 1978a. Middle Indo-Aryan studies XIII: The recensions of the Aśokan rock edicts. *JOIB* 27/3–4:78–85.

———. 1978b. The role of Pāli in early Sinhalese Buddhism. In Bechert 1978, 28–47.

———. 1979a. Two Pali etymologies. *BSOAS* 42:321–28.

———. 1979b. Māgadhisms in the Kathāvatthu. In Narain 1979, 279–87.

———. 1979c. Middle Indo-Aryan studies XIV–XV. *JOIB* 29:37–49.

———. 1980a. Four etymologies from the Sabhiya-sutta. In Balasooriya 1980, 173–84.

———. 1980b. The dialects in which the Buddha preached. In Bechert 1980, 61–77.

———. 1980c. Dhammapada 97: A misunderstood paradox. *Indologica Taurinensia* 7:325–31.

———. 1981a. The Pali Text Society: 1881–1981. *The Middle Way* 56/2:71–75.

———. 1981b. Notes on the Vessantara-jātaka. In Bruhn and Wezler 1981, 163–74.

———. 1981c. Devas and adhidevas in Buddhism. *JPTS* 9:145–55.

———. 1981d. A note on *attā* in the Alagaddūpama-sutta. In *Studies in Indian*

Philosophy: A memorial volume in honour of Pandit Sukhlalji Sanghvi, 19–29. L. D. Series 84. Ahmedabad: L. D. Institute of Indology.

———. 1982a. The Four Noble Truths: A problem of Pāli syntax. In Hercus et al. 1982, 377–91.

———. 1982b. Aśokan *silā-thaṃbha-s* and *dhamma-thaṃbha-s*. In *Ācārya-vandanā: D. R. Bhandarkar Birth Centenary Volume,* 311–18. Calcutta: University of Calcutta.

———. 1983a. *Pāli literature, including the canonical literature in Prakrit and Sanskrit of all the Hīnayāna schools of Buddhism.* Vol. 7, fasc. 2 of *A history of Indian literature.* Wiesbaden: O. Harrassowitz.

———. 1983b. The Pratyeka-Buddha in Buddhism and Jainism. In Denwood and Piatigorsky 1983, 92–106.

———. 1983c. The nine treasures of a cakravartin. *Indologica Taurinensia* 11:183–93.

———. 1984b. The value of the Pali tradition. *Jagajjyoti Buddha Jayanti Annual,* 1–9. Calcutta: Bauddha Dharmankur Sabha (Bengal Buddhist Association).

———. 1984c. The metres of the Lakkhaṇa-suttanta. In Dhammapāla et al. 1984, 176–88.

———. 1984d. On translating from Pāli. *One Vehicle,* 77–87. Singapore: National University of Singapore Buddhist Society.

———. 1985a. The influence of the Pāli commentators and grammarians upon the Theravādin tradition. *Buddhist Studies* 15:109–23.

———. 1985b. A report on Pāli dictionaries. *Buddhist Studies* 15:145–52.

———. 1985–90. Pāli lexicographical studies. Parts 3-8. *JPTS* 10:23–36; 11:33–49; 12:49–63; 13:219–27; 14:219–25; 15:145–54.

———. 1987. An epithet of Nibbāna. *Śramaṇa Vidyā. Studies in Buddhism. Prof. Jagannath Upadhyaya Commemoration Volume* I, 23–31. Sarnath: Central Institute of Higher Tibetan Studies.

———. 1987–88. The metres of the Lakkhaṇa-suttanta (II). *Indologica Taurinensia* 14:285–94.

———. 1988a. An aspect of external Sandhi in Pāli. *Buddhist Studies* 17:89–95.

———. 1988b. The origin of Pāli and its position among the Indo-European languages. *Journal of Pāli and Buddhist Studies* 1:1–27.

———. 1989a. Dialect forms in Pāli. In Caillat 1989, 369–92.

———. 1989b. Notes on the Patna Dharmapada. *Amalā Prajñā: Aspects of Buddhist studies,* ed. N. H. Samtani and H. S. Prasad, 431–44. Delhi: Sri Satguru.

———. 1990a. Aspects of early Buddhism. In Seyfort Ruegg and Schmithausen 1990, 24–35.

———. 1990b. Collected papers. Vol. 1. Oxford: Pali Text Society.

Norman, K. R., tr. 1969. *The Elders' Verses I, Theragatha.* Pali Text Society Translation Series 38. London: Luzac.

———. 1971b. *The Elders' Verses II, Therigatha.* Pali Text Society Translation Series 40. London: Luzac.

———. 1984a. *The Group of Discourses* (Sutta-nipāta). Vol. 1. London: Pali Text Society. (Paperback ed., 1985)

Oberhammer, Gerhard, ed. 1968. *Beiträge zur Geistgeschichte Indiens: Festschrift für Erich Frauwallner.* Vols. 12–13 of *WZKSO.* Leiden: E. J. Brill.

———. 1976a. Erich Frauwallner (28.12.1898–5.7.1974). *WZKS* 20:5–17.

———. 1976b. Verzeichnis der Schriften Erich Frauwallners. *WZKS* 20:19–36.

———. 1978. *Transzendenzerfahrung, Vollzugshorizont des Heils: Das Problem in indischer und christlicher Tradition.* Publications of the De Nobili Research Library 5. Vienna: Gerold & Co..

———. 1979. Ludwig Alsdorf. *Almanach der Österreichischen Akademie der Wissenschaften* 129:368–77.

———. 1982. *Epiphanie des Heils: Zur Heilsgegenwart in indischer und christlicher Religion.* Publications of the De Nobili Research Library 9. Vienna: Gerold & Co.

Obermiller, Eugène. 1932. The doctrine of Prajñā-pāramitā as exposed in the Abhisamayālaṃkāra of Maitreya. *Acta Orientalia* 11:1–133, 334–54.

———. 1933–43. *Analysis of the Abhisamayālaṃkāra.* 3 fascs. (1933, 1936, 1943). Calcutta Oriental Series 27. London: Luzac & Co.

Obermiller, E., tr. 1931. The Sublime Science of the Great Vehicle to Salvation, being a manual of Buddhist monism. *Acta Orientalia* 9:81–306.

Oetke, Claus. 1988a. *"Ich" und das Ich: analytische Untersuchungen zur buddhistisch-brahmanischen Ātmankontroverse.* Stuttgart: F. Steiner.

———. 1988b. Die metaphysische Lehre Nāgārjunas. *Conceptus: Zeitschrift für Philosophie* 22, no. 56:47–56.

———. 1989. *Rationalismus und Mystik in der Philosophie Nāgārjunas. *StII* 15:1–40.

———. 1990. On some non-formal aspects of the proofs of the Madhyamakakārikās. In Seyfort Ruegg and Schmithausen 1990, 91–109.

Okada, Yukihiro, ed. 1990. *Die Ratnāvalīṭīkā der Ajitamitra.* Indica et Tibetica 19. Bonn: Indica et Tibetica Verlag.

Ōkubo, Yūsen, ed. 1982. The *Ekottara-āgama* fragments of the Gilgit manuscript—romanized text. *Bukkyōgaku Seminā* 35:120–91.

Okuzumi, Takeki, tr. 1988. **Chūronchūshakusho no kenkyū: Chandorakīrti "Purasannapadā."* Tokyo: Daizō Shuppan.

Oldenberg, Hermann. 1881. *Buddha: Sein Leben, seine Lehre, seine Gemeinde.* Berlin: W. Hertz. (2d ed., 1890; 3rd ed. 1897)

———. 1882. Über den Lalita Vistara. In *Verhandlungen des 5. Internationalen Orientalisten-Congresses,* vol. 2, 2d half, 107–22. Berlin. (= *Kleine Schriften,* 873–88)

———. 1898. Buddhistiche Studien. *ZDMG* 52:613–94. (= *Kleine Schriften,* 889–970)

———. 1912a. Studien zur Geschichte des buddhistischen Kanons. *NGGW:* 155–218. (= *Kleine Schriften,* 973–1036)

———. 1912b. Studien zum Mahāvastu. *NGGW:* 123–54. (= *Kleine Schriften,* 1037–68)

———. 1917. Zur Geschichte der Sāṃkhya-Philosophie. *NGGW:* 218–53. (= *Kleine Schriften* 2:1423–58; on Buddhism and Sāṃkhya see esp. 1445–52)

———. 1923. *Die Lehre der Upanishaden und die Anfänge des Buddhismus*. Göttingen: Vandenhoeck & Ruprecht. (1st ed., 1915)

———. 1967. *Kleine Schriften*. Ed. Klaus Ludwig Janert. Wiesbaden: F. Steiner.

Oldenberg, Hermann, ed. 1879–83. *The Vinaya Piṭakaṃ*. 5 vols. London: Williams and Norgate. Reprint, London: Pali Text Society, 1964.

Oldenberg, H., ed. and tr. 1879. *The Dîpavaṃsa: An ancient Buddhist historical record*. London: Williams and Norgate.

Oldenburg (Ol'denburg), Sergeji Federovič. 1892. Kašgarskaja rukopis N. F. Petrovskogo. *ZVORAO* 7:81–82.

———. 1893a. On the Buddhist Jātakas. *JRAS* 25:301–56.

———. 1893b. The Buddhist source of the (Old Slavonic) legend of the twelve dreams of Shahaïsh. *JRAS* 25:509–16.

———. 1894a. K kašgarskim buddijskim tekstam. *ZVORAO* 8:151–53.

———. 1894b. Ešče po povodu kašgarskix tekstov. *ZVORAO* 8:349–51.

———. 1894c. Otryvki kašgarskix sanskritskix rukopisej iz sobranija N. F. Petrovskogo. *ZVORAO* 8:47–67.

———. 1897a. *Predvaritel'naja zamjetka o buddijskoj rukopisi, napisannoj pis'menami kharoṣṭhī*. St. Petersburg: Akademija Nauk.

———. 1897b. Notes on Buddhist art. Tr. Leo Wiener. *JAOS* 18 (pt. 1):183–201.

———. 1898. A propos du Mahābhārata dans la littérature bouddhique. *RHR* 37:342–43.

———. 1899. Otryvki kašgarskix ... Petrovskogo. *ZVORAO* 11:207–67.

———. 1902–3. Otryvki kašgarskix ... Petrovskogo. *ZVORAO* 15:0113–0122.

———. 1910. Pamjati Nikolaja Fedoroviča Petrovskogo 1837–1908. *ZVORAO* 20:01–08.

Olson, Robert F. and Masao Ichishima, trs. 1979. The third process of meditative actualization by Kamalaśīla. *Annual of the Institute for Comprehensive Studies of Buddhism, Taisho University* [*Taishō Daigaku Sōgō Bukkyō Kenkyūjo Nempō*] 1:241(17)–205(53).

Pandey, Raghunath, ed. 1984. *Ācāryaratnakīrtiviracitam Udayananirākaraṇam*. Bibliotheca Indo-Buddhica 10. Delhi: Sri Satguru.

Pandeya, Raghunatha, ed. 1988–89. *The Madhyamakaśāstram of Nāgārjuna*. With the commentaries *Akutobhayā* of Nāgārjuna, *Madhyamakavṛtti* of Buddhapālita, *Prajñāpradīpavṛtti* of Bhāvaviveka, *Prasannapadāvṛtti* by Candrakīrti critically reconstructed. 2 vols. Delhi: Motilal Banarsidass.

Pandeya, Ramchandra, ed. 1989. *Pramāṇavārttika with Svopajñavṛtti and Manorathanandin's Pramāṇavārttikavṛtti*. Delhi: Motilal Banarsidass.

Pāsādika (aka Prāsādika), Bhikkhu, 1986. Review of S. Dietz's *Fragmente des Dharmaskandha*. *Buddhist Studies Review* 3/1: 65–71.

———. 1989. *Kanonische Zitate im Abhidharmakośabhāṣya des Vasubandhu* (SWTF, Beiheft I). Göttingen: Vandenhoeck & Ruprecht.

Pāsādika, Bhikkhu, ed. 1989. *Nāgārjuna's Sūtrasamuccaya: A critical edition of Mdo kun las btus pa*. København: Akademisk Forlag.

Pāsādika, Bhikkhu, tr. 1977–79. Kāśyapaparivarta. *"Linh-Son"—Publications d'études bouddhiques*. Nos. 1–9. Joinville-le-Pont.

———. 1978–82. Sūtrasamuccaya. *"Linh-Son"—Publications d'étude bouddhiques.* Nos. 2–20. Joinville-le-Pont.

Pāsādika (Prāsādika), B. and Lal Mani Joshi, eds. 1981. *Vimalakīrtinirdeśasūtra: Tibetan version, Sanskrit restoration, and Hindī translation.* Bibliotheca Indo-Tibetica 5. Sarnath: Central Institute of Higher Tibetan Studies.

Paulinus a Sancto Bartholomaeo (alias J. P. Wesdin). 1791. *Systema brahmanicum.* Rome: Antonium Fulgonium.

———. 1793. *Musei Borgiani Velitris codices manuscripti Avenses, Peguani, Siamici, Malabarici, Indostani....* Rome: Antonium Fulgonium.

Pauly, Bernard, ed. 1964. Matériaux pour une édition définitive du Varṇārhavarṇastotra de Mātṛceṭa. *JA* 252: 197–271.

———. 1965. Fragments sanskrits de Haute Asie (Mission Pelliot). *JA* 253:83–121.

———. 1965–67. Fragments sanskrits de Haute Asie (Mission Pelliot). *JA* 253:116–19, 183–87; 254:245–304; 255:231–41.

Pelliot, Paul. 1905. Review of volume 1 of Thomas Watters's *On Yuan Chwang's travels in India, 629–645 A.D. BEFEO* 5:423–57.

———. 1931. Review of J. Przyluski's "Açvaghoṣa et la Kalpanāmaṇḍitikā." *T'oung Pao* 28:196–97.

Pereira, José and Francis Tiso, trs. 1987. A Buddhist classification of reality: A translation of the first chapter of the *Abhidharmakośa* of Vasubandhu. *A.R.I. Kiyō* 6:51–84.

Pérez-Remón, Joaquin. 1980. *Self and Non-Self in early Buddhism.* The Hague/Paris/New York: Mouton.

Peri, Noël. 1911. A propos de la date du Vasubandhu. *BEFEO* 11:339–90.

———. 1918. Les femmes du Çākya-Muni. *BEFEO* 18:1–37.

Petech, Luciano. 1952–53. *I missionari Italiani nel Tibet e nel Nepal.* Vols. 1–4. Rome: Libreria dello Stato.

———. 1954–56. *I missionari Italiani nel Tibet e nel Nepal.* Vols. 5–7. Rome: Libreria dello Stato.

Petech, Luciano and Fabio Scialpi. 1984. Bibliography of works of Giuseppe Tucci. *East and West* 34:23–42.

Pfandt, Peter, comp. 1983. *Mahāyāna texts translated into Western languages: A bibliographical guide.* Cologne: Brill. (Rev. and enl. ed. 1986)

Pischel, Richard. 1904. Bruchstücke des Sanskritkanons der Buddhisten aus Idykutshari, Chinesisch-Turkestan. *SPAW:* 807–27.

———. 1906. *Leben und Lehre des Buddha.* Leipzig: Teubner.

Pjatigorskij, Aleksandr Moiseevič. 1971. O. O. Rozenberg i problema jazyka opisanija v buddologii [O. O. Rosenberg and the problem of the language of description in Buddhology]. *Trudy po znakovym sistemam* 5 (Tartu): 423–36.

Pollet, Gilbert, ed. 1987. *India and the ancient world: History, trade and culture before A.D. 650. Professor P. H. L. Eggermont jubilee volume presented on the occasion of his seventieth birthday.* Leuven: Peeters.

Postel, Guillaume. 1552. *Des Merveilles du monde.* Paris.

Potter, Karl H. 1970. *Bibliography of Indian Philosophies.* Delhi: Motilal Banarsidass.

———. 1972. Supplement to *Bibliography of Indian Philosophies. Journal of Indian Philosophy* 2:65–112.

Pradhan, Prahlad, ed. 1950. *Abhidharmasamuccaya of Asaṅga.* Visva-Bharati Studies 12. Śāntiniketan: Visva-Bharati.

———. 1967. *Abhidharm-Koshabhāṣya of Vasubandhu.* Tibetan Sanskrit Works 8. Patna: K. P. Jayaswal Research Institute. Reprint, 1975.

Pruden, Leo M. 1988–90. *Abhidharmakośabhāṣyam.* 4 vols. Eng. translation of La Vallée Poussin 1923–31. Berkeley: Asian Humanities Press.

Przyluski, Jean. 1914. Le Nord-ouest de l'Inde dans le Vinaya des Mula-sarvāstivādin et les textes apparentés. *JA* 1914-2:493–568.

———. 1918–20. Le parinirvāṇa et les funérailles du Bouddha. *JA* 1918-1:485–526; 1918-2:401–56; 1919-1:365–430; 1920-1:5–54.

———. 1920. *Le parinirvāṇa et les funérailles du Buddha.* Paris: Imprimerie Nationale.

———. 1923. *La légende de l'empereur Açoka.* Paris: P. Geuthner.

———. 1926–28. *Le concile de Rājagṛha: Introduction à l'histoire des canons et des sectes bouddhiques.* Paris: P. Geuthner.

———. 1931. Açvaghoṣa et la Kalpanāmaṇḍitikā. *BCL*, 5th ser., 16:425–34.

———. 1932. Sautrāntika et Dārṣṭāntika. *Rocznik Orientalistyczny* 8:14–24.

———. 1936. Le partage des reliques du Buddha. *MCB* 4:341–67.

———. 1940. Dārṣṭāntika, Sautrāntika and Sarvāstivādin. *Indian Historical Quarterly* 16:246–54.

Puini, Carlo. 1904. *Il Tibet (geografia, storia, religione, costumi) secondo la Relazione del viaggio del p. Ippolito Desideri (1715–1721).* Rome: Società Geografica Italiana.

Python, Pierre, O.P., ed. and tr. 1973. *Vinaya-viniścaya-upāli-paripṛcchā.* In the appendix: *Sugatapañcatriṃśatstotra.* Paris: Jean Maisonneuve.

Qvarnström, Olle, tr. 1989. *Hindu philosophy in Buddhist perspective: The Vedāntatattvaviniścaya chapter of Bhavya's Madhyamakakārikā.* Lund: Plus Ultra.

Raghu Vira and Lokesh Chandra, eds. 1959–74. *Gilgit Buddhist manuscripts (facsimile edition).* Śata-Piṭaka Series: Indo-Asian Literatures 10, 1–10. New Delhi: International Academy of Indian Culture. (Reprint 1995, in 3 vols., Delhi: Sri Satguru)

Rahula, Walpola, tr. 1971. *Le compendium de la super-doctrine (philosophie) (Abhidharmasamuccaya) d'Asaṅga.* PEFEO 78. Paris: École Française d'Extrême-Orient. Reprint, 1980.

Raper, T. C. H., comp. 1983. *Catalogue of the Pāli printed books in the India Office Library.* London: The British Library.

Rau, Wilhelm. 1982. Friedrich Weller (1889–1980). *ZDMG* 132:1–21.

Reese, Wilhelm. 1914. *Die griechischen Nachrichten über Indien bis zum Feldzuge Alexanders des Grossen.* Leipzig: B. G. Teubner.

Regamey, Constantin. 1954. Randbemerkungen zur Sprache und Textüberlieferung des Kāraṇḍavyūha. In Schubert and Schneider 1954, 514–27.

———. 1957. Le problème du bouddhisme primitif et les derniers travaux de Stanislaw Schayer. *Rocznik Orientalistyczny* 21:37–58.

Reigle, David. 1986. *The lost Kālacakra Mūla Tantra on the Kings of Śambhala.*

Kālacakra Research Publications 1. Eastern School, P.O. Box 684, Talent, Oregon 9754.

Rémusat, Jean Pierre Abel, tr. 1836. *Foé Koué Ki; ou, Relation des royaumes bouddhiques de Fa hian.* Rev., completed, and augmented by J. H. Klaproth and E. A. X. Clerc de Landresse. Paris: Imprimerie Royale.

Renou, Louis. 1956. *Histoire de la langue sanskrite.* Lyon: Éditions IAC.

———. 1957. Jakob Wackernagel. *Altindische Grammatik: Introduction générale.* Göttingen: Vandenhoeck & Ruprecht.

Renou, Louis, ed. 1937. *Mémorial Sylvain Lévi.* Paris: P. Hartmann.

Rhys Davids, Caroline Augusta Foley, tr. 1909. *Psalms of the sisters.* Pali Text Society Translation Series 1. London: H. Frowde.

———. 1937. *Psalms of the brethren.* Pali Text Society Translation Series 4. London: Luzac.

———. 1964. *Psalms of the early Buddhists.* Reprint of C. A. F. Rhys Davids 1909 and 1937, pub'd as 1 vol. London: Luzac.

Rhys Davids, Thomas William. 1877. *Buddhism, being a sketch of the life and teachings of Gautama the Buddha.* London: Society for Promoting Christian Knowledge. (14th ed., 1890)

Rhys Davids, T. W., ed. 1890–1911. *The Dīgha-nikāya.* London: Pali Text Society. (With J. Estlin Carpenter)

Rhys Davids, T. W., tr. 1890–94. *The Questions of King Milinda.* Sacred Books of the East 35 and 36. Oxford: Clarendon Press.

———. 1899. *Dialogues of the Buddha.* Vol. 1. Sacred Books of the Buddhists 2. London: Oxford University Press.

Rhys Davids, T. W. and Hermann Oldenberg, trs. 1881–85. *Vinaya texts.* Sacred Books of the East 13, 17, 20. Oxford: Clarendon Press. Reprint, Delhi: Motilal Banarsidass, 1965.

Rockhill, William Woodville, tr. 1883. *Udānavarga: A collection of verses from the Buddhist canon.* London: Trübner & Co.

———. 1884. *The life of the Buddha, and the early history of his order.* London: Trübner & Co.

———. 1886. *Prâtimoksha sutra.* Paris: E. Leroux.

Roerich, George N. (Rerix, Ju. N.). 1983–93. *Tibetsko-Russko-Anglijskij slovar' s sanskritskimi paralleljami.* Parts 1–11. Moscow: Izdatel'skaja Firma "Vostočnaja Literatura".

Rosenberg, Otto (Otton Ottonovič Rozenberg). 1918. *Problemy buddijskoj filosofii.* Petrograd. (German trans.: *Die Probleme der buddhistischen Philosophie.* Heidelberg: O. Harrassowitz, 1924)

Roth, Gustav. 1970. *Bhikṣuṇī-vinaya.* Patna: K. P. Jayaswal Research Institute.

———. 1986. *Indian Studies: Selected papers.* Delhi: Sri Satguru.

Roth, G., ed. 1977. Observations on the first chapter of Asaṅga's Bodhisattvabhūmi. *Indologica Taurinensia* 3–4:403–12.

———. 1980. Particular features of the language of the Ārya-Mahāsāṃghika-Lokottaravādins and their importance for early Buddhist tradition. In Bechert 1980, 78–135.

Rozen, Victor R. 1947. *Povesti o Barlaame i Iosafe.* Edited by Ignatij Kračkovskij (Krachkovsky). Moscow: Akademiya Nauk SSSR.

Rudoj, V. I., tr. 1990. *Abxidxarmakoša (Ènciklopedija Abxidxarmy): Razdel pervyj, analiz po klassam èlementov.* Moscow: Nauka.

Saddhātissa, Hammalava. 1974. Pāli literature of Thailand. In Cousins et al. 1974, 211–25.

———. 1976. The dawn of Pali literature in Thailand. In *Malalasekera Commemoration Volume,* 315–24. Colombo.

———. 1979. Pāli literature from Laos. In Narain 1979, 327–40.

———. 1980. Pāli studies in Cambodia. In Balasooriya 1980, 242–50.

———. 1981. Pāli literature in Cambodia. *JPTS* 9:178–97.

Saigusa, Mitsuyoshi, ed. and tr. 1985. *Chūrongejusōran (Nāgārjuna's Mūlamadhyamakakārikā-s; texts and translations).* Tokyo: Dai-san Bunmeisha.

Saitō, Akira. 1984. *A study of the Buddhapālita-Madhyamaka-vṛtti.* Ph.D. dissertation, The Australian National University.

———. 1985. Textcritical remarks on the *Mūlamadhyamakakārikā* as cited in the *Prasannapadā. Indogaku Bukkyōgaku Kenkyū* 33:846(24)–842(28).

———. 1986. A note on the *Prajñā-nāma-mūlamadhyamakakārikā* of Nāgārjuna. *Indogaku Bukkyōgaku Kenkyū* 35:487(15)–484(18).

———. 1987. "Konpon chūron" tekisuto kō. In Takasaki ... Kinenkai 1987, 764(75)–755(84).

Sakai, Shinten. 1984–88. *Sakai Shinten Chosakushū.* Kyoto: Hōzōkan.

Sakuma, Hidenori S. 1990. *Die Āśrayaparivṛtti-Theorie in der Yogācārabhūmi.* 2 parts. Stuttgart: F. Steiner.

Sander, Lore. 1985. Ernst Waldschmidt (15.7.1897–25.2.1985): A personal tribute. *Buddhist Studies Review* 2:73–79.

Sander, Lore and Ernst Waldschmidt, eds. 1980–85. *Sanskrithandschriften aus den Turfanfunden.* 2 vols. (4: 1980; 5: 1985). Wiesbaden: F. Steiner.

Sanskrit-Wörterbuch der buddhistischen Texte aus den Turfan-Funden und der kanonischen Literatur der Sarvāstivāda-Schule. Begonnen von Ernst Waldschmidt. Im Auftrage der Akademie der Wissenschaften in Göttingen, herausgegeben von Heinz Bechert. 1973–. Volume 1, covering the vowels, completed with fascicule 8 in 1994. Göttingen: Vandenhoeck & Ruprecht.

Schayer, Stanislav (Stanislaw, Stanislaus). 1931. *Ausgewählte Kapitel aus der Prasannapadā.* Cracow: Polska Akademia Umiejetności.

———. 1935. Precanonical Buddhism. *Archív Orientální* 7:121–32.

———. 1937. New contributions to the problem of pre-Hinayanistic Buddhism. *Polish Bulletin of Oriental Studies* 1:8–17.

Scherrer-Staub, Cristina Anna. 1987. D'un manuscript tibétain des Pratītyasamutpādahṛdayakārikā de Nāgārjuna. *Cahiers d'Extrême-Asie* 3:102–11.

Schiefner, Franz Anton von. 1868. *Târanâthae de doctrinae buddhicae in India propagatione narratio.* St. Petersburg. Reprint, Tokyo: Suzuki Research Foundation, 1963.

———. 1869. *Târanâtha's Geschichte des Buddhismus in Indien.* St. Petersburg: Eggers & Co. Reprint, Tokyo: Suzuki Research Foundation, 1963.

———. 1882. *Tibetan tales derived from Indian sources.* Tr. by W. R. S. Ralston. London: Trübner & Co. (New ed., London: G. Routledge, 1926)

Schierlitz, Ernst. 1938. In memory of Alexander Wilhelm Baron von Staël-Holstein. *Monumenta Serica* 3: 286–91.

Schlingloff, Dieter. 1968. *Die Buddhastotras des Mātṛceṭa: Faksimilewiedergabe der Handschriften.* Berlin: Akademie-Verlag.

———. 1971. Das Lebensrad in Ajanta. *Asiatische Studien* 25:324–34.

———. 1972a. Jātakamālā-Darstellungen in Ajanta. *WZKS* 16:55–65.

———. 1972b. Die Erforschung altindischer Wandmalereien. *Christina Albertina* 13:32–38.

———. 1973a. A battle-painting in Ajanta. *Indologen-Tagung 1971,* ed. Herbert Härtel and Volker Moeller, 196–203. Wiesbaden: F. Steiner.

———. 1973b. Prince Sudhana and the kinnarī. *Indologica Taurinensia* 1:155–67.

———. 1973c. The unicorn: Origin and migrations of an Indian legend. In *German Scholars on India,* ed. Cultural Department of the Embassy of the Federal Republic of Germany, vol. 1, 294–307. Varanasi: The Chowkhamba Sanskrit Series Office.

———. 1975a. Aśvaghoṣa's Saundarānanda in Ajanta. *WZKS* 19:85–102.

———. 1975b. Die Erzählung von Sutasoma und Saudāsa in der buddhistischen Kunst. *Altorientalische Forschungen* 2:93–117.

———. 1976. Kalyāṇakārin's adventures: The identification of an Ajanta painting. *Artibus Asiae* 38:5–28.

———. 1977a. Der König mit dem Schwert: Die Identifizierung einer Ajantamalerei. *WZKS* 21:57–70.

———. 1977b. Zwei Malereien in Höhle 1 von Ajanta. *ZDMG*. Supplement III.2, XIX. Deutscher Orientalistentag, 912–17. Wiesbaden: Steiner.

———. 1977c. Die Jātaka-Darstellungen in Höhle 16 von Ajanta. In Museum für Indische Kunst 1977, 451–78.

———. 1977d. Zwei Antiden-Geschichten im alten Indien. *ZDMG* 127:369–97.

———. 1981a. Die älteste Malerei des Buddhalebens. In Bruhn and Wezler 1981, 181–98.

———. 1981b. The Mahābodhi-jātaka in Bharhut. In *Abhinandana-grantha: Ludwik Sternbach Felicitation Volume,* 745–49. Lucknow: Akhila Bharatiya Sanskrit Parishad.

———. 1981c. Erzählung und Bild: Die Darstellungsformen von Handlungsabläufen in der europäischen und indischen Kunst. In *Beiträge zur allgemeinen und vergleichenden Archäologie* 3, ed. Hermann Müller-Karpe, 87–213. Munich: Oscar Beck.

———. 1982. Aśoka or Māra? On the interpretation of some Sāñcī reliefs. In Hercus et al. 1982, 441–55.

Schmidt, Isaak Jakob. 1832. Über einige Grundlehren des Buddhaismus. *Mémoires de l'Acad. Imp. d. Sc. de St. Pétersbourg,* 6th ser., *Sc. Polit., Hist. et Philol.* 1:90–120, 222–62.

———. 1834a.Über die sogenannte dritte Welt der Buddhaisten. *Mémoires de l'Acad. Imp. d. Sc. de St. Pétersbourg,* 6th ser., *Sc. Polit., Hist. et Philol.* 2:1–39.

———. 1834b. Über die Tausend Buddhas einer Weltperiode der Einwohnung oder gleichmässigen Dauer. *Mémoires de l'Acad. Imp. d. Sc. de St. Pétersbourg*, 6th ser., *Sc. Polit., Hist. et Philol.* 2:41–86.

———. 1837. Über das Mahâjâna und Pradschnâ Pâramita der Bauddhen. *Mémoires de l'Acad. Imp. d. Sc. de St. Pétersbourg*, 6th ser., 4:123–228.

———. 1843. *Dsanglun, oder der Weise und der Tor.* St. Petersburg: W. Graff's Erben.

Schmidt, Klaus T., ed. 1988. *Der Schlussteil des Prātimokṣasūtra der Sarvāstivādins: Text in Sanskrit und Tocharisch A verglichen mit den Parallelversionen anderer Schulen.* Sanskrittexte aus den Turfanfunden, vol. 13. Göttingen: Vandenhoeck & Ruprecht.

Schmithausen, Lambert. 1967. Sautrāntika-Voraussetzungen in Viṃśatikā und Triṃśikā. *WZKSO* 11:109–36.

———. 1969a. *Der Nirvāṇa-Abschnitt in der Viniścaya-saṃgrahaṇī der Yogācārabhūmiḥ.* Vienna: Verlag der Österreichischen Akademie der Wissenschaften.

———. 1969b. Zur Literaturgeschichte der älteren Yogācāra-Schule. *ZDMG* Supplement 1, XVII. Deutscher Orientalistentag, Vorträge, Pt. 3. Wiesbaden: Steiner.

———. 1970. Zu den Rezensionen des Udānavargaḥ. *WZKS* 14:47–124.

———. 1971. Philologische Bemerkungen zum Ratnagotravibhāgaḥ. *WZKS* 15:123–77.

———. 1972. The definition of pratyakṣam in the Abhidharmasamuccayaḥ. *WZKS* 16:153–63.

———. 1973. Zu D. Seyfort Rueggs Buch *La théorie du tathāgatagarbha et du gotra.* *WZKS* 17:123–60.

———. 1976a. Zu Rahula Walpolas Übersetzung von Asaṅgas Abhidharmasamuccaya. *WZKS* 20:111–22.

———. 1976b. On the problem of the relation of spiritual practice and philosophical theory of Buddhism. In *German scholars on India,* edited by Cultural Department of the Embassy of the Federal Republic of Germany (Bombay: Nachiketa Publications, vol. 2 [vol. 1 pub'd in 1973]).

———. 1976c. Die vier Konzentrationen der Aufmerksamkeit. *ZMR* 60:241–66.

———. 1977. Zur buddhistischen Lehre von der dreifachen Leidhaftigkeit. *ZDMG* Supplement III.2, XIX. Deutscher Orientalistentag, 918–31. Wiesbaden: Steiner.

———. 1978. Zur Struktur der erlösenden Erfahrung im indischen Buddhismus. In Oberhammer 1978, 97–119.

———. 1981. On some aspects of descriptions of theories of "Liberating Insight" and "Enlightenment" in Early Buddhism. In Bruhn and Wezler 1981, 199–250.

———. 1982a. Die letzten Seiten der Śrāvakabhūmi. In Hercus et al. 1982, 457–89.

———. 1982b. Versenkungspraxis und erlösende Erfahrung in der Śrāvakabhūmi. In Oberhammer 1982, 59–85.

———. 1987. *Ālayavijñāna: On the origin and early development of a central concept of Yogācāra philosophy.* 2 parts. Tokyo: International Institute for Buddhist Studies.

Schneider, Ulrich, ed. and tr. 1978. *Die grossen Felsen-Edikte Aśokas: Kritische Ausgabe, Übersetzung und Analyse der Texte.* Wiesbaden: Harrassowitz.

Schopen, Gregory, ed. and tr. 1989. The manuscript of the Vajracchedikā found at Gilgit. In Gómez and Silk 1989, 89–139.

Schroeter, Friedrich Christian Gotthelf. 1826. *A dictionary of the Bhotanta or Boutan language*. Serampore.

Schubert, Johannes. 1935–36. Berthold Laufer. *Artibus Asiae* 4:265–70; 5:83; 6:169.

Schubert, Johannes and Ulrich Schneider, eds. 1954. *Asiatica: Festschrift Friedrich Weller*. Leipzig: O. Harrassowitz.

Schuh, Dieter. 1973–81. *Tibetische Handschriften und Blockdrucke*. Parts 5 (1973), 6 (1976), and 8 (1981). Wiesbaden: Steiner. (Also see Wilhelm and Panglung 1979)

Schurhammer, Georg. 1932. *Die zeitgenössischen Quellen zur Geschichte Portugiesisch-Asiens ... zur Zeit des hl. Franz Xaver, 1538–1552*. Leipzig: Verlag Asia Major.

Schurhammer, Georg and Iosephus Wicki. 1945. *Epistolae S. Francisci Xaverii ... nova editio*. Vol. 2. Rome: Monumenta Historica Soc. Iesu.

Schwarz, Franz F. 1972. Neue Perspektiven in den griechisch-indischen Beziehungen. *Orientalistische Literaturzeitung* 67, col. 18-21.

Schwentner, Ernst. 1959. *Tocharische Bibliographie 1890–1958*. Berlin: Akademie-Verlag.

Semičov, B. V. and M. G. Brjanskij, eds. and trs. 1980. Abxidxarmakoša: Blizkij k tekstu perevod s tibetskogo na russkij jazyk, podgotovka tibetskogo teksta... . 2 vols. Vol. 1, chaps. 1 and 2; vol. 2, chap. 3. Ulan-Udè: Burjatskoe Knižnoe Izdatel'stvo.

Senart, Émile Charles Marie. 1873–75. *Essai sur la légende du Buddha, son caractère et ses origines*. *JA*, 7th ser., 2:43–303; 3:249–456; 6:97–234. (Also pub'd in 1 vol. in 1875 [Paris: Imprimerie Nationale])

———. 1879. Notice sur le premier volume du Corpus Inscriptionum Indicarum. *JA*, 7th ser., 13:522–45.

———. 1882. *Essai sur la légende du Buddha*. 2d, rev. ed., with an index. Paris: E. Leroux.

———. 1883. Une inscription bouddhique du Cambodge. *Rev. Archéol.*, 3d series, vol. 1.

———. 1889. Un roi de l'Inde au IIIe siècle avant notre ère: Açoka et le bouddhisme. *Revue des Deux Mondes* 92 (March): 67–108.

———. 1896. A propos de la théorie bouddhique des douze Nidānas. In *Mélanges Charles de Harlez*, 281–97. Leyden: E. J. Brill.

———. 1898. Le manuscrit Kharoṣṭhī du Dhammapada: Les fragments Dutreuil de Rhins. *JA* 1898-2:193–308, 545–48.

———. 1900. Bouddhisme et Yoga. *Revue de l'histoire des religions* 42:345–64.

———. 1903. Nirvāṇa. In *Album-Kern*, 101–104. Leiden: E. J. Brill.

———. 1907. Origines bouddhiques. *AMG, B.V.* 25:115–58.

Senart, É, ed. 1882–97. *Le Mahāvastu: Texte sanscrit...* . 3 vols. Paris: Impr. Nationale.

———. 1920–29. *Kharoṣṭhī inscriptions...* . (See Boyer et al. 1920–29)

Senart, É, ed. and tr. 1871. *Grammaire pâlie de Kaccayana*. Paris: Ernest Leroux. (Also found in *JA* 1871: 193–540)

———. 1881–86. *Les inscriptions de Piyadasi.* 2 vols. Paris: Imprimerie Nationale.

Seneviratne, A. C., ed. 1939. *Memoirs and desultory writings of the late James D'Alwis.* Colombo: "Ceylon Observer" Press.

Seyfort Ruegg, David. 1969. *La théorie du tathāgatagarbha et du gotra.* PEFEO 70. Paris: École Française d'Extrême-Orient.

———. 1977. The uses of the four positions of the *catuṣkoṭi* and the problem of the description of reality in Mahāyāna Buddhism. *Journal of Indian Philosophy* 5:1–71.

———. 1981. *The literature of the Madhyamaka school of philosophy in India.* Wiesbaden: Harrassowitz.

———. 1982. Towards a chronology of the Madhyamaka school. In Hercus et al. 1982, 505–30.

———. 1990. On the authorship of some works ascribed to Bhāvaviveka/ Bhavya. In Seyfort Ruegg and Schmithausen 1990, 59–71.

Seyfort Ruegg, D., tr. 1973. *Le traité du tathāgatagarbha de Bu ston Rin chen grub.* PEFEO 88. Paris: École Française de l'Extrême-Orient.

Seyfort Ruegg, D. and Lambert Schmithausen, eds. 1990. *Earliest Buddhism and Madhyamaka.* Vol. 2 of *Panels of the VIIth World Sanskrit Conference: Kern Institute, Leiden, August 23–29, 1987* (Gen. ed., Johannes Bronkhorst). Leiden: Brill.

Shastri, Acharya Paramanandan. 1979. *Tarkarahasya.* Tibetan Sanskrit Works 20. Patna: K. P. Jayaswal Research Institute.

Shastri, Haraprasad, ed. 1927. *Advayavajrasaṃgraha.* Baroda: Oriental Institute.

Shukla, Karunesha, ed. 1973. *Śrāvakabhūmi of Ācārya Asaṅga.* Tibetan Sanskrit Works 14. Patna: K. P. Jayaswal Research Institute.

Shukla, Narayan S., ed. 1979. *The Buddhist Hybrid Sanskrit Dharmapada.* Patna: K. P. Jayaswal Research Institute.

Simson, Georg von , ed. 1986. *Prātimokṣa der Sarvāstivādins: Teil I, Wiedergabe bisher nicht publizierter Handschriften in Transkription.* Sanskrittexte aus den Turfanfunden, vol. 11, pt. 1. Göttingen: Vandenhoeck & Ruprecht.

Skačkov, Petr E. 1934. Materialy dlja bibliografija trudov S. F. Oldenburga. In *Sergeju Fedoroviču Ol'denburgu k pjatidesjatiletiju naučno-obščestvennoj dejatel'nosti 1882–1932* (Leningrad), 625–37.

Skorupski, Tadeusz. 1983. *The Sarvadurgatipariśodhana Tantra: Elimination of all evil destinies.* Delhi: Motilal Banarsidass.

———. 1990b. The life and adventures of David Snellgrove. In Skorupski 1990a, 1–21.

Skorupski, T., ed. 1990a. *Indo-Tibetan studies: Papers in honour and appreciation of Professor David L. Snellgrove's contribution to Indo-Tibetan studies.* Tring: The Institute of Buddhist Studies.

Smith, Helmer. 1950. *Les deux prosodies du vers bouddhique.* Lund.

———. 1954. *Analecta rhythmica.* Helsinki.

———. 1953–55. En marge du vocabulaire sanskrit des bouddhistes. *Orientalia suecana* 2:119–28; 3:31–35; 4:109–13.

Smith, Vincent Arthur. 1896. *The remains near Kasia.* Allahabad: North-Western Provinces and Oudh Govt. Press.

Snellgrove, David Llewellyn. 1987. *Indo-Tibetan Buddhism: Indian Buddhists & their Tibetan successors.* London: Serindia Publications/Boston: Shambhala.

Snellgrove, D. L., ed. and tr. 1959. *The Hevajra tantra: A critical study.* 2 vols. London: Oxford University Press.

Sopa, Geshe Lhundub. 1985a. The Kalachakra Tantra initiation. In Sopa and Jackson 1985, 91–117.

———. 1985b. The subtle body in Kalachakra. In Sopa and Jackson 1985, 139–58.

Sopa, Geshe L. and Roger Jackson, eds. 1985. *The Wheel of Time: The Kalachakra in context.* Madison: Deer Park Books.

Sørensen, Per K., ed. and tr. 1986. *Candrakīrti: Triśaraṇasaptati. The septuagint of the three refuges.* Wiener Studien zur Tibetologie und Buddhismuskunde 16. Vienna: Arbeitskreis für Tibetische und Buddhistische Studien.

Speyer, Jacob Samuel, ed. 1902–9. *Avadānaçataka, a century of edifying tales belonging to the Hīnayāna.* Bibliotheca Buddhica 3. St.-Pétersbourg: Commissionaires de l'Académie Impériale des Sciences.

Speyer, J. S., tr. 1895. *The Jâtakamâlâ, or Garland of Birth-Stories, by Ārya Śûra.* London: Henry Frowde. Reprint, Delhi: Motilal Banarsidass, 1971.

Spiegel, Friedrich von. 1841. *Kammavākyaṃ: Liber de officiis sacerdotum buddhicorum.* Bonn: H. B. Koenig.

———. 1845. *Anecdota Pâlica.* Leipzig: W. Engelmann.

Sprung, G. Mervyn, ed. 1973. *The problem of two truths in Buddhism and Vedānta.* Dordrecht: Reidel.

Sprung, G. Mervyn, tr. 1979. *Lucid exposition of the Middle Way: The essential chapters from the Prasannapadā of Candrakīrti.* London: Routledge and Kegan Paul.

Staal, Frits. 1985. Substitutions de paradigmes et religions d'Asie. *Cahiers d'Extrême-Asie* 1:42–44.

Stache-Rosen, Valentina. 1968. *Dogmatische Begriffsreihen im ältern Buddhismus.* Vol. 2: *Das Saṅgītisūtra und sein Kommentar Saṅgītiparyāya.* Berlin: Deutsche Akademie der Wissenschaften zu Berlin, Institut für Orientforschung.

Staël-Holstein, Alexander Wilhelm Baron von, ed. 1926. *The Kāśyapaparivarta, a Mahāyānaūtra of the Ratnakūṭa class.* Shanghai: The Commercial Press.

———. 1933. *A commentary to the Kāśyapaparivarta: Edited in Tibetan and in Chinese.* Peiping: Nat. Library and Nat. Tsinghua University.

Stcherbatsky, Theodor (Fedor Ippolitovič Shcherbatskoj). 1903–9. *Teorija poznanija i logika po ucheniju pozdnejšix buddistov.* 2 vols. S.-Peterburg: Tip-Lit. Gerol'd.

———. 1923. *The central conception of Buddhism and the meaning of the word "dharma".* London: Royal Asiatic Society. (4th ed., Delhi: Indological Book House, 1970)

———. 1924. *Erkenntnistheorie und Logik nach der Lehre der späteren Buddhisten.* Trans. Otto Strauss. Munich-Neubiberg: O. Schloss.

———. 1926. *La théorie de la connaissance et la logique chez les bouddhistes tardifs.* Trans. I. de Manziarly and Paul Masson-Oursel. Paris: P. Geuthner.

———. 1927. *The conception of Buddhist Nirvāṇa.* Leningrad: Publ. Office of the Acad. of Sc. of the USSR. (Rev. and enl. ed., Varanasi: Bharatiya Vidya Parkashan, 1968, 1 vol., various pagination; 2d rev. and enl. ed., Delhi: Motilal Banarsidass, 1977)

———. 1930–32. *Buddhist logic.* 2 vols. Bibliotheca Buddhica 26. Leningrad: Akademia Nauk SSSR. Reprints, New York: Dover, 1962; Osnabrück: Biblio Verlag, 1970.

———. 1936a. Dr. E. Obermiller, obituary notice. *Journal of the Greater India Society* 3:211–13. (Also in *Indian Historical Quarterly* 12, no. 2 [June 1936]:380– 82)

———. 1969. *Papers of Th. Stcherbatsky: Translated for the first time into English by Harish C. Gupta.* Edited with an introduction by Debiprasad Chattopadhyaya. Soviet Indology Series 2. Calcutta: K. L. Mukhopadhyaya.

———. 1971. *Further papers of Stcherbatsky: Translated for the first time from the Russian by Harish Chandra Gupta.* Ed. by Debiprasad Chattopadhyaya. Soviet Indology Series 6. Calcutta: K. L. Mukhopadhyaya.

Stcherbatsky, Theodor, tr. 1936b. *Madhyānta-vibhaṅga: Discourse on discrimination between middle and extremes.* Leningrad: Reprint, Osnabrück, Biblio Verlag, 1970.

Steinkellner, Ernst. 1968. Die Entwicklung des kṣanikatvānumānam bei Dharmakīrti. *WZKSO* 12–13:361–77.

———. 1971. Wirklichkeit und Begriff bei Dharmakīrti. *WZKS* 15:179–211.

———. 1976. Der Einleitungsvers von Dharmottaras Apohaprakaraṇam. *WZKS* 20:123–24.

———. 1977a. *Verse-index of Dharmakīrti's works (Tibetan versions).* Vienna: Arbeitskreis für Tibetische und Buddhistische Studien, Universität Wien.

———. 1977b. Jñānaśrīmitra's Sarvajñasiddhiḥ. In Lancaster 1977, 383–93.

———. 1978. Yogische Erkenntnis als Problem im Buddhismus. In Oberhammer 1978, 121–34.

———. 1979b. Miszellen sur erkenntnistheoretisch-logischen Schule des Buddhismus. *WZKS* 23:141–54.

———. 1980. Some Sanskrit fragments of Jinendrabuddhi's Viśālāmalavatī. In Basham 1980, 96–105.

———. 1981b. Philological remarks on Śākyamati's Pramāṇavārttikaṭīkā. In Bruhn and Wezler 1981, 283–95.

———. 1982. The spiritual place of the epistemological tradition in Buddhism. *Nanto Bukkyō* 49:1–18.

———. 1984. Anmerkungen zu einer buddhistischen Texttradition: Paralokasiddhi. *Anzeiger der phil.-hist. Kl. der Österreichischen Akademie der Wissenschaften* 121:79–94.

———. 1985. Paralokasiddhi-texts. In *Buddhism and its relation to other religions: Essays in honour of Dr. Shōzen Kumoi on his seventieth birthday,* 215–24. Kyoto: Heirakuji Shoten.

Steinkellner, E., ed. 1973. *Dharmakīrti's Pramāṇaviniścayaḥ, Zweites Kapitel: Svārthānumānam,Teil I: Tibetischer Text und Sanskrittexte.* Vienna: Verlag der Österreichischen Akademie der Wissenschaften.

Steinkellner, E., ed. and tr. 1967. *Dharmakīrti's* Hetubinduḥ. 2 vols. Vienna: Verlag der Österreichischen Akademie der Wissenschaften.

———. 1986. *Dharmottaras* Paralokasiddhi: *Nachweis der Wiedergeburt zugleich eine Widerlegung materialistischer Thesen zur Natur der Geistigkeit.* Vienna: Verlag der Österreichischen Akademie der Wissenschaften.

———. 1988. *Nachweis der Wiedergeburt: Prajñāsena's* 'Jig rten pha rol sgrub pa. 2 vols. Vienna: Verlag der Österreichischen Akademie der Wissenschaften.

Steinkellner, E., tr. 1979a. *Dharmakīrti's Pramāṇaviniścayaḥ, Teil II: Übersetzung und Anmerkungen.* Vienna: Verlag der Österreichischen Akademie der Wissenschaften.

———. 1981a. *Śāntideva: Eintritt in das Leben zur Erleuchtung* (Bodhicaryāvatāra). Düsseldorf/Cologne: Eugen Diederichs.

Steinkellner, E. and Helmut Krasser, eds. and trs. 1989. *Dharmottaras Exkurs zur Definition gültiger Erkenntnis im Pramāṇaviniścaya.* Vienna: Verlag der Österreichischen Akademie der Wissenschaften.

Streng, Frederick John. 1967. *Emptiness: A study in religious meaning.* Nashville: Abingdon Press.

Strickmann, Michel. 1977. A survey of Tibetan Buddhist studies. *Eastern Buddhist* 10/1:128–49.

Strolz, Walter and Shizuteru Ueda, eds. 1982. *Offenbarung als Heilserfahrung im Christentum, Hinduismus und Buddhismus.* Publications of the De Nobili Research Institute Library 2. Vienna: De Nobili Research Library.

Sutton, Florin Giripescu. 1990. *Existence and enlightenment in the Laṅkāvatārasūtra: A study in the ontology and epistemology of the Yogācāra school of Mahāyāna Buddhism.* Albany: SUNY Press.

Swellengrebel, Jan Lodewijk. 1980. In memoriam C. Hooykaas 26th December 1902–13th August 1979. *BKI* 136:190–214.

Tabata, Tetsuya and Hoshiko Tabata, comps. 1986–90. Index of Yaśomitra's Abhidharmakośavyākhyā. *A.R.I. Kiyō* 5–9.

Tabata, Tetsuya, Satoshi Nonome, and Shōkū Bandō, comps. 1987. *Index to the Dhammasaṅgaṇi.* London: Pali Text Society.

Tabata, Tetsuya, Satoshi Nonome, Toyoaki Uesugi, Shōkū Bandō, and Genshoh Unoke, comps. 1982. *Index to the Kathāvatthu.* London: Pali Text Society.

Takahashi, Moritaka. 1970. *Kengukyō: Zō-Kan taiyaku.* Osaka: Kansai Daigaku Tōzai Gakujutsu Kenkyūjo.

Takakusu, Junjirō, comp. 1935-41. *Nanden Daizōkyō.* 65 vols. Tokyo: Taishō Shinshū Daizōkyō Kankō-kai.

Takakusu, Junjirō and Kaigyoku Watanabe, comps. 1924-34. *Taishō Shinshū Daizōkyō.* 85 vols. (texts), 12 vols. (illustrations), and 3 vols. (catalogues). Tokyo: Taishō Issaikyō Kankō-kai.

Takasaki, Jikidō. 1965. Remarks on the Sanskrit fragments of the Abhidharmadharmaskandhapādaśāstra. *Indogaku Bukkyōgaku Kenkyū [Journal of Indian and Buddhist Studies]* 13/1:403(33)–411(41).

———. 1966. *A study on the Ratnagotravibhāga (Uttaratantra): Being a treatise on the Tathāgathagarbha theory of Mahāyāna Buddhism.* Serie orientale Roma 33. Rome: IsMEO.

———. 1988–89. *Nyoraizō shisō.* 2 vols. Kyoto: Hōzōkan.

Takasaki, J., ed. 1981. *A revised edition of the Laṅkāvatāra-sūtra, Kṣaṇika-Parivarta.* Tokyo.

Takasaki, J., tr. 1989. *Hōshōron.* Tokyo: Kōdansha.

Takasaki Jikidō Hakushi Kanreki Kinenkai, eds. 1987. *Indogaku Bukkyōgaku ron-*

shū: Takasaki Jikidō Hakushi kanreki kinen ronshū. Tokyo: Shunjūsha.

Tanji, Teruyoshi. 1988a. *Chūronshaku: Akiraka na kotoba I*. Osaka: Kansai Daigaku.

———. 1988b. *Chimmoku to kyōsetsu*. Osaka: Kansai Daigaku.

Tatia, Nathmal, ed. 1975. *Lokottaramahāsāṃghikānāṃ Prātimokṣasūtram*. Tibetan Sanskrit Works 16. Patna: K. P. Jayaswal Research Institute.

———. 1976. *Abhidharmasamuccayabhāṣya*. Tibetan Sanskrit Works 17. Patna: K. P. Jayaswal Research Institute.

Tatz, Mark, tr. 1986. *Asaṅga's chapter on ethics with the commentary by Tsong-Kha-Pa: The basic path to awakening, the complete bodhisattva*. Lewiston: Edwin Mellen.

Tauscher, Helmut, tr. 1981. *Candrakīrti: Madhyamakāvatāraḥ und Madhyamakāvatārabhāṣyam (Kapitel VI, Vers 166–226)*. Vienna: Arbeitskreis für Tibetische und Buddhistische Studien, Universität Wien.

Thakur, A. L., ed. 1974. *Aśokanibandau*. Tibetan Sanskrit Works 15. Patna: K. P. Jayaswal Research Institute.

Thurman, Robert A. F., tr. 1976. *The holy teaching of Vimalakīrti: A Mahāyāna scripture*. University Park: Pennsylvania State University Press.

Timmer, Barbara Catharina Jacoba. 1930. *Megasthenes en de indische Maatschappij*. Amsterdam: H.J. Paris.

Toda, Hirofumi. 1984a. Hokekyō no seiritsu—bonbun shahon no shoyōsō [Some remarks about the text of the Saddharmapuṇḍarīkasūtra]. *Tōyō Gakujutsu Kenkyū* 23/1:141–81.

———. 1984b. Pekin Minzoku Bunkakyū Toshokan shozō bonbun Hokkekyō baiyō shahon [On the Peking manuscript of the Saddharmapuṇḍarīka-sūtra]. *Tōyō Gakujutsu Kenkyū* 23/2:260(1)–247(14).

———. 1984–96. A classification of the Nepalese manuscripts of the Saddharmapuṇḍarīkasūtra. *Tokushima Daigaku Kyōyōbu Kiyō (Jimbun Shakai-Kagaku) [Journal of Cultural and Social Science]* 19–28; *Tokushima Daigaku Sōgō Kagakubu, Ningen shakai bunka kenkyū*, I–III.

———. 1985. Hokekyō bonbun shahon no shoyōsō; Pekin shahon o megutte. *Hokke Bunka Kenkyū* 11:67–90.

Toda, Hirofumi, ed. 1977–78. Saddharmapuṇḍarīkasūtra, Kashgar manuscript. *Tokushima Daigaku Kyōyō-bu Rinri Gakka Kiyō* 1–5.

———. 1979. Saddharmapuṇḍarīkasūtra Gilgit manuscripts (groups B and C). *Tokushima Daigaku Kyōyōbu Kiyō (Jimbun Shakai-Kagaku) [Journal of Cultural and Social Science]* 14:249–304.

———. 1980. Saddharmapuṇḍarīkasūtra Nepalese manuscript (K′) (X–XVII). *Tokushima Daigaku Kyōyōbu Kiyō (Jimbun Shakai-Kagaku) [Journal of Cultural and Social Science]* 15:299–347.

———. 1980–85. Saddharmapuṇḍarīkasūtra Nepalese manuscript (K′), I–XXVII [including a rev. ed. of X–XVII]. *Tokushima Daigaku Kyōyō-bu Rinri Gakka Kiyō* 8–11.

———. 1981. *Saddharmapuṇḍarīkasūtra: Central Asian manuscripts*. Romanized text. Tokushima: Kyōiku Shuppan Center.

———. 1984c. Bonbun Hokekyō kō (2). *Bukkyōgaku* 17: 1–21.

———. 1986–96. Saddharmapuṇḍarīkasūtra. Romanized text. *Tokushima Daigaku*

Kyōyō-bu Rinri Gakka Kiyō 12–16, 22–24; *Tokushima Daigaku Sōgō Kagaku-bu, Kenkyū Hōkokusho* 1–3.

———. 1988. Romanized text of the Saddharmapuṇḍarīkasūtra (Purvayogaparivarta). In *Naritasan Bukkyō Kenkyū Kiyō* 11: *Bukkyō Shisōshi Ronshū*, 247–91.

———. 1989. Romanized text of the Saddharmapuṇḍarīkasūtra (Purvayogaparivarta) (2). In *Indo tetsugaku to Bukkyō: Fujita Kōtatsu Hakushi kanreki kinen ronshū* (Kyoto: Heirakuji Shoten, 1989), 263–94.

Tola, Fernando and Carmen Dragonetti, eds. and trs. 1980. The Hastavālanāmaprakaraṇavṛtti. *The Journal of Religious Studies* 8/1:18–31.

———. 1982. Dignāga's Ālambanaparīkṣāvṛtti. *Journal of Indian Philosophy* 10:105–34.

———. 1983. The Trisvabhāvakārikā of Vasubandhu. *Journal of Indian Philosophy* 11:225–66.

———. 1985. Nāgārjuna's Catustava. *Journal of Indian Philosophy* 13: 1–54.

———. 1987. Śūnyatāsaptati: The seventy *kārikās* on voidness (according to the svavṛtti of Nāgārjuna). *Journal of Indian Philosophy* 15: 1–55.

Tomomatsu, Entai. 1931. Sūtrālaṃkāra et Kalpanāmaṇḍitikā. *JA* 1931-2:135–74, 245–337.

Tosaki, Hiromasa, tr. 1979–85. *Bukkyō ninshikiron no kenkyū—Hosshō-cho Pramāṇavārttika no genryōron.* 2 vols. Tokyo: Daitō Shuppansha.

Toscano, Giuseppe M. 1951. *La prima missione cattolica nel Tibet.* Parma: Istituto Missioni Estere.

Trenckner, Vilhelm, ed. 1880. *The Milindapañho, being dialogues between King Milinda and the Buddhist sage Nāgasena.* London: Williams and Norgate.

Tsukamoto, Keishō. 1985. Notes on the Saddharmapuṇḍarīka-stavas. *Hokke Bunka Kenkyū* 11:23–66.

———. 1987. A study of Sanskrit manuscripts of Saddharmapuṇḍarīkasūtra. *Hokke Bunka Kenkyū* 13:39–77.

Tsukamoto, Keishō, Yukei Matsunaga, and Hirofumi Isoda, eds. 1989–. *A descriptive bibliography of the Buddhist literature.* Vol. 3 (1990): Abhidharma, Madhyamaka, Yogācāra; vol. 4 (1989): *The Buddhist Tantra.* Kyoto: Heirakuji Shoten.

Tsukamoto, Zenryū, ed. 1955. *Jōron kenkyū* [Studies in the *Chao-lun*]. Kyoto: Hōzōkan.

Tucci, Giuseppe. 1928a. Is the Nyāyapraveśa by Diṅnāga? *JRAS:* 7–13.

———. 1928b. The Vādavidhi. *Indian Historical Quarterly* 4:630–36.

———. 1929a. *Pre-Diṅnāga Buddhist texts on logic from Chinese sources.* Gaekwad's Oriental Series 49. Baroda: Oriental Institute.

———. 1929b. Buddhist logic before Diṅnāga. *JRAS:* 451–88, 870–71.

———. 1930a. Bhāmaha and Diṅnāga. *Indian Antiquary* 59:142–47.

———. 1931. Notes on the Nyāyapraveśa by Śaṅkarasvāmin. *JRAS:* 381–413.

———. 1949. *Tibetan painted scrolls.* 3 vols. Rome: Libreria dello Stato.

———. 1971. *Opera minora.* Vol. 1. Rome: Giovanni Bardi.

Tucci, G., ed. 1956–71. *Minor Buddhist texts.* Part 1, 1956; part 2, 1958; part 3, 1971. Rome: IsMEO.

Tucci, G., ed. and tr. 1956. Triśatikāyāḥ prajñāpāramitāḥ Kārikā Saptatiḥ. In *Minor Buddhist texts,* pt. 1, 1–128.

Tucci, G., tr. 1930b. *The Nyāyamukha of Dignāga: The oldest Buddhist text on logic.* Heidelberg: Harrassowitz.

Turnour, George. 1836. Examination of some points of Buddhist chronology. *JASB* 5:521–36.

———. 1837–38. An examination of the Pāli Buddhistical annals. *JASB* 6:501–28; 717–37; 8:686–701, 789–817, 919–33, 991–1014.

Turnour, G., ed. and tr. 1837. *The Mahāwanso, in roman characters, with the translation subjoined.* Vol. 1. Colombo.

Tuxen, Poul. 1928. *Buddha: Hans Läre, dens Overlevering og dens Liv i Nutiden.* Copenhagen.

———. 1936. *Indledende Bemærkninger til buddhistisk Relativisme.* Copenhagen: B. Lunos Bogtrykkeri a/s.

———. 1937. In what sense can we call the teachings of Nagarjuna negativism? *JOR Madras* 9:231–42.

Upadhyaya, Jagannatha, ed. 1986. *Vimalaprabhāṭīkā of Kalki Śrī Puṇḍarīka on Śrī Laghukālacakratantrarāja by Śrī Mañjuśrīyaśa.* Vol. 1. Sarnath: Central Institute of Higher Tibetan Studies.

van Bijlert, Victor A. 1989. *Epistemology and spiritual authority: The development of epistemology and logic in the old Nyāya and the Buddhist school of epistemology, with an annotated translation of Dharmakīrti's Pramāṇavārttika II (Pramāṇasiddhi) vv. 1–7.* Wiener Studien zur Tibetologie und Buddhismuskunde 20. Vienna: Arbeitskreis für Tibetische und Buddhistische Studien.

van den Broeck, José. 1977a. *La Progression dans la Méditation* (Bhāvanākrama de Kamalaśīla). Brussels: Institut Belge des Hautes Études Bouddhiques.

———. 1977b. *La Saveur de l'Immortel* (A-p'i-t'an Kan Lu Wei Lun): *La version chinoise de l'*Amṛtarasa *de Ghoṣaka (T. 1553).* Louvain-la-Neuve: Institut Orientaliste.

Vasil'ev, Vasilij Pavlovič. 1857. *Buddizm, ego dogmaty, istorija i literatura.* St. Petersburg.

———. 1860. *Der Buddhismus, seine Dogmen, Geschichte und Literatur.* St. Petersburg: Kaiserliche Akademie des Wissenschaften.

———. 1865. *Le Bouddhisme, ses dogmes, son histoire et sa littérature.* Tr. by M. G. A. Comme. Paris: A. Durand.

Vasil'kov, Jaroslav V. 1989. Vstreča Vostoka i Zapada v naučnoj dejatel'nosti F. I. Ščerbatskogo: Vstupitel'naja stat'ja, sostavlenie i primečanija. *Vostok-Zapad: Issledovanija, perevody, publikacii* 4:178–223. (Moscow: Nauka)

Velthem, Marcel van. 1977. *Le traité de la descente dans la profonde loi* (Abhidharmāvatāraśāstra) *de l'Arhat Skandhila.* Louvain-la-Neuve: Université Catholique de Louvain, Institut Orientaliste.

Ver Eecke, Jacqueline, ed. and tr. 1976. *Le Dasavatthuppakaraṇa.* PEFEO 108. Paris: École Française d'Extrême-Orient.

———. 1980. *Le Sīhalavatthuppakaraṇa: Texte Pāli et traduction.* PEFEO 133. Paris: École Française d'Extrême-Orient.

Vetter, Tilmann. 1964. *Erkenntnisprobleme bei Dharmakīrti.* Vienna: Verlag der Österreichischen Akademie der Wissenschaften.

———. 1982a. Die Lehre Nāgārjunas in den Mūla-Madhyamaka-Kārikās. In Oberhammer 1982, 87–108.

———. 1982b. Zum Problem der Person in Nāgārjuna's Mūla-Madhyamaka-Kārikās. In Strolz and Ueda 1982, 167–85.

———. 1983. Review of J. Pérez-Remón's *Self and Non-Self in early Buddhism. WZKS* 27:211–15.

———. 1985. Recent research on the most ancient form of Buddhism: A possible approach and its results. In *Buddhism and its relation to other religions: Essays in honour of Dr. Shōzen Kumoi on his seventieth birthday*, 67–85. Kyoto: Heirakuji Shoten.

———. 1988. *The ideas and meditative practices of early Buddhism.* Translated from Dutch by Marianne Oort. Leiden: Brill.

———. 1990. Some remarks on older parts of the Suttanipāta. In Seyfort Ruegg and Schmithausen 1990, 36–56.

Vetter, T., tr. 1966. *Dharmakīrti's Pramāṇaviniścayaḥ: 1. Kapitel: Pratyakṣam.* Vienna: Verlag der Österreichischen Akademie der Wissenschaften.

———. 1984. *Der Buddha und seine Lehre in Dharmakīrti's Pramāṇavārttika.* Vienna: Arbeitskreis für Tibetische und Buddhistische Studien, Universität Wien.

Vogel, Claus. 1966. On the first canto of Aśvaghoṣa's *Buddhacarita. IIJ* 9/4:266–90.

Vogel, Claus and Klaus Wille, eds. 1984. *Some hitherto unidentified fragments of the Pravrajyāvastu portion of the Vinayavastu manuscript found near Gilgit. NAWG* 1984, No. 7. Göttingen: Vandenhoeck & Ruprecht.

Vogel, Jean Philippe. 1934. *Op het voetspoor van Boeddha.* Haarlem: H. D. Tjeenk Willink.

Vostrikov, Andrej. 1962. *Tibetskaja istoričeskaja literatura.* Bibliotheca Buddhica 32. Moscow: Izd-vo Vostočnoj Lit-ry.

Wackernagel, Jakob. 1896. *Altindische Grammatik.* Vol. 1. Göttingen: Vandenhoeck & Ruprecht.

Waldschmidt, Ernst. 1944–48. *Die Überlieferung vom Lebensende des Buddha.* Göttingen: Vandenhoeck & Ruprecht.

———. 1982. Valentina Stache-Rosen (1925–1980). *ZDMG* 132:22–28.

———. 1989. *Ausgewählte kleine Schriften.* Ed. Heinz Bechert. Wiesbaden: Steiner.

Waldschmidt, E., ed. 1926. *Bruchstücke des Bhikṣuṇī-Prātimokṣa der Sarvāstivādins.* Leipzig: F. A. Brockhaus.

———. 1932. *Bruchstücke buddhistischer Sūtras aus dem zentralasiatischen Sanskritkanon I.* Leipzig: Deutsche Morgenländische Gesellschaft in Kommission bei F. A. Brockhaus.

———. 1950–51. *Das Mahāparinirvāṇasūtra.* Berlin: Akademie-Verlag.

———. 1951. Vergleichende Analyse des Catuṣpariṣatsūtra. In *Beiträge zur indischen Philologie und Altertumskunde: Walther Schubring zum 70. Geburtstag...* , 84–122. Hamburg: Cram, de Gruyter & Co.

———. 1953–56. *Das Mahāvadānasūtra: ein kanonischer Text über die sieben letzten Buddhas.* 2 vols. Berlin: Akademie-Verlag.

———. 1963. *Faksimile-Wiedergaben von Sanskrit-Handschriften aus den Berliner Turfanfunden*. Vol. 1. The Hague: Mouton.

———. 1965–71. *Sanskrithandschriften aus den Turfanfunden*. 3 vols. (1: 1965; 2: 1968; 3: 1971). With Walter Clawiter and Lore Holzmann. Wiesbaden: F. Steiner. (See also Sander and Waldschmidt 1980–85 and Bechert 1989–)

———. 1967. *Von Ceylon bis Turfan*. Göttingen: Vandenhoeck & Ruprecht.

———. 1980. *Sanskrithandschriften aus den Turfanfunden*. Vol. 4. Wiesbaden: Steiner.

Waldschmidt, E., ed. and tr. 1952–62. *Das Catuṣpariṣatsūtra*. Berlin: Akademie-Verlag.

Watanabe, Shōkō, ed. 1972. *Saddharmapuṇḍarīka manuscripts found in Gilgit*. 2 vols. Tokyo: The Reiyukai.

Watters, Thomas. 1904–5. *On Yuan Chwang's travels in India, 629–645 A.D.* 2 vols. Ed. after his death by T. W. Rhys Davids and S. W. Bushell. London: Royal Asiatic Society. Reprint, New York: AMS, 1971.

Wayman, Alex. 1961. *Analysis of the Śrāvakabhūmi manuscript*. Berkeley: U. of California Press.

———. 1973. *The Buddhist tantras: Light on Indo-Tibetan esotericism*. New York: S. Weiser.

———. 1977. *Yoga of the Guhyasamājatantra: The arcane lore of forty verses*. Delhi: Motilal Banarsidass.

Wayman, Alex and Hideko Wayman, trs. 1974. *The Lion's Roar of Queen Śrīmālā*. New York: Columbia University Press.

Webb, Russell. 1975. *An analysis of the Pali canon*. With a bibliography. Kandy: Buddhist Publication Society. (The Wheel Publication nos. 217/218/219/220)

———. 1983–84. Giuseppe Tucci. *Buddhist Studies Review* 1:157–63.

———. 1986. A. L. Basham (24.6.14–27.1.86). *Buddhist Studies Review* 3:45–47.

———. 1987. Hermann Kopp (1902–1987). *Buddhist Studies Review* 4:143.

Weber, Albrecht Friedrich. 1853. Die neuesten Forschungen auf dem Gebiete des Buddhismus. *Indische Studien* 3:117–95.

———. 1858. Über das Makasajâtakam. *Indische Studien* 4:387–92.

Weber, A. F., tr. 1860. Das Dhammapadam: Die älteste buddhistische Sittenlehre. *ZMDG* 14:29–86. (Also in *Indische Streifen* 1 [1868]:112–85)

Welbon, Guy Richard. 1968. *The Buddhist Nirvāṇa and its Western interpreters*. Chicago: University of Chicago Press.

Weller, Friedrich. 1933. *Index to the Tibetan translation of the Kāçyapaparivarta*. Harvard Sino-Indian Series 1. Cambridge: Harvard University Press.

———. 1935. *Index to the Indian text of the Kāçyapaparivarta*. Harvard Sino-Indian Series 2, Pt. 1. Cambridge: Harvard University Press.

———. 1952–55. *Tibetisch-sanskritischer Index zum Bodhicaryāvatāra*. 2 vols. Berlin: Akademie-Verlag.

———. 1987. *Kleine Schriften*. 2 vols. Stuttgart: F. Steiner.

Weller, F., ed. 1962. *Zum Kāśyapaparivarta*. Vol. 1. *Mongolischer Text*. Berlin: Akademie-Verlag.

Weller, F., ed. and tr. 1926–28. *Das Leben des Buddha von Aśvaghoṣa*. Leipzig: Eduard Pfeiffer.

Weller, F., tr. 1964. Kāśyapaparivarta nach der Tjin-Übersetzung verdeutscht.

Wiss. Z. der Karl-Marx Universität Leipzig 13. *Gesellschafts- und Sprachwissenschaftliche Reihe* (fasc. 4): 771–804.

———. 1965. *Zum Kāśyapaparivarta.* Vol. 2. *Verdeutschung des sanskrit-tibetischen Textes.* Berlin: Akademie-Verlag.

———. 1966a. Kāśyapaparivarta nach der Djin-Fassung verdeutscht. *Mitteilungen des Instituts für Orientforschung* 12:379–462.

———. 1966b. Die Sung-Fassung des Kāśyapaparivarta. *Monumenta Serica* 25:207–361.

———. 1970. Kāśyapaparivarta nach der Han-Fassung verdeutscht. In *Buddhist Yearly 1968/69,* 57–221. Halle: Buddhist Centre Halle.

Wessels, Cornelius, SJ. 1924. *Early Jesuit travellers in Central Asia, 1603–1721.* The Hague: M. Nijhoff.

———. 1940. New documents relating to the journey of Fr. John Grueber. *Archivum historicum S. J.* 9:281–302.

Westergaard, Niels Ludwig. 1846. *Codices indici Bibliothecae Regiae Havniensis jussu ... enumerati et descripti.* Copenhagen: Kongelige Bibliotek.

Wilhelm, Friedrich and Jampa Losang Panglung. 1979. *Tibetische Handschriften und Blockdrucke.* Part 7. Wiesbaden: Steiner.

Wille, Klause, ed. 1990. *Die handschriftliche Überlieferung des Vinayavastu der Mūlasarvāstivādin.* Stuttgart: Steiner.

Willemen, Charles. 1974. *Dharmapada: A concordance to Udānavarga, Dhammapada, and the Chinese Dharmapada literature.* Brussels: Institut Belge des Hautes Études Bouddhiques.

———. 1975a. *Udānavarga: Chinese-Sanskrit glossary.* Tokyo: Hokuseido.

———. 1978. The Chinese Udānavarga. *MCB* 19.

Willemen, C., tr. 1975b. *The essence of metaphysics:* Abhidharmahṛdaya. Brussels: Institut Belge des Hautes Études Bouddhiques.

Williams, Paul. 1984. Chr. Lindtner, Nāgārjuniana: Studies in the writings and philosophy of Nāgārjuna. *Journal of Indian Philosophy* 12:73–104.

———. 1989. *Mahāyāna Buddhism: The doctrinal foundations.* London/New York: Routledge.

Willis, Janice Dean, tr. 1979. *On knowing reality: The Tattvārtha chapter of Asaṅga's* Bodhisattvabhūmi. New York: Columbia University Press.

Windisch, Ernst Wilhem Oskar. 1895. *Māra und Buddha.* Leipzig: S. Hirzel.

———. 1908. *Buddha's Geburt und die Lehre von der Seelenwanderung.* Leipzig: B. G. Teubner.

———. 1909. *Die Komposition des Mahāvastu: Ein Beitrag zur Quellenkunde des Buddhismus.* Leipzig: B. G. Teubner. (= *Abh. d. K. Sächsischen Ges. d. Wiss.,* Philol.-hist. Kl., 27 [1909]: 467–511)

———. 1917–20. *Geschichte der Sanskrit-Philologie und indischen Altertumskunde.* 2 vols., paged consecutively. Vol. 1, Strassburg: Trübner (1917). Vol. 2, Berlin/Leipzig: Walter de Gruyter & Co. (1920).

———. 1921. *Philologie und Altertumskunde in Indien: Drei nachgelassene Kapitel des III. Teils der Geschichte der Sanskrit-Philologie und indischen Altertumskunde.* Leipzig: F. A. Brockhaus.

Wyngaert, Anastaas van den, OFM. 1929. *Itinera et relationes Fratrum Minorum saec. XIII et XIV*. Sinica Franciscana 1. Quaracchi-Firenze: Collegium S. Bonaventurae.

Yamada, Ryūjō. 1959. *Bongo butten no shobunken*. Kyoto: Heirakuji Shoten.

Yamaguchi, Susumu, ed. 1934–37. *Madhyāntavibhāga-ṭīkā de Sthiramati: Exposition systématique du Yogācāravijñāptivāda*. 3 vols. Nagoya: Hajinkaku. Reprint, Tokyo: Suzuki Research Foundation, 1966.

Yamaguchi, Tsutomu. 1984. On the *Pañcaviṃśatisāhasrikā Prajñāpāramitā* discovered in Sri Lanka. *Bukkyōgaku* 18:1–25.

Yamakami, Shōdō, Yasuke Ikari, and Muneo Tokunaga, eds. 1989. *Hattori Masaaki hakushi taikan kinen ronshū*. Vol. 6 of *Indoshisōshi Kenkyū*. Kyoto: Indoshisōshi Kenkyūkai.

Yuyama, Akira. 1987. Remarks on the Kōkiji fragment of the Lokaprajñapti. In Pollet 1987, 215–27.

Yuyama, Akira, comp. 1970. *A bibliography of the Sanskrit texts of the Saddharmapuṇḍarīkasūtra*. Oriental Monograph Series 5. Canberra: Australian National University, Faculty of Asian Studies.

———. 1973. *A grammar of the* Prajñā-pāramitā-ratna-guṇa-saṃcaya-gāthā *(Sanskrit Recension A)*. Canberra: Australian National University.

———. 1979. *Systematische Übersicht über die buddhistische Sanskrit-Literatur*. Part 1: *Vinaya-Texte*. Wiesbaden: F. Steiner.

Yuyama, A., ed. 1976. *Prajñā-pāramitā-ratna-guṇa-saṃcaya-gāthā (Sanskrit Recension A)*. Cambridge: Cambridge University Press.

———. 1988. *Sanskrit fragments of the Mahāyāna Mahāparinirvāṇasūtra*. Tokyo: Reiyukai Library.

Zimmermann, Heinz. 1975. *Die Subhāṣita-ratna-karaṇḍaka-kathā (dem Āryaśūra zugeschrieben) und ihre tibetische Übersetzung: Ein Vergleich zur Darstellung der Irrtumsrisiken bei der Auswertung tibetischer Übersetzungen*. Wiesbaden: Harrassowitz.

Zongtse, Champa Thupten, ed. 1990. *Udānavarga*. Vol. 3. With the collaboration of Siglinde Dietz. Göttingen: Vandenhoeck & Ruprecht.

Žukovskaja, N. L. 1970. Sovetskaja buddologija (bibliografičeskij obzor za 1959–1969 gody). *Narody Azii i Afriki* 1970/6:148–56.

Zürcher, Erik. 1959. *The Buddhist conquest of China: The spread and adaptation of Buddhism in early medieval China*. 2 vols. Sinica Leidensia 11. Leiden: E. J. Brill. (Reprinted with additions and corrections, 1972)

INDEX A

Names of Scholars

The page numbers of footnote references are italicized.

INDEX B

Titles of Texts